D1338942

ry and

Gre oration

ILL
DUE BACK
1/10/21

# CULTURAL MEMORIES

VOL. 2

SERIES EDITOR

Katia Pizzi
Director, Centre for the Study of Cultural Memory
Institute of Modern Languages Research, University of London

PETER LANG

Oxford · Bern · Berlin · Bruxelles · Frankfurt am Main · New York · Wien

# Nation, Memory and Great War Commemoration

Mobilizing the Past in Europe, Australia and New Zealand

Shanti Sumartojo and Ben Wellings (eds)

**PETER LANG**

Oxford · Bern · Berlin · Bruxelles · Frankfurt am Main · New York · Wien

Bibliographic information published by Die Deutsche Nationalbibliothek
Die Deutsche Nationalbibliothek lists this publication in the Deutsche Nationalbibliografie;
detailed bibliographic data is available on the Internet at http://dnb.d-nb.de.

A catalogue record for this book is available from the British Library.

Library of Congress Cataloging-in-Publication Data

Nation, memory and Great War commemoration : mobilizing the past in Europe, Australia
and New Zealand / Shanti Sumartojo and Ben Wellings (editors).
     pages cm. -- (Cultural memories)
  Includes bibliographical references and index.
  ISBN 978-3-0343-0937-0 (alkaline paper)
  I. World War, 1914-1918--Social aspects--Europe. 2. World War, 1914-1918--Social
aspects--Australia. 3. World War, 1914-1918--Social aspects--New Zealand. 4. War memo-
rials--Europe. 5. War memorials--Australia. 6. War memorials--New Zealand. 7. Collective
memory--Europe. 8. Collective memory--Australia. 9. Collective memory--New Zealand.
10. Great Britain. Army. Australian and New Zealand Army Corps--History. I. Sumartojo,
Shanti. II. Wellings, Ben, 1971-
  D524.7.E85N38 2014
  940.4'6--dc23

                          2014007850


Cover image: Fifth Australian Division Memorial, Polygon Wood, Zonnebeke, Belgium.
Photo by Shanti Sumartojo.

ISSN 2235-2325
ISBN 978-3-0343-0937-0


© Peter Lang AG, International Academic Publishers, Bern 2014
Hochfeldstrasse 32, CH-3012 Bern, Switzerland
info@peterlang.com, www.peterlang.com, www.peterlang.net

This publication has been peer reviewed.

Printed in Germany

# Contents

# Acknowledgements

This volume has been informed by a sense of collegial inquiry that has made it a real pleasure to compile. It is based on papers presented in April 2012 at a symposium at the Australian National University called *Politics of the Past*, an event that was generously supported by the then Head of the ANU's School of Politics and International Relations, Professor John Ravenhill, and the Director of the ANU's Centre for European Studies, Professor Jacquie Lo. Our thanks must first go to John and Jacquie who provided the support for this collaborative venture. To a person, the authors in this volume, both at the initial symposium and in the subsequent work in bringing their contributions to publication, have been a pleasure to work with. We thank them for their ongoing enthusiasm and intellectual creativity.

We would also like to thank the Ambassador of France to Australia, His Excellency Stéphane Romatet, and the former Ambassador of Belgium to Australia, His Excellency Patrick Renault, both of whom engaged openly at the symposium. The Embassy of France materially supported the participation of some of our French colleagues and Ambassador Romatet's subsequent intellectual support has been welcome. Brigadier Will Taylor from the British High Commission in Australia also made a very welcome contribution at the symposium, and we thank him for his participation. At the Royal Belgian Embassy, Ms Sophie Hottat's initial enthusiasm helped start the project.

A lot of invisible labour goes into the success of such academic work. In particular our thanks go to Ms Caroline Wood, formerly Executive Officer of the School of Politics and International Relations at ANU and Jane Coultas, senior administrator at the ANUCES, who ensured a smooth running of the symposium. Not least, we thank Ms Megan Harbridge at the ANU branch of STA Travel for herding the academic cats from Europe to Australia and back again. The production of this book straddled our move from Canberra to Melbourne and thanks go to supportive ANU colleagues and the wonderful ANU students whom Ben had the privilege to teach over the past ten years: the 'Last Lecture' remains a career highlight. Professor Pascaline Winand at the Monash European and EU Centre and Associate Professor Quentin Stevens at RMIT University also supported the project in its latter stages. At Peter Lang, Laurel Plapp has been terrific to work with and Katia Pizzi's guiding hand as series editor has been most welcome.

Further invisible labour was provided by our friends in Canberra who took care of our children as the symposium unfolded during and after Anzac Day 2012. Jo and Michael, Megan and David, Di and Tim, Helen and Daniel and the all the Kindy and Year 4 parents at Majura Primary School who helped us deserve our thanks. As ever, Ivan and Claire's 'Richmond Suite' was a very comfortable London *pied à terre*. In the subsequent research stemming from the symposium, Jean-Charles and Sarah in Brussels provided the wine that ensured we got on the wrong train to Germany the following morning and Ralf and Anke picked up the pieces in Oberkessel. Esther and Yo suffered from Maastricht to Amiens, providing opportunities to research European doctors' views on Australian Great War commemoration in France, while Nick's seventy-fifth birthday was one to remember. In V-B Agnes Bertoux taught our children more than they realized, while back in England Joyce and Joan took the children to Harry Potter World in Watford (just) when their parents were pursuing work and life elsewhere in Europe.

Most of all our thanks go to our two children. The research for this book took them to Flanders, Picardy, Provence, the banks of the Rhine and beyond. We hope that the embarrassing impromptu talks to French school children and an unwanted introduction to the German classroom were compensated for by Uncle Mick's garage, dead rats and live snakes on the Somme and the discovery of Nutella and *steak haché*. This book is dedicated to Adi and Ria.

— SHANTI SUMARTOJO AND BEN WELLINGS
Melbourne, March 2014

ANDREW MYCOCK, SHANTI SUMARTOJO AND BEN WELLINGS

# 'The centenary to end all centenaries': The Great War, Nation and Commemoration

In 2008, largely thanks to the initiative of Melbourne schoolteacher Lambis Englezos, a number of mass graves were discovered in Pheasant Wood near Fromelles, a village in northern France on the former Western Front. The graves contained the remains of approximately 250 British and Australian servicemen who had been hastily buried by their German adversaries following a disastrous diversionary attack during the opening stages of the Battle of the Somme in July 1916. As the remains were recovered and reburied forensic investigators attempted to identify the individuals, aided by DNA testing of potential family members located after historical and genealogical research in Australia. The graves also revealed personal items that helped identify the dead soldiers, including uniform buttons, buckles and insignia; a pipe and toothbrush; and, poignantly, a return train ticket from Fremantle to Perth in Western Australia, with only one leg of the journey marked as used.[1]

This discovery led to the creation and consecration of the first Great War cemetery since the 1960s, an event attended by high level dignitaries, not least His Royal Highness Prince Charles, the Australian Governor-General Ms Quentin Bryce and the mayor of Fromelles, Monsieur Hubert Huchette. At the cemetery's dedication in July 2010, Quentin Bryce described the treatment of the bodies:

---

1    See Julie Summers, ed., *Remembering Fromelles: A new cemetery for a new century* (Maidenhead: CWGC Publishing, 2010).

Each and every one of them: gently, expertly, reverently cradled and carried from where they were last thrust side by side, already fallen, more than nine decades ago to a new resting place, this place, a place of resolution and peace.[2]

The discovery of the gravesite and the official ceremony received a high degree of media coverage, building on decades of interest (personal, official and from within civil society) in what is referred to in Australia simply as 'Anzac', a term that implies a set of national values derived from the social and political significance of military service in Australia's past and present. Thus although the Great War took place almost one hundred years ago, its commemoration is very much a contemporary concern, exemplified in both the discovery of the previously unknown gravesite at Pheasant Wood, and the painstaking attempts to link those individuals buried at the site to their living relatives.

Commemoration of the Great War is thus simultaneously deeply personal and completely public, subject to both family and state rituals that link the individual to the nation. As such, the ceremony at Fromelles was an example of Jay Winter's 'historical remembrance', a 'discursive field, extending from ritual to cultural work of many different kinds [... with a] capacity to unite people who have no other bonds drawing them together'.[3] For Benedict Anderson 'no more arresting emblems of the modern culture of nationalism exist than cenotaphs and the tombs of Unknown Soldiers' and in this way, remembrance and commemoration help generate the nation as 'an imagined political community'.[4] Events such as the ceremony at Fromelles link the individual and the nation through the figure of the reinterred combatants whom we are invited to mourn almost one hundred years after their deaths.

---

2    The full text of this speech is available at <http://www.gg.gov.au/speech/dedication-fromelles-pheasant-wood-military-cemetery-and-burial-250th-unnamed-soldier> accessed 16 August 2013.

3    Jay Winter, *Remembering War: The Great War Between Memory and History in the Twentieth Century* (New Haven: Yale University Press, 2006), 11.

4    Benedict Anderson, *Imagined Communities. Reflections on the origins and spread of nationalism* (London: Verso, 1991), 6–9.

At the same time as they are personal and national, however, the commemorations are also inescapably global. This is not only because of the multinational nature of the conflict one hundred years ago, but also due to the international relationships that have transformed over the past century from adversarial to cooperative, in the case of the European combatants, or from intimately linked to fully independent, as in the case of former empires. But this is not the only global dimension to such commemoration. International collaboration at Fromelles ensured the bodies were discovered and identified, a new Commonwealth War Grave opened and high level official participation in the consecration of the cemetery. This involved multi-agency cooperation and coordination between British, Australian and French diplomatic corps and veterans affairs' departments, local government in the Pas de Calais region, British universities and Australian media networks – an intensification of (peaceable) international collaborative effort far removed from that of a hundred years ago.

This example also demonstrates the simultaneous fragility and strength of Great War narratives – fragile in the personal memories of family members that can be lost with generational change, but robust in the repeated use of historical narrative for many different purposes – to cohere co-nationals around a unifying set of 'values'; to try to define the extent and diversity of the contemporary nation; to shape the tone of international relationships and to build political support for contemporary ends. The examples in this volume, written by established and emerging scholars, examine these processes in detailed case studies, organized into four sections animated by the following questions:

- How is war remembered in what is often characterized as a 'global' and 'post-national' era?
- How does commemoration of the Great War inflect questions of national belonging in developed societies today?
- To what extent has the memory of the Great War been consciously or unconsciously mobilized as part of a wider politics of legitimacy?
- How are specific locations of commemoration and commemorative acts designed to shape individual and collective understandings of the past and present?

This volume has been produced to coincide with the centenary of the beginning of the Great War in August 2014, a period of intense planning and reflection around commemorative activity. The centenary is part of a wider phenomenon whereby commemorative activity has grown in the past three decades. This has expanded to the extent that former Australian Prime Minister Paul Keating gave a speech in 2013 to mark the twentieth anniversary of his speech at the internment of the Unknown Solider at the Australian War Memorial in 1993. This convoluted occasion was effectively a commemorative event commemorating a commemorative event.

The volume's scope is necessarily international, comparative and multi-disciplinary. The contributions carefully examine how the research themes operate in Australia, New Zealand, the United Kingdom, Ireland, France, Germany and Belgium, as well as the French overseas territory of New Caledonia. An international approach is necessary given that the Great War centenary will involve no less that seventy-two states across four years of commemoration from 2014 to 2018, a prospect that led Henry Porter describe this as 'the centenary to end all centenaries'.[5] This is a case when one can truly say that for reasons of space only a small proportion of examples could be included.

This book grew from a symposium held at the Australian National University's Centre for European Studies in April 2012 called *Politics of the Past*. Given the editors' location in Australia, the initial motivation behind this project was to place the significant activity associated with war memory in Australia in an international context. Comparative analysis is especially important in the study of nationalism, because nations and nationalisms exist in a tension between the particular and the universal. All nations by their very definition are unique and particular collective manifestations of what are often described as 'values' or 'culture'. On the other hand, nations are a universal category: although the content of particular nationalisms may differ, the form is instantly recognizable throughout the world. Thus, comparative analysis can avoid the trap of over-stressing what may appear significant within the mental universe created by living in a world of nations,

---

5    Henry Porter, 'When we first knew destruction', *Guardian Weekly* (9 August 2013), 21.

by asking if such phenomena are important or significant elsewhere. If, as the Russians say, 'every duck is proud of his pond', then a comparative approach enables us to see beyond the banks of our own murky ditches.

The subject matter of this collection also required the breadth of a multi-disciplinary approach to do justice to the subject matter. National belonging and memory are simultaneously public and intimate, collective and private modes of being. At times the relationship between the individual and memory of the past can be close, but often this activity is mediated by governments, civil society organizations and the media. The contributions to this volume accordingly sit at the intersections of history, politics, geography and cultural studies as a means to interpret the diverse ways that nations and national belonging are experienced and reproduced.

The deaths of the last members of the generation that fought in the Great War have offered significant opportunities for political, academic and public deliberation concerning the legacies of the conflict. When the last surviving British combatants of the First World War, Harry Patch and Henry Allingham, died in 2009, *The Economist* declared a farewell to the conflict, claiming that it had shifted 'from memory to history' (although some historians in this volume question whether it has moved decisively from personal memory to collective memory, by-passing history as a method of inquiry along the way).[6] Nevertheless, *The Economist*'s headline revealed the inter-relationship between history and memory. Both were seen as having the potential to connect the past with the present and the future. The assumption was that collective and individual life would be enriched if such connections were made. The anxiety, perhaps, was that most people (especially the young) knew little and cared less about the events in question.

This anxiety taps into concerns about the value of remembrance and the necessity of commemorative practices. Nora's seminal notion of *lieux de mémoire* is useful here: broadly defined sites, rituals or artefacts of national memory where the past is explicitly, if selectively, evoked and represented.

6    'Farewell to WWI: From Memory to History', *The Economist* (17 December 2009), <http://www.economist.com/node/15108655> accessed 14 February 2013. Note however that the last surviving veteran (as opposed to combatant) was a woman named Florence Green who died in 2012 (see Cadot, this volume).

However, *lieux de mémoire* foreground only some aspects of the past, demonstrating a tension between official history, or a 'representation of the past', and vernacular or popular memory, 'a perpetually acting phenomenon, a bond tying us to the eternal present'.[7] Nora's identification of these two aspects speaks to the relationship between history and memory: the power of institutions to shape national narratives on the one hand, and the resistance, adherence or even indifference to these narratives by the public on the other. The centenary of the Great War occurs at a time when the connections between history, memory, nation, state and the individual have been significantly reframed in comparison with one hundred years ago. The critical, analytical ordering and articulation of the past by historians and politicians who have often sought to elevate the nation through the production of 'grand' national narratives has, during the past thirty years or so, become increasingly fragmented.[8] According to Jay Winter a 'memory boom', embraced by states and citizens alike, has gradually superseded history in the past three decades, pitting a method of inquiry against deeply felt empathy.[9] Although this tension started with the First World War and was subsequently underpinned by Holocaust remembrance, it was intensified by new ways of thinking about the role of history and the past in contemporary society that reflected the impact of 'identity politics' and the 'recovery of voices that had been there all along'.[10] In this situation, 'memory' is not the same as historical inquiry into the past. Aleida Assmann argues that history has been transformed into socially constructed memory cultures through public discourse about how past events are remembered, interpreted and articulated.[11] This has meant historical narratives have

7    Pierre Nora, 'Between Memory and History: *Les Lieux de Mémoire*', *Représentations* 26 (1989), 8.

8    Stefan Berger and Chris Lorenz, 'National Narratives and their "Others": Ethnicity, class, religion and the gendering of national histories', *Storia della Storiografia* 50 (2006), 59–98.

9    Winter, *Remembering War*.

10    Jay Winter, 'The Generation of Memory: Reflections on the "Memory Boom" in Contemporary Historical Studies', *GHI Bulletin* 21 (2000), 374.

11    Aleida Assmann, 'Memory, Individual and Collective', in Robert E. Goodin and Charles Tilly, eds, *The Oxford Handbook of Contextual Political Analysis* (Oxford: Oxford University Press, 2006), 210–26, 216.

been reconfigured into emotionally charged versions of 'our history', thus providing reference points for complementary and at times contradictory forms of identity. Thus, official 'history' and vernacular 'memory' have been selectively mixed in the arena of identity politics by a range of actors who choose aspects of the historical past to buttress their own political goals.

This fragmentation is apparent in attempts by governments to deploy historical narratives to repair or occlude perceived instances of social and political cleavage. Accordingly, the state is crucial in facilitating this conceptual shift from official monolithic history towards something more discursive and fluid, and in mediating the memories of its citizens. Comparison over time reveals that state agencies were crucial in creating the first wave of commemoration in the wake of the Great War. As Bruce Scates and Bart Ziino have shown in the case of Australia, shared national consciousness was encouraged and facilitated by the state, offering opportunities to construct 'collective memories' from the recent conflict via personal pilgrimages and journeys.[12] Citizens were also encouraged to participate in national acts of collective remembrance through the shared experience of state-sponsored memorials, libraries, museums and mass education programmes, something they willingly did across Europe and its imperial possessions in great numbers.[13] However, today's state is different from the one that led people to war in 1914. In many ways it is both stronger and weaker than its forebear of a hundred years ago, which generates a different dynamic for the politics of national belonging. Globalization and the shift from government to governance have required different narratives to bind state and citizen in a historical context of social and political fragmentation. Remembrance and commemoration play a part in this renewal of national narratives.

---

12　Bruce Scates, *Return to Gallipoli: Walking the Battlefields of the Great War* (Cambridge: CUP, 2006); Bart Ziino, *A Distant Grief: Australians, War Graves and the Great War* (Crawley: UWA Press, 2007).

13　Małgorzata Pakier and Bo Stråth, 'A European Memory?', in Małgorzata Pakier and Bo Stråth, eds, *A European Memory? Contested Histories and the Politics of Remembrance* (Oxford: Berghahn Books, 2010), 1–24.

## War and memory in a 'post-national' era

The historical and political context of globalization and European inte-gration frames Part I of this volume. The three authors in this section understand Great War commemoration as activity shaped by international and global forces, but they nevertheless question the claim that we have entered a truly 'post-national' era as envisioned by Jürgen Habermas.[14] John Hutchinson's broad historical-sociological analysis situates contemporary remembrance in the wider structures of global change of the past thirty years, in particular noting the impossibility of remembering the First World War without remembering the Second. He examines the claim that the two world wars can be regarded together as a 'second Thirty Years' War' that eroded belief in European national identities and enabled the rise of global and regional identities. In challenging this conclusion, he finds that such ideas project post-national longings as a universal phenomenon and gravely misunderstand the ways that nationalism continues to inform everyday experience and commemorative practices in the developed world.

Like Hutchinson, Ben Wellings analyses the increasing cultural and political prominence accorded to war commemoration in the past thirty years by way of the intersection of nationalism and globalization. He too argues that far from eroding nationalism, globalization has led to new attempts to link state to citizen as a self-weakened state searches for new legitimizing narratives in a global era of dislocation and uncertainty. Wellings argues that although nationalists usually present the nation in terms of cultural, political and social continuity, nationalism itself is a response to change. His is the first of several contributions to take the example of the Anzac narrative in Australia and shows how it has come to dominate the national imagination, providing cues to the content of Australian 'values' and how Australians should understand themselves and their government's place in the world.

14    Jürgen Habermas, *The Post-national Constellation: political essays* (Cambridge, MA: MIT Press, 2001).

Roger Hillman extends Hutchinson's link between the two world wars, demonstrating how knowledge of the First is refracted through contemporary memory of the Second. Hillman shows how cinematic interpretations of the Great War have been generated by what he calls (*pace* McKenna) a 'sentimental supra-nationalism',[15] arguing that 'film is better suited than written history to honing symbolic history'. To make his case, Hillman analyses four films made ninety years after the end of the Great War, noting the retelling of Great War narratives in light of contemporary European concerns. In speaking of the ending to one of his examples, Christian Carion's *Joyeux Noël* (2005), Hillman argues that the 'home' envisioned at its conclusion is vindicated by the award of the Nobel Peace Prize to the European Union in 2012: the film 'has far more to do with the strivings of the New Europe', he concludes, 'than with the events of Christmas 1914'. The European identity project revealed by this analysis of film makes an important point. Regional integration, notably in Europe itself, has created a new context for the articulation of national identities and nationalisms. We must, however, be careful not to over-state the impact of this; as Helen Thompson notes, 'new transnational sites of governance have the same political problem as states, albeit manifested in different forms'.[16] In other words, European integration can help initiate nationalism as well as providing narratives for its containment (and even suppression) and the development of a 'European memory' in film is part of this broad process. The difficulty in building such a narrative is also examined in Christine Cadot's contribution in Part IV.

15   Mark McKenna, 'Patriot Act', *The Australian Literary Review* (6 June 2007), 15.
16   Helen Thompson, 'The Character of the State' in Colin Hay, ed., *New Directions in Political Science: Responding to the challenges of an interdependent world* (Basingstoke: Palgrave, 2010), 136.

Commemoration and the politics of national belonging

Part II also grapples with the extent to which the state can construct or manipulate national identity. The primary role of the state in shaping war commemoration highlights its fundamental and politicized role in the formation of national identity in the century after the Great War. War commemoration has emphasized sacrifice and loss in either victory or defeat as a means of preserving and reinforcing particular national projects and ideologies that involve memory as a means of cohering a putative national group and, at times, distinguishing that group from others. The nation-state, with all the resources and power at its disposal, has been the primary agent for the articulation of war remembrance, which has meant that commemoration has often been founded on hegemonic and state-approved historical narratives. In the contemporary era, just as one hundred years ago, war commemoration remains primarily a political project whereby the state mediates and orders both formal and informal collective remembrance in the promotion of a unitary national identity.

But the state is not the only actor in generating collective memory, although it usually has the most power. Deliberative public exchanges can reflect dynamic and unequal power structures between elites and groups within states that are realized through official attempts to propagate particular interpretations of the past.[17] As memory operates at both individual and group levels, personalized and subordinate forms of analysis of the national past can come into conflict with state-sponsored forms of collective memory. According to Pierre Nora, this indicates that politics, which covers both memory and ideology, is in an ongoing conflict with history.[18] If, one hundred years ago, history could be understood as a *political* activity

17    James E. Young, *The Texture of Memory: Holocaust memorials and meaning* (New Haven: Yale University Press, 1993), 3–10.
18    Pierre Nora, 'Recent history and the new dangers of politicization', *Eurozine* (24 November 2011) <http://www.eurozine.com/articles/2011-11-24-nora-en.html> accessed 12 January 2013.

in support of the nation, it is now *politicized* in support of multiple, divergent or even competing ideological constructions of the national present at a time when governments seek to establish simple narratives in support of sometimes fragile national unity.

Accordingly, Part II turns to the links between commemoration, belonging and national unity, asking how Great War commemoration might alternately exacerbate or obscure cleavages within the communities in question. In his analysis of Anzac, Frank Bongiorno begins his analysis by pointing to some unintended consequences in the development of the Anzac narrative of the past thirty years. Bongiorno begins to explore the social and political complexities of Great War commemoration in Australia's multicultural context, arguing that 'once a tradition is defined in more inclusive terms, those who refuse to participate can readily be represented as beyond the pale. To question, to criticize – even to analyse – can become un-Australian'. He argues that the generalizing and inclusive nature of the narrative occludes real social and political differences and silences questions about inequality in contemporary Australia, and that this occurs not only despite, *but because of*, attempts to render it inclusive.

Problems of inclusion also complicate the United Kingdom government's attempts to commemorate the First World War, as Andrew Mycock illustrates. He shows how, having belatedly started preparations for the centenary given commitments to the Olympics up to 2012, the Cameron-led coalition set itself an ambitious remit. While the aim was to capture and express 'our national spirit', the boundaries of the nation in question (England, Britain or the United Kingdom and its former Empire) were not clear. The scope of activities included all the nations of the United Kingdom, the ethnically diverse population of Britain and particularly England, as well as the countries of the Commonwealth and beyond that had fought alongside Great Britain. This has been occurring at a time when the future of the United Kingdom has itself been in doubt given the referendum on Scottish independence in September 2014, only one month after the first centenary event marking the outbreak of hostilities. This wide remit, national and post-imperial, led to a situation whereby the UK government was unable to provide a clear articulation of the aims of the commemorations. Mycock concludes that recognition of the 'entangled histories of the citizens and nations of the UK and its former Empire during the First World War, and the pluralities and complex configurations that result from it' would be a far better approach than seeking to pursue an elusive sense of unity at a time of austerity and the potential break-up of the United Kingdom.

Across the Irish Sea, nation and memory are particularly entangled, unity is unlikely and belonging is highly contentious. In comparing the politics of Great War commemoration and memory in Ireland (north and south) James W. McAuley argues that the moment of division between 1916 and 1923 conditioned the historical memory of the Great War amongst unionist and nationalist communities in sharply divergent ways. However, such divisions were given greater intensity and political significance by the onset of The Troubles from the mid-1960s, particularly for Unionists and Loyalists. In contrast with the state-organized memorials of many of the other case studies in this volume, Loyalist Great War memory and commemoration is popular, vernacular and at times 'unauthorized'. This is because, as McAuley states, 'since the outbreak of the Troubles, Ulster Loyalists have expressed overlapping senses of identity, which at the macro level emphasized a distinct sense of Britishness, while at the micro level often rested on a very localized sense of belonging'. In comparison with other nationalisms, the Nationalist memory of a war *against* an imperial power as a foundational and legitimizing national mythology, however historically distorted, contrasts with Loyalist and indeed Australian 'blood sacrifice' *for* an imperial power occurring far from the national territory.

Like Ireland, the multi-national state of Belgium contains politically charged memories of the Great War and as such has encountered significant challenges in agreeing how best to commemorate the centenary. In the final chapter of Part II, Laurence van Ypersele traces how an official Belgian memory of the war had become plural by the 1930s: 'Flemish and French-speaking historical versions of the past began to diverge; the official version of history no longer corresponded exactly with local versions'. The implications of this divergence, an ongoing source of tension, had an ambiguous impact on how people perceived and acted in the Second World War. It also continued to shape contemporary political responses to centennial commemorations that challenged the official and no longer hegemonic narrative of Belgium as a 'heroic victim' that emerged following the Locarno Pact in 1925. In analysing plans for organized war commemorations, van Ypersele disentangles the cultural, regional and national identities in Belgium and shows how divergent memories of the Great War in Flanders and Wallonia have created diplomatic difficulties for Belgium's central role as a location of commemorative activities beginning in 2014.

## Mobilizing the Great War

Part III develops the theme of the politics of commemoration and interrogates the way that the Great War has been used in the past century for various political projects, democratic or otherwise. As the preceding section has shown, the past is not an area of innocent inquiry. As John Coakley claims, the sense of a shared past is 'is necessarily based on selection and over-simplification, if not misinterpretation and fabrication'. The form that this package takes', he continues, 'will be determined by the current needs of the state or of the elites that have placed themselves at the head of a national movement'.[19] The past, therefore, can be mobilized by what the literature on nationalism characterizes as 'civic' and 'ethnic' or 'statist' and 'cultural' nationalists. But we must not make too much of these ideal-typical distinctions. Chaim Gans argues that 'statist nationalism is cultural [because] it requires that citizenries of states share not merely a set of political principles, but also a common language, tradition and a sense of common history', adding that 'within statist nationalism, the national culture is the means, and the values of the state are the aims'.[20] This begins to illustrate why the past is so important to states and governments today.

19    John Coakley, 'Mobilizing the Past: nationalist images of history', *Nationalism and Ethnic Politics*, 10/1 (2004), 533.
20    Chaim Gans, *The Limits of Nationalism* (Cambridge: Cambridge University Press, 2003), 16 and 7.

Jonathan Hearn has argued that nationalism is not just the pursuit of state-hood; well-established states and their populations continually engage in nationalism too.[21] Echoing Michael Billig's conclusion about 'banal nationalism', also referred to by Michael Skey as the intersection between 'national belonging and everyday life', Hearn claims that:

> [I]n stable democratic regimes, this process of nationalism is very deeply embedded in civil society and electoral systems and [is] not simply an elite or state-led process. It is part of the normal functioning of democratic regimes.[22]

Furthermore, the mobilization of collective memory by the contemporary state renders it implicitly political. Paul Daley calculated that total Australian spending on the Great War centenary was in the region of Australian $140 million, a sum that contrasted notably with the UK government's allocation of $94 million for its commemorations, a country three times bigger than Australia. From this, Daley concluded that 'the disparity reflects Australia's ever-strengthening cultural and political attachment to Anzac'.[23] It may also be that Australia, relatively unscathed by the global financial crisis that began in 2008, simply had more money to spend than 'Austerity Britain' (itself a culturally specific memory of the years following the Second World War).

However, the contemporary mobilization of the Great War is not just political in the sense that governments, via state agencies, have the power to allocate scarce resources. This is not to say that the allocation of such resources is not important or contentious, even though public dissent in

---

21    Jonathan Hearn, *Rethinking Nationalism: A Critical Introduction* (Basingstoke: Palgrave, 2006), 165.

22    Hearn, *Rethinking Nationalism*, 165. See also Michel Billig, *Banal Nationalism* (London: Sage, 1995) and Michael Skey, *National Belonging and Everyday Life: The Significance of Nationalism in an Uncertain World* (Basingstoke: Palgrave, 2011).

23    Paul Daley, 'Australia spares no expense as the Anzac legend nears its century', 15 October 2013 <http://www.theguardian.com/world/2013/oct/14/australia-anzac-legend-centenary-war> accessed 19 January 2014. Note that the official Australian Government figure for centenary spending was $83m.

the case of war commemoration is rare.[24] In reflecting on the politics of memory and national belonging, a definition of politics must be wider than who gets what, when and how. In particular, bipartisan support for a policy or set of activities must not be misunderstood as an apolitical area of deliberation. Colin Hay advances a definition of politics that is based on content rather than a delineated domain of activity. For Hay, politics is:

> [T]he capacity for agency and deliberation in situations of genuine collective or social choice [...] Politics does not, and cannot, arise in situations in which human purpose can exert no influence. Politics is synonymous with contingency; its antonyms are fate and necessity.[25]

This is what creates certain misgivings about the political impact of Anzac and other forms of Great War commemoration. Critics of Anzac, for example, are wary of the invocation of the dead that occurs in times of war because it narrows the possibility for the type of deliberative public debate that is seen to be the lifeblood of democracy. Christopher Clark writes of concerns about how the use of the war dead can have the effect of narrowing contemporary politics: 'It is important that we challenge manipulative or reductive readings of the past when these are mobilized in support of present day political objectives'. He continues:

> The recourse to history is most enlightening when we understand our conversations about the past are as open-ended as our reflections on the present should be. History is 'the great instructor of public life', as Cicero said. But history's wisdom comes to us not as pre-packaged lessons but as oracles, whose relevance to our predicaments has to be puzzled over.[26]

24   See James Brown, 'Anzac's Long Shadow: the Cost of Our National Obsession', <http://www.lowyinstitute.org/publications/anzacs-long-shadow-cost-our-national-obsession> accessed 21 February 2014.
25   Colin Hay, *Why We Hate Politics* (Cambridge: Polity Press, 2007), 77.
26   Christopher Clark, 'Is history telling us something?', *The Guardian Weekly* (7 February 2014).

This suggests that the past, as an element in various political projects, can at times act as a democratic depressant as much as a civic stimulant. This contention is examined in Part III.

Mark McKenna begins by focusing on the central role of war remembrance in Australia and New Zealand, identifying both its significance and the uncritical 'ahistorical remembering' that characterizes its political use. In the case of Australia, he shows how Anzac has been used to distract attention from the foundational internal conflict of white settlement and Indigenous disempowerment: 'Against this history, the Anzac legend has appeared less controversial and divisive, a far more malleable history for the purposes of national communion than competing demands of invasion, settlement and sovereignty'. As with Bongiorno's discussion of how Anzac's inclusivity can actually work to exclude, McKenna's critique of Anzac relies on the way it is ahistorical and has been sentimentalized, with the result that popular memory is not required to engage with difficult, painful or complex national history.

A different type of political project, 'memorial diplomacy', or the use of commemorative sites and practices as the location for international relations, is the subject of Matthew Graves's contribution. He points out that the 'inauguration or rededication of sites of memory […] has long served as a platform for reinforcing relations between governments'. He discusses this development as a feature of the second 'memory boom', particularly in relation to Franco-Australian relations. Like Hutchinson, he identifies an intensification of commemorative activities in the past thirty years, arguing that memorial diplomacy represents an extension of the considerable political and social resources of commemorative sites. Such diplomatic efforts represent a mobilization of commemoration that rests on hegemonic and state-based interpretations of military history, the same interpretations set to shape the tenor of much domestic commemorative activity during the 2014–18 period.

But what happens when there is resistance to such state approved narratives, particularly in a colonial context? Narratives or memories that are seen as peripheral or that potentially compromise official versions can be actively marginalized or even purposefully excluded by the state. Experiences of empire or other transnational forms of political, economic and/or cultural union can also extend to forms of war commemoration beyond the boundaries of the state to include other former or current allies. For former colonial states, commemoration can include colonies that contributed soldiers and resources to previous conflicts. It can also highlight, however, the unequal and sometimes exploitative nature of colonial relationships, encouraging post-colonial revisionism that challenges dominant modes of commemoration. Elizabeth Rechniewski tackles this question in relation to remembering and forgetting the contribution of New Caledonian Kanak (indigenous) soldiers to the French Great War effort. She shows how 'institutional amnesia, strategic forgetting, ideological dissonance and conflict over material interests' combined with structural inequality in the French colony combined to shape the 'forgetting' of Kanak soldiers. Just as McKenna identifies Indigenous Australian displacement as the 'forgetting' that underpins Anzac remembrance, Rechniewski pinpoints conflict between French colonial authorities and indigenous fighters as the crux of a more nuanced account of Kanak war service. In this case, the unsettling memories of the hundred years that separates contemporary societies from those that went to war in 1914 intrudes on commemorative activities despite official attempts to determine otherwise.

Of all the cases contained in this volume, the place where the occulsion of the First and Second World Wars in collective memory has been the greatest is Germany. It is also the place where the past has been mobilized with truly important historic results, such as the delegitimization of the Weimar Republic and the rehabilitation of the Federal Republic after 1949. Matthew Stibbe's chapter places German academic writing and public discourses about the Great War within the framework of broader changes in perceptions of the national past from 1919 to the present day, taking in Weimar, the Nazi period, the Fischer controversy and the *Vergangenheitsbewältigung* [coming to terms with the past] that preceded and was in some sense supplanted by reunification in 1990. As Stibbe argues, 'the Great War has been refought in Germany at many different stages in the twentieth century and beyond, reflecting shifting political priorities, generational expectations, geopolitical realities and cultural trends'. Although derived from the German experience, this conclusion pertains to all of the cases studied in this volume.

All of this implies that political power continues to fuel how the Great War is remembered. Rebecca Graff-McRae argues that war commemoration is always political in that it reflects and reproduces unequal power relations that can be shaped by race, ethnicity, class, gender and other social hierarchies within states.[27] If, as Assmann proposes, political memory is stronger in ethnically homogeneous groups and nations, this suggests that poly-ethnic or multicultural societies, particularly those with sizeable migrant groups, have greater challenges in establishing inclusive modes of war commemoration which are founded on collective narratives or memories. Concomitantly, diversity can produce a stronger response from governments and civil society groups concerned with the maintenance of a form of national unity. In this project, the state and civil society groups whose values and ideologies align with those of governments have more power and influence than dissenting voices in shaping national narratives – and hence political outcomes – based on visions of the past.

## Locations of commemoration

Despite this asymmetry in power relationships, states are not the only actors with a stake in commemoration. Part IV adopts a focus on how, where and by what means the Great War will be remembered. The five chapters in this section discuss memorials, museums and other commemorative sites, engaging closely with the politics and complexities of such *lieux de mémoire*. The empirical examples in this section illustrate how historical narratives and the memory of war, including the Great War, are also contextual and subject to continual reinterpretation by subsequent generations and different actors. As such, they are situated in the national 'mythscape', 'the discursive space in which the various myths of the collective are forged, transmitted and

27    Rebecca Graff-McRae, *Remembering and Forgetting 1916: Commemoration and Conflict in Post-Peace Process Ireland* (Dublin: Irish Academic Press, 2010), 6–10.

challenged'.[28] In such commemorative locations, 'representational practices are thus inherently bound up in the process of national identity formation'.[29] Nira Yuval-Davis also notes the hegemonic and contingent elements in the production of national cultures, a social phenomenon that is more than just an arbitrary collection of values and modes of behaviour. When considered together, Yuval-Davis argues, these values, symbols and modes of behaviour 'acquire, to a greater or lesser extent, "stabilizing properties" which are inherent in the practices of their social reproduction [...]. As a result, cultural models become resonant with subjective experience. They become the ways individuals experience themselves, their collectivities and the world'.[30] The chapters in Part IV all engage with how audiences experience and respond in different ways to such 'cultural models', including by resisting, challenging or ignoring them.

Sarah Christie begins this section with an analysis of the cultural production of memory at the intersection of gender and nation. She analyses the example of the *Marquette*, a troop ship torpedoed in the Aegean Sea in October 1915, when ten nurses form the No. 1 New Zealand Stationary Hospital were drowned. Christie examines how initial constructions of gender and community identity influenced the subsequent creation of the collective memory of the event, including challenges to the construction of the nurses as 'honorary men'. She goes on to investigate the resurgence in popularity of the *Marquette* story and its renewed relevance in light of contemporary ideas about gender roles and national identity in post-imperial New Zealand. But the past is not entirely malleable. Her conclusion, that the initial framing of the event becomes part of collective memory and is then important in defining the subsequent parameters of public discussion, mirrors that of McAuley's in the case of Nationalist and Unionist memories of the Great War.

---

28    Duncan Bell, 'Agonistic Democracy and the Politics of Memory', *Constellations* 15/1 (2008), 151.
29    Duncan Bell, 'Mythscapes: memory, mythology and national identity', *British Journal of Sociology* 54/1 (2003), 69.
30    Nira Yuval-Davis, *Gender and Nation* (London: Sage, 1997), 42.

The section returns to Australia with Guy Hansen's discussion of the treatment of the Anzac story in the National Museum of Australia (NMA) after its opening in 2001. Hansen, who was a Head Curator at the NMA, argues that museums play a central role in promulgating the Anzac myth, although as public institutions they have limited room for manouevre. He situates Anzac as 'a set of cultural practices rather than as a type of verifiable history', which creates tensions for those who might want to deconstruct or complicate it. Despite the apparent flexibility of cultural practice, Hansen shows how 'Anzac stands in the centre of popular narratives of Australian history impervious to the debate that surrounds it', in part due to the politicization of the museum sector, a sector that sits somewhere between an arm of government and civil society.

Christine Cadot remains on the topic of museums, although this time a trans- or supranational one, focusing on the historiographical processes that are at stake in building a history of European integration. She discusses the role that museums play in this understanding of Europe's past and examines the possibilities for museums and memorials as European sites in which historical memory can develop. Like others in this volume, she finds that remembering the First World War without considering the Second has become publicly impossible. Cadot concludes, however, that at a historical juncture where member-states still jealously guard their national histories for reasons outlined in this volume, a *European* memory remains 'political wishful thinking' rather than 'a proven reality'.

Despite the range of cultural institutions and media outlets urging otherwise, individuals exercise a great deal of agency in collective remembrance and commemorative practices. Anthony Cohen warns that, when examining 'nationalist ritual', to distinguish between 'the intentions of their producers and the readings made of them by their audiences'.[31] Indeed, there are vernacular attempts at many levels apart from the state to redefine or reclaim commemorative activity, as many of the chapters in this volume assert. This can mean that collective war memories and patterns

---

31    Anthony Cohen, 'personal nationalism – a Scottish view of some rites, rights, and wrongs', *american ethnologist* 23/4 (1996), 804.

of commemoration are both hegemonic *and* contentious, the result of complex exchanges between the state and a diverse range of social groups. Contemporary responses to past conflicts can see popular expression, such as mourning traumatic loss, complicate attempts by the state to manipulate commemoration.[32]

The contest over commemorative practice and national memory that coheres this section is the explicit focus of Romain Fathi's chapter, as he illustrates the interaction between state and civil society actors in the (over) production of commemorative activity. He analyses the history of Australian commemorative activity in Villers-Bretonneux, the site of the Australian National Memorial on the former Western Front. Fathi brings new French sources into English in a detailed examination of the impact of international processes on local identities, some welcome, others less so. He shows how time and space are collapsed in the creation of Australian national 'values', expanding on the point made by Hutchinson and Wellings in Part I, and tracing Australian governments' engagement with this small town in northern France.

Finally, Shanti Sumartojo builds on the theme of the negotiation between official and vernacular aspects of commemoration, and between personal and family memory and national remembrance. In her study of the Australian Remembrance Trail (ART) on the former Western Front in France and Belgium, she responds to Todman's warning that we should be wary of 'obscuring the persistence of individual memories that may contradict the prevalent shared beliefs'.[33] She focuses on how such sites are both represented and experienced and shows how individual and personal commemorative practices encouraged on the Trail can help shape 'Anzac nationalism'. Sumartojo argues that commemorative rituals at ART sites are linked to specific landscapes and practices that so far remain resistant to transformation, or even complexity of use. This contributes to a version

---

32    Debra Marshall, 'Making Sense of Remembrance', *Social and Cultural Geography* 5/1 (2004), 37–54.

33    Dan Todman, 'The Ninetieth Anniversary of the Battle of the Somme' in Michael Keren and Holger Herwig, eds, *War Memory and Popular Culture: Essays on Modes of Remembrance and Commemoration* (Jefferson NC: McFarland and Co, 2009), 25.

of Australia as a nation with a strong sense of kinship at its core, a focus that can sit uneasily with the 'civic' and multicultural qualities with which Australia is usually associated. She touches on similar themes to Bongiorno, McKenna and Hansen, concluding that visitors' practices of remembrance on the Trail work to reinforce the existing limits of the Anzac narrative, and therefore Australian identity more broadly.

## Conclusion

One hundred years after the Great War, the impact of the conflict is still evident in its mobilization for contemporary political and nationalist projects: hence the title of this volume. The collection is intended to help establish a starting point for ongoing research on Great War commemoration during the centenary period. In doing so, its comparative framework has revealed four initial findings that we suggest merit further exploration.

The first is the link between national events and international trends, not least the relationship between globalization and specific national narratives. Although one's own national commemorations may be compelling and seemingly unique (they are, after all, designed to be), similar pressures and imperatives are generating demands for commemorative activity across the developed world. A related point is that there is an increasing use of 'memorial diplomacy' as part of this trend and as a deliberate activity of government. Cooperative multi-national commemorative activity affects the tenor of domestic commemoration, but will also be an important stage for bilateral and multilateral relationships up to 2018.

A second finding is that despite common international and global themes (indeed, maybe because of them) national and local specificities loom large in the form and content of Great War commemorations considered in this volume. Commemorative and remembrance activities are performed by individuals and groups with the crucial support – or at least the inevitable intrusion of – the state. The overall themes of commemoration must resonate at the personal as well as national level and be politically useful in order to continue to enjoy official support. We anticipate that commemorative activity during the centenary period will provide useful case studies for ongoing analyses of the relationship between the individual and the state. However, the question of the flexibility and malleability of Great War remembrance remains unclear – to what extent can the current discourse accommodate complication, for example, multiplicity, or even disagreement?

Thirdly, it has become extremely difficult – if not impossible – to remember the First World War without remembering the Second. This has been particularly the case in Germany but is no less true in Belgium and is evident in broader 'European' narratives. It is also difficult to imagine the Great War in Northern Ireland and the Republic of Ireland without a memory of 'The Troubles' intruding. Even in Australia, the centenary of the Great War has become an occasion to celebrate or commemorate the 'Anzac Centenary', a reframing of time that encourages participants not to compare 1915 with 2015, but which collapses a century of military service into a single date, 25 April. This links the Australian nation today with soldiers and their reputed values from a hundred years ago. Such a general process also incurs 'forgetting' as part of the collapse of time: how the Armenian genocide, for example, will be remembered and forgotten in the forthcoming centenary remains to be seen.

Finally, contemporary commemorative politics and culture remain firmly lodged in a 'national imaginary' despite (and again because of) globalization and European integration. This is a very basic point but one that needs stating. The politics of nationalism has a profound impact on the shape of Great War commemoration in each of the countries studied in this volume. In some places, nationalist politics may preclude a deep connection with state narratives, for example as happens in Flanders in relation to the rest of Belgium. In other multinational states, like the United Kingdom, the politics of nationalism and multiculturalism produce state narratives that seek to include an almost impossibly wide national and international group of communities. In England and France, imperial memories intrude on national commemorations. Even in places such as France and Australia where more unitary national narratives exist, commemoration provides an opportunity for the state to endorse values it holds dear. Nationalism, whether 'statist' or 'cultural', still plays a large part in animating and determining the ways we relate to each other as individuals and groups, and how we understand ourselves and our place in the world collectively. Remembrance and commemoration amplify these modes of being. This is certainly partially due to interventions such as government funding of commemorative activity, but it is also shaped by cultural, familial and personal activities and attitudes. One thing remains clear: however enormous the death toll of the Great War, the nation itself was not on the casualty list.

PART I

# War and Memory in a 'Post-national' Era

JOHN HUTCHINSON

# National Commemoration after the 'Second Thirty Years' War'

## Introduction

When analysing Great War commemoration one hundred years after the event, it is difficult not to refer to its successor, since the Second World War arose out of the instabilities created by the Versailles settlement. This chapter will examine if the two world wars can be regarded together as a 'second Thirty Years' War' that has eroded belief in European national identities and enabled the rise of global and regional identities, in which the politics of reconciliation and restitution replaces that of martial *realpolitik*. In many countries the commemorative rituals of the First and Second World Wars are the frame through which the sacrifices of all subsequent wars are recognized. But from another perspective, the wars laid the basis of a post-national world, creating first in the League of Nations, then in 1945 the United Nations, organizations that sought to establish universal norms to regulate disputes within a new global system of nation-states.

To speak of the two world wars as a 'second Thirty Years' War' is to make analogies with the religious conflicts that devastated Central Europe in the seventeenth century. The memory of this catastrophe haunted German nationalist thinkers through the nineteenth century and during the existential conflicts of the two world wars.[1] Historians have assessed this parallel, in considering if the world wars should be viewed as a single

---

1    Kevin Cramer, 'Religious war, German war, total war: the shadow of the Thirty Years' War on German war making in the twentieth century' in Jenny Macleod, ed., *Defeat and Memory* (Basingstoke: Palgrave Macmillan, 2008), 81–95.

interrupted struggle between the great powers for European dominance or as separate conflicts.[2] My purpose, however, is not to enter into a discussion of this historical debate, but to consider if the world wars had a functional equivalence to their predecessor. The fanaticism, huge loss of life and threat to political and social order during Thirty Years' War are generally regarded as generating a moral and political revulsion against religious claims, reflected in the Westphalian settlement that subordinated religion to state imperatives, and later in the Enlightenment project of establishing a civil society and polity founded on rational principles. This analogy raises an interesting question: if twentieth-century wars between the European states produced a similar shift away from national identity, how is national commemoration affected by this today?

I shall address this question by assessing four interrelated claims about the effect of the wars on the generally positive connection made in the nineteenth century between the warfare and European national identities. First, they have produced an antipathy towards nationalism, now perceived as a threat to the peace of Europe. Second, since 1945 technological developments have combined with a general revulsion against war to produce a 'civilianization' of society and a focus on the welfare state as the basis of national cohesion. Third, the world wars resulted in a collapse of European overseas empires and undermined the prestige of Europe in the eyes of its own populations. 'Wars of intervention' in former colonial territories have tended to further corrode a sense of national identity. Finally, the wars have encouraged a postmodernist scepticism about national progress stories. However, after outlining the case for a fundamental shift, I will argue these perspectives are west-Eurocentric and fail to recognize the embedded character of national war memories in popular culture.

2    P. H. M. Bell, *The Origins of the Second World War in Europe* (London: Cambridge University Press, 1986); Michael Howard, 'A Thirty Years' War? The Two World Wars in Historical Perspective', *Transactions of the Royal Historical Society, Sixth Series* 3 (1993), 171–84.

## The end of martial heroism?

Central to many nationalisms is the ritual cult of the fallen hero, who by dying in battle for the nation achieves immortality by being remembered forever.[3] This has been interpreted in Durkheimian terms as socially regenerating, through which the living are bound in obligation to the memory of the dead to sacrifice their individual egos for the collective good of the nation.[4] The cult developed from the late eighteenth century onwards, finding strong early expression in commemorative ceremonies of the French Revolution in which the martial dead were celebrated as 'martyrs'.[5] Some young would-be nation-states have viewed large-scale sacrifice in war as an essential rite of passage, as Americans viewed their Civil War.[6]

However, the cumulative effect of the two world wars may have reversed the positive relationship between war and nation formation. These were total wars that, instead of revitalizing nations, threatened to destroy them.[7] They evoked not a sense of heroic agency, but of anonymous victimhood. In 1914, war became a mass technological phenomenon: static, anonymous and alienating except for the camaraderie of the trenches, and it produced death on an unprecedented scale.[8] The Second World War completed the destruction of the romantic myth by blurring the vital distinction between fighters and civilians in the aerial devastation of cities, the Holocaust and the introduction of (nuclear) armaments that indicated that future wars

3   Reinhart Koselleck, 'War Memorials: Identity Formations of the Survivors', in Reinhart Koselleck, *The Practice of Conceptual History: Timing History, Spacing Concepts* (Stanford: Stanford University Press, 2002), 285–326.
4   Anthony D. Smith, *Chosen Peoples* (Oxford: Oxford University Press, 2003), 23.
5   George Mosse, *Fallen Soldiers* (Oxford: Oxford University Press, 1990), ch. 2.
6   Susan Mary Grant, 'When was the first new nation? Locating America in a national context', in Atsuko Ichijo and Gordana Uzelac, eds, *When is the Nation? Towards an Understanding of Theories of Nationalism* (London: Routledge, 2004), 157–76.
7   Mosse, *Fallen Soldiers*, ch. 4.
8   Christopher Coker, *The Future of War* (Oxford: Blackwell, 2004), 14.

might annihilate nations.[9] Since 1945 there has been a profound revulsion in much of Europe, the birth-place of the nation-state, against nationalism, now blamed for the origins and excesses of these wars.

This has taken several forms. One response was to establish global organizations to prevent conflict between the great powers and contain nationalist tensions within states. After the First World War the League of Nations was established to police treaty agreements and protect the many national minorities in the new states of Central Europe. Its failure and the subsequent outbreak of the Second World War resulted in the founding of the United Nations, as an instrument of global governance, based on universal principles of human rights, to moderate the old *realpolitik* of warring states and prevent crimes against humanity. A second response was the emergence of the European Union as a supranational project to resolve the rivalries of the great nation-*states*, which had triggered the two wars and which were now perceived as threatening the very existence of national *peoples*. Inspired by liberal democratic ideals, the apostles of the EU have dreamed of transcending the nation-state and converting the continent into a zone of peace and democratic progress.[10]

This latter project is supported by historical 'memories', negative and positive. The negative is the evocation of the horrors of the world wars to overcome resistance to the expansion of EU powers at the expense of the states. The positive is the post-1945 success of the EU as the realization of a new international politics of reconciliation, begun by the agreement of two historic rivals, France and Germany, to co-operate in building a new Europe. It has been given concrete form by Germany's willingness to make material and symbolic restitutions to its victims. Bernhard Giesen maintains that trauma has become the basis of a new European identity, and Europe's means of mastering its violent past by rituals of apology and restitution

9    Mosse, *Fallen Soldier*, ch. 4.
10   A. C. d'Appolonia, 'European nationalism and the European Union', in Anthony Pagden, ed., *The Idea of Europe: From Antiquity to the European Union* (Cambridge: Cambridge University Press, 2002), 171–90.

provides a model for overcoming historic conflicts world wide.[11] It offers a more humble and pacific alternative to the militaristic and messianic USA in the global advancement of human rights and democracy. This has led Elazar Barkan to refer to the 'guilt of nations', and to maintain that the emergence of this restitutive politics marks a replacement of martial *realpolitik* by morality in the conduct of international relations.[12]

## Marginalization of the military

The idea of the citizen in arms, forged in the French Revolution, has been a key component of the nation-state and linked to the institution of the mass conscription army.[13] It asserted the duties of citizens to defend the nation. The world wars, as total and people's wars, were a culmination of this principle. However, the First World War also induced a powerful mood of war weariness and pacifism in much of Europe. Although this was countered by fascist movements, the outbreak of the Second World War in 1939 was greeted even by the German population with apprehension. Its consequences were to reinforce a strong anti-war mentality Europe. This mood, combined with technological and organizational revolutions in war-making since the 1940s, has loosened the close relationship between the military and the national collective.

Michael Howard has argued that with the rise of nuclear and high-precision weaponries, the onus of national defence is now imposed on skilled professional militaries rather than mass conscription armies. War

11  Bernhard Giesen, 'The collective identity of Europe: Constitutional practice or community of memory?' in Willfried Spohn and Anna Triandafyllidou, eds, *Europeanisation, National Identities and Migration* (London: Routledge, 2003), 21–35.
12  Elazar Barkan, *The Guilt of Nations* (Baltimore: Johns Hopkins University Press, 2000), xvi.
13  B. R. Posen, 'Nationalism, the Mass Army and Military Power', *International Security* 18/2 (1993), 80–124.

or its prospect no longer provides a source of mass cohesion and states now do not feel the need to nationally mobilize their populations. There has been a general demilitarization of mature western democracies, particularly in Europe, where the welfare state has become the social cement of the democratic nation-state.[14]

The result is a decline in the salience of nationalism, particularly among an educated middle class who were pioneers of the original romantic cult of heroic sacrifice but who are increasingly alienated from the martial values of the past. Modern middle class democracies, it is claimed, are suspicious of military campaigns and casualty averse, all the more so because fertility decline reduces the surplus of young men (and now women) available to fight.[15] Moreover, with the end of empire European states have lost a large source of military conscripts. The First and Second World Wars were imperial as well as national wars. As European societies have turned to a culture of consumerism and individualism, Michael Howard has warned that this is likely to undermine in the long run the morale of a military, committed to hierarchy, discipline and self-sacrifice, as part of a distinctive mission to the nation-state.[16]

## Post-heroic wars?

The effect of the world wars has also been to transform both the context and the character of war. The barbarism of the First World War had shaken the legitimacy of European mandates in the eyes of their colonial peoples

---

14   See Michael Howard, *War in European History* (Oxford: Oxford University Press, 1976), 140–3.

15   Edward Luttwak, 'Towards Post-Heroic Warfare', *Foreign Affairs* 73/4 (1995), 109–20. See also Gil Merom, *How Democracies Lose Small Wars* (Cambridge: Cambridge University Press, 2003).

16   Michael Howard, *The Invention of Peace and the Re-invention of War* (London: Profile Books, 2001), ch. 5.

and in the Second World War the Japanese humiliation of imperial armies in Asia paved the way for a general decolonization after 1945, out of which came the present order of avowedly nation-states. The United Nations, in search of security, sanctified existing state boundaries and prohibited military interference in recognized states except in limited circumstances, thereby robbing nation-states of one of their generating rituals. Yet many of these new states are unstable, and after the end of the Cold War the great powers have been impelled to intervene in failed states that are perceived to be a security threat, since their internal conflicts may overspill to neighbours or they may become a haven for international terrorist groups. To justify military intrusions, the great powers cannot appeal to national civilizing missions as in the nineteenth century. Instead, they must generally now obtain a mandate from a world community justifying their campaigns on universalist principles such as the prevention of human rights violations (notably genocide) or on grounds of international security. The tasks of intervening states and their militaries are now very different, not territorial conquest and glory, but conflict-resolution and peace-keeping.

Most wars since the Second World War, therefore, have a different character and, some argue, require a new 'post-heroic' ethos.[17] Unlike earlier existential conflicts that inspired mass nationalist passions, these are preventative 'wars of choice', fought by professional armies often against local insurgencies. Their 'asymmetrical' character, pitting soldiers against non-uniformed combatants, imposes great strains on the self-disciplines of militaries. The military campaigns are in service of a broader mission of 'peace-keeping' or 'state-building'. Mary Kaldor argues that western states face above all a political rather than a military challenge. The major problem is the breakdown of legitimacy in the zones of war, and we need a new cosmopolitan politics to reconstruct this.[18]

Participating states and their militaries, then, cannot look to nationalist sentiments in order to sustain long-term support for diffuse political

17   Edward Luttwak, 'Towards Post-Heroic Warfare'.
18   Mary Kaldor, *New and Old Wars: Organized Violence in a Global Era* (Cambridge: Polity, 2006), ch. 4.

goals. Many of these wars are fought in former imperial territories and are conducted against the backdrop of postcolonial guilt. This is exacerbated by the increasing diversity of European societies as a result of migration from former colonies in Asia and the Middle East, evoking fears about the loyalty of these new populations when militaries intervene in Muslim lands.

## Demythologizing nations

These changes have, it is asserted, in turn undermined the heroic ethos of war and increasingly transformed the way it is conceived and commemorated. We now live in a global age in which the nation-states have allegedly lost sovereignty and their cultural homogeneity. Their progress stories, embodied in great public monuments to the glorious dead, are being challenged by immigrant communities and national minorities.[19] The focus is on the victims of war, one expression of which is the institutionalization of Holocaust Days, articulating a universalist condemnation of genocides and mass ethnic cleansings.

Paul Fussell found the origins of this shift in the modernist culture of the intellectuals at the time of the First World War, exemplified in the war poets, who conveyed a sense of disillusionment with European civilization.[20] Christopher Coker dates 'de-heroization' to the mechanized mass death of the First World War. The monuments to the Unknown Soldier indicated that with the triumph of industrial technology, war had become agentless. In Britain, Edward Lutyens's Cenotaph to the dead was notably unheroic. Hence soldiers are no longer warriors given individuality and

19    See John Gillis, 'Introduction' in J. Gillis, ed., *Commemorations* (Princeton: Princeton University Press, 1994).
20    Paul Fussell, *The Great War and Modern Memory* (Oxford: Oxford University Press, 1975).

meaning by a shared national *telos* but have become victims.[21] Indeed the pervasive religious symbolism of mass public ceremonies after the two world wars expressed a need to make sense of overwhelming loss rather than a triumphant nationalism.[22] According to Mosse, after the Second World War there was a further shift from a monumental sacralization of the dead towards the utilitarian provision of recreational facilities for the people.[23] The Vietnam Veterans' Memorial wall continued this long-term trend by viewing war through the prism of 'trauma'. The architect of the wall, an Asian-American woman, deliberately rejected masculinist 'phallic' celebratory forms of nationalism to focus on individual mortality and loss. Eschewing a didactic national context, it aimed to encourage an individualistic and constructivist stance to the past that undermines the idea of a moral collective that should be worshipped.[24] This aligns with Winter's thesis about the 'second memory boom' that emerged in the 1970s arising from an awareness of the enormity of the Holocaust and the degree of collaboration in occupied Europe. Whereas the first boom in the later nineteenth century sanctified the emerging mass nation-states, the second boom now focuses on the traumas and losers of history, often crushed by great powers. Whereas once there were national unities, there is now social fragmentation and a proliferation of identity groups.

Recent responses to British military casualties seem to confirm this analysis. In 'homecoming' rituals at Wootton Bassett, a small military town in Wiltshire where coffins draped in Union Jacks process through the main street, participants emphasized the local, communal, 'non-political' and performative character of the occasion. Military press releases set the dead as individuals with close-knit family relationships and loyalties to soldier comrades, and references are conspicuously lacking to any overarching patriotic

---

21 Coker, *The Future of War*.
22 Jay Winter, *Sites of Memory, Sites of Mourning* (Cambridge: Cambridge University Press, 1995), chs 4, 8.
23 Mosse, *Fallen Soldiers*, ch. 10.
24 Jenny Edkins, *Trauma and the Memory of Politics* (Cambridge: Cambridge University Press, 2003), ch. 3.

purpose.[25] For this reason, many have questioned the continued symbolic and emotional resonance of national events such as Remembrance Day.

Although there is force to these claims, they require heavy qualification. I will argue that they are west-Eurocentric, and in many areas of the world nationalism and military commitment remain strong. Western casualty aversion is related to the legitimacy of given wars, not of war itself. Even far distant 'humanitarian' wars, though less likely to obtain popular support, may reinforce a sense of national allegiance. Finally, constructionist perspectives underestimate the extent to which the memories of war are embedded in the practices of everyday life and provide the terrain for the performance of 'sacred' commemorative occasions, which regain their salience at times of crises.

## Varying responses to world wars

Michael Howard, after considering the 'Thirty Years' War' thesis, heavily qualified it. If Hitler had declared victory in 1941, he would have achieved Germany's First World War aims of hegemony in Europe. His decision, however, to attack the USSR and to attempt a racial 'purification' of Europe meant that the Second World War much more than its predecessor was an ideological war, rather than one of great power politics, a total war justified by ultimate values.[26]

Furthermore, much depends not on the experience of mass death and destruction itself, but on the interpretation of it, something that is shaped by the outcome of war. The First World War was more devastating in its losses for the French than for the British people. The conventional depiction in Britain has been of a war of futility and suffering, a view heavily

---

25    Michael Freeden, 'The politics of ceremony: The Wootton Bassett phenomenon', *Journal of Political Ideologies* 16/1 (2011), 1–10; Anthony King, 'The Afghan war and "postmodern" memory: Commemoration and the dead of Helmand', *British Journal of Sociology* 61/1 (2010), 1–25.

26    Howard, 'Thirty Years' War', 182–4.

influenced by the later war poets as noted above. In contrast, in France historians viewed it in more heroic terms, albeit suffused with torment, as an existential war on their own territory that ended with the defeat of the invaders and the recovery of their lost provinces of Alsace and Lorraine.[27] Undoubtedly the continental Western European perception of modern industrial war was coloured by subsequent shared experiences during the Second World War of catastrophic loss, occupation and defeat. It was particularly demoralizing because the continental peoples had to be liberated by external actors. Although General de Gaulle tried to manufacture a redeeming myth of the French Resistance, the sense of humiliation at the defeat and Vichy collaboration was profound.

Although deeply affected by the wars, winners took a different stance. The British (like their US and Soviet allies) invoked the Second World War as a heroic age that justified claiming leadership in world politics and in engaging in military interventions in alliance with the USA, in spite of the loss of Empire and their precipitate military decline. For the nationalities of Central and Eastern Europe the First World War was the midwife of their freedom, and after the collapse of communism, in search for an alternative value system on which to establish the new post-Soviet states, they recalled popular resistance in the Second World War against Germans and Russians in museums of occupation (in Estonia) and commemorative ceremonies (for example of the Warsaw Rising).

In this regard, Western Europe, both in historical terms and as a region in the contemporary world, was peculiar. Its relative pacifism was made possible by the US nuclear umbrella, which maintained an unusually long period of peace in Europe in spite of the Soviet threat. The European rejection of militarism since 1945 also serves as a differentiating device. Its leaders have presented themselves as having a continued civilizing role in the world, via a European Union that employs soft power in contrast to the USA in advancing human rights and democracy. The European peculiarity, however, may not last as we move into an increasingly unstable, multi-polar world.

27    Jay Winter and Antoine Prost, *The Great War in History* (Cambridge: Cambridge University Press, 2005), vii.

## The loss of military virtues and contemporary wars

What of arguments that the decline of conscription is both a cause and an index of the marginalization of military virtues in the life of the nation-state? If we examine the experience of the nineteenth century, supposedly the classic era of the nation-state, we find the institution of conscription as mired in controversy. The imposition of conscription in peace time could provoke strong local resistance in parts of France, and traditionally, in Britain the institution of a permanent standing army was perceived to be a threat to the liberties of the nation.

Although the horrors of war did induce an anti-militarist mood in Europe, in time of war what gives status or otherwise to armed services is not their particular formation but whether conflicts are perceived to be legitimate. In the age of nationalism, to gain consent politicians almost invariably justify wars as defensive.[28] Wars that are perceived to be imperialist are problematic, especially when they run into trouble. Where there are national disagreements about the legitimacy of a war, attempts to impose conscription reinforce cleavages. Hence during the Vietnam War, the draft itself became an object of divisions as in Australia in 1916–17. Indeed, the Vietnam controversies resulted in the US government abandoning the draft in favour of a professional volunteer army. This raises questions about how foreign military missions in the contemporary period can be sustained if traditional war cults are possibly outmoded and whether the maintenance of international law and humanitarian ideals can inspire military sacrifice and popular backing for the foreign interventions that typify the warfare of developed states today.

In practice, universalist goals (such as the prevention of genocide) are too frail to galvanize long term sacrifice on the part of troops and populations. Such aims are necessary to legally justify military interventions. But

---

28    P. C. Stern, 'Why do people sacrifice for their nations?' in John Comaroff and Paul Stern, eds, *Perspectives on Nationalism and War* (Amsterdam: Gordon and Breach Publishers, 1995).

effective campaigns are made by coalitions of *nation*-states which are able to mobilize support among their population by appeals to national interests, ideal and material. The opacity of many international missions (to engage in 'state-building' or more broadly still in 'nation-building') has created difficulties for soldiers, especially when they find themselves engaged in asymmetric warfare that has inevitably produced large-scale civilian casualties. A source of public and military concern is how to prevent soldiers, trained to be disciplined killers in conventional rule-governed combat, from morally degenerating when faced with non-uniformed adversaries employing unrestrained violence.

Recently, these problems have been faced by US and British troops in Iraq and Afghanistan, where excesses erode both military discipline and the justifications for the interventions made to the national publics. Those, like Kaldor, who consider the military as emissaries of a cosmopolitan political project look for solutions in an extension of *universal* legal and human rights norms into the battlefield. Christopher Coker, however, has argued that rationally-based external strategies to regulate the conduct of soldiers in battle zones will always break down in stress situations. To be effective, norms have to be internalized in *particular* codes of honour, and militaries are increasingly seeking these in ancient martial sources.[29] These are likely also to be shaped by the norms of the national community they serve.

In practice, the stresses of the military in such difficult combat zones are recognized by the public. These foreign missions have become increasingly unpopular, more so in Europe and less in the USA, where the 9/11 attacks enabled governments to depict the Afghan campaigns in defensive terms. But criticism is directed more at politicians rather than the armed forces who are depicted as 'victims' of ill thought out government policies. Although there may be reactions against the government or even the state, popular sympathy for the predicaments of the armed services means that soldiers can be pictured simultaneously as victims of the state and heroes of the nation.

---

29    Christopher Coker, *The Warrior Ethos* (London: Routledge, 2007), ch.7.

## The end of nationalist memorialization?

This may indicate there has been a significant shift in public memorialization of war, from national celebration to mourning and a sense of victimhood. Undoubtedly, the Holocaust has turned the focus onto the victims of war, even if memories of the Holocaust have been used by Israeli politicians to justify their domestic and foreign policies. However, we should not exaggerate this historic turn. A concern for the losers of history can be found in early romanticism, and trauma and catastrophe have been frequently been used by nationalists to justify claims to independence and territorial rights.

Nevertheless, the charge is that the character of national memorialization has indeed changed, that war has lost its power to sacralize and substantiate the nation as a moral collectivity and that there has been a concomitant rejection of monumental and official 'didactic' occasions exemplified by First World War commemorations in favour of a more individualistic and diffuse memorialization. Although the pervasive religious symbolism of mass public commemorations after the two world wars expressed a need to make sense of overwhelming loss rather than a triumphal nationalism, such symbolism (in France, the iconographical cult of St Joan, and in England the images of the village graveyard) often contained strong national connotations. The willingness of large numbers of people to come together to mourn and to support permanent memorials to the war dead inevitably implied that the suffering was common rather than simply individual or sectional.[30] Moreover, the siting of monuments like the Cenotaph in the political heart of the national capital and later of the Vietnam Veterans' Memorial close to the Washington and Lincoln monuments inevitably gave them a national significance. Even the Vietnam memorial, whose design avoided the national, increasingly took on such meaning as heroic statuary was added and when national flags and personal messages were left on the

---

30  John Hutchinson, 'Warfare and the sacralisation of nations: the meanings, rituals and politics of national remembrance', *Millennium: Journal of International Studies* 38/2 (2009), 412.

monument by individual mourners.[31] Indeed, by recognizing the sacrifice of soldiers in a war previously viewed with deep ambivalence, it came to be seen as a necessary instrument of national reconciliation.

Such memorials have become foci for collective mourning that are both national and individual although not always personal. It may be that ceremonies in Wootton Bassett in England for the returning dead from Afghanistan and Iraq may express a local and depoliticized form of homage. In fact, the regular televising of the Wootton Bassett processions made them national as well as local events to the extent that they attracted 'pilgrims' from far and wide. Visits by Prince Charles and the renaming of the town as Royal Wootton Bassett is evidence of the local and demotic being absorbed into the public iconography of the nation-state.[32] Such combination of local pride and national allegiance is far from new. The development of the Nelson cult after 1805 came from below, promoted by middle class patriots in rising regional ports such as Liverpool, Glasgow, and Edinburgh, dependent on the navy's control of the seas.[33] Although some British officers have expressed concern at what they perceive as a process of 'Diana-ization', that is 'excessive' popular mourning of the dead as 'victims', such emotions may arise because of confusion about the validity of the war rather than of the nation and state for which it is fought. As the language of the popular press testifies, there is a popular thirst for heroes, although this heroism may be couched in varied terms.

The great public commemorations of the dead of long gone wars retain their power not just despite, but rather because of the secular changes in contemporary societies. Concern was expressed that institutions such as Remembrance Day in Britain and Anzac Day in Australia would wither as the last survivors of the First World War disappeared, but the awareness of the increasingly fragile physical links brought a resurgence of popularity. One reason for their persistence is that they are 'revitalized' by blood and

31    Edkins, *Trauma and the Memory of Politics*, 78, 86.
32    Freeden, 'The politics of ceremony', 4, 6, 7.
33    J. MacKenzie, 'Nelson goes global: The Nelson myth in Britain and beyond' in David Cannadine, ed., *Admiral Lord Nelson: Context and Legacy* (Houndsmill: Palgrave Macmillan, 2005), 148–9.

sacrifice of the dead of subsequent wars. This of course begs the question of why their commemorative repertoire still seems appropriate as a vehicle through which the public pays homage to the military dead, in the way that commemorations of Waterloo or Trafalgar, for example, do not.

Such public ceremonies 'work' because they are underpinned by a popular awareness of the events to which they refer. They rest on the everyday mnemonic activities in national life. There are many bridging mechanisms at work in social practices, whereby a martial past is channelled into the present.[34] In Britain there is a never-ending thirst for documentaries, comedies and fictional stories about the two world wars. Images of the great events of war – of the Blitz, Dunkirk and El Alamein are regularly cited by politicians to justify policies and mobilize support, and journalists 'playfully' evoke memories of 'the Huns' on the eve of sporting occasions featuring the Germans. In Australia, Prime Minister Paul Keating linked the 'betrayals' of Gallipoli (vividly depicted in Peter Weir's film of 1981) and of Singapore to subsequent repudiations of British obligations to Australia in order to justify his republican stance. In the banal nationalism of daily life the images of war provide a store of meaning through which individuals and communities reflect on the everyday problems of their lives. This provides the soil in which public commemorations live.

There is a deeper reason for why such national commemorations persist during periods of extensive social change. Collective identities rest on a sense of common history, one that tells individuals who they are, from where they come and where they are going. National commemorative days, in so far as they are calendrical, give a 'natural' rhythm to a national life, and are a way of overcoming the attrition of time. Wars can be foundational events of nations or mark 'critical junctures', and hence operate as major reference points for populations. Their power may rest not just on the events and the memory of the sacrifices with which they are associated but on perceptions of their broader consequences. In much of Europe the First World War ushered in the mass democratic nation-state and it can be viewed as dividing line that ushered in much of the modern world. The

34    Eviatar Zerubavel, *Time Maps* (Chicago: University of Chicago Press, 2003), ch. 2.

Second World War is invoked to support British pretensions to remain a world actor (with a seat on the UN Security Council) in spite of its relative decline as a great power.

Finally, wars are recalled because of the unpredictability of the modern world, in which many states and their populations have been periodically subject to crises. At these points, populations are forced regularly to consider *existential* questions of who they are and what they stand for. Inevitably, leaders and intellectuals are drawn to consider the relevance of the stock of older myth-images, where they are available, in order to reformulate programmes and mobilize populations in defence of the nation. 'Memories' of great crises such as war that the collectivity has faced and overcome in the past are then invoked to provide hope and lessons for their future.

## Conclusion

In this chapter I have argued that the modes of war commemoration have indeed changed since the end of the Great War to incorporate a sense of the tragedies of war. This can be related to changes in the nature of war itself, in global politics and a new focus on the individual. In the developed west, the military is now a professional minority, as opposed to the mass conscript armies deployed in the first half of the twentieth century and maintained during the Cold War. Europe's empires have gone and structures of global governance have challenged, although certainly in no way superseded, the nation-state in Europe and beyond. Importantly, the commemoration of 'wars of choice' since 1945 presents a more complex and ambiguous notion of heroism that, although valorizing individual sacrifice, rejects didactic nationalism and may also view the dead at times as 'victims'.

Nonetheless, large scale and public commemoration still plays an important role on the perpetuation of national identities in many countries, particularly in periods of crisis when they offer inspiration to populations facing existential challenges. Therefore, whilst acknowledging a fundamental shift in the global political context of commemorative activity, an important qualification is in order. Memory and commemoration are deployed by states in times of uncertainty as restatements of national values, designed to provide reassuring lessons for citizens. Given this purpose, and despite the dislocating effects of the 'Second Thirty Years' War' from which contemporary commemoration emerged, national memory and national commemorations will continue to be valued by governments and consumed by citizens.

BEN WELLINGS

# Lest You Forget: Memory and Australian Nationalism in a Global Era

## Introduction

The central contention of this chapter is that Great War commemoration in Australia is conditioned by globalization, although in ways that have yet to be fully explored. This hypothesis is a result of analysing Anzac via the lens of nationalism studies and rests upon an understanding of nationalism as a phenomenon that was and is generated by change rather than continuity. This being said, in periods of accelerated change, elements of continuity are necessary to provide a form of stability during times of dislocation and novelty. Thus memory, or more specifically acts of collective remembrance, provide that element of stability in developed countries in the so-called global era.

Australia is no exception. With the development of policies designed to facilitate and enhance a set of practices referred to as 'globalization', the past thirty years in Australia have been years of persistent and accelerated change. In this context, new national narratives were articulated as political projects designed to link state and citizen at a moment when that relationship was undergoing fundamental revision. Of all the visions of nationhood set out in this period – multiculturalism, republicanism, Reconciliation – it was 'Anzac' that became the dominant form of Australian nationalism by the beginning of the twenty-first century. This version of Australian nationalism links a foundational moment during the Great War with a repertoire of what are promoted as enduring national values. What we might call Anzac nationalism, however, has become much more than this. Part of the success of Anzac since the early 1990s has been related not just to changes within Australia domestically, but to the utility of Australia's participation in the Great War as a tool of international 'middle power' diplomacy. These are the dual foundations underpinning the basic argument of this chapter: that the promotion of Anzac nationalism and the public remembrance of the Great War since the 1990s is a response to the accelerated change brought about by globalization. Despite suggesting a comforting continuity of national values over the past century, the most recent manifestations of Great War memory and Anzac nationalism are in fact the products of globalization and change.

## Memory, nationalism and globalization

Nationalism and globalization have often being conceptualized as antithetical phenomena. Certain important historical developments from the end of the Second World War helped to give this idea some force. The rise of economic and military superpowers, the strain on the Westphalian state system and the apparent high water mark of liberation nationalisms in the Third World led some observers to conclude by the end of the 1980s that the age of nationalism was at an end.[1] These trends were compounded by the adoption of neo-liberalism in the developed west and the eventual triumph of this political ideology in the former Soviet bloc and the global South from the 1990s. From this vantage point the beginning of what was increasingly referred to as the 'global' era automatically spelled the end of the nationalist one. This conclusion was, however, premature.

---

1    For such ideas, contrast the first and second editions of Benedict Anderson's *Imagined Communities: Reflections on the Origins and Spread of Nationalism* from 1983 and 1991 respectively; Eric Hobsbawm famously wrote off nationalism in 1990 in *Nations and Nationalism since 1780* (Cambridge: Cambridge University Press, 1990).

More recent scholarship has stressed the compatibility between the two phenomena.[2] Kim Huynh has argued that 'in an increasingly globalized world national identity will continue to fulfill a deep need in people to belong and to be recognized as belonging – to a place, a moment, a culture'.[3] The value of such structural understandings of nationalism is that they correctly locate the source of nationalism not in cultural *continuity* but in social, political and economic *change*. Thus nationalism was and remains a political response to economic, social and political disruption and dislocation, even if it presents itself as expressing the timeless, durable essence of a particular collectivity.

In this context, the past became a crutch that could support individuals and communities being brought – often unwillingly – into these new global structures. For Anthony Smith this was one of the reasons that nations came into existence: pre-modern *ethnies* were forged into modern nations during the transition to modernity.[4] Tom Nairn illustrated the link between the past and the present in nationalism when he argued the following:

> [...] It is through nationalism that societies try to propel themselves forward to certain kinds of goals (industrialisation, prosperity, equality with other peoples, etc.) *by a certain sort of regression* – by looking inwards, drawing more deeply on their indigenous resources, resurrecting past folk-heroes and myths about themselves and so on.[5]

Such analysis helped establish the origins of the era of nationalism (as distinct from the origins of nations) in the period of accelerated social, political and economic change of modernity. Thus if we consider globalization to be 'the intensification of connections between different parts of

2    See Claire Sutherland, *Nationalism in the Twenty-first Century* (Basingstoke: Palgrave, 2011); and Daphne Halikiopoulou and Sophia Vasilopoulou, eds, *Nationalism and Globalization* (Abingdon: Routledge, 2011).

3    Kim Huynh, 'Us and Them: National Identity and the Question of Belonging', in Jim George and Kim Huynh, eds, *The Culture Wars: American and Australian Politics in the Twenty-first Century* (South Yarra: Palgrave Macmillan Australia, 2009), 76.

4    Anthony Smith, *The Ethnic Origins of Nations* (London: Blackwell, 1986).

5    Tom Nairn, *The Break-up of Britain: Crisis and Neo-nationalism* (London: Verso, 1981), 348.

the world *and* our increasing consciousness of this development', then we can see that what has been labeled as 'globalization' since the 1990s has a far longer provenance than is commonly admitted.[6] The important point here is that the generation and continuation of nationalism as a historical phenomenon is linked to global processes of change. As long as change remains a feature of human society, nationalism is unlikely to disappear.

This emphasis on change and dislocation suggests reasons why nationalism has not withered amidst the latest round of globalization. Far from receding into political history, changes that we associate with globalization such as increased population flows, the triumph of the lightly regulated market economy and the self-proclaimed weakening of the state in certain areas of activity have led to the persistence of nationalist politics in the developed west. Policies introduced to bring about 'globalization' since the 1980s have seen a return to the type of changes associated with the liberal political economy that helped generate the first round of nationalism associated with the transition to modernity. Importantly, we should not see nationalism in the past or present as aberrant, a political phenomenon that happens 'elsewhere' and only outside the developed west. As Jonathan Hearn notes, nationalism can be characterized as 'routinized nationalism'. Hearn argues that liberal democracies 'do not so much transcend nationalism, as domesticate it, routinizing its dynamic, by channelling it through core political institutions'.[7] When it comes to contemporary nationalism in the developed west, he continues:

> [...] What is at stake is contending visions of how a population within a given territory should be governed, and such visions are normally underwritten by a certain conception of the population's common *identity*, embodied in shared beliefs and values [...] The state must continually reach down into this process of contentious national identity-building in order to renew its legitimacy.[8]

6    Graham Day and Andrew Thompson, *Theorizing Nationalism* (Basingstoke: Palgrave, 2004), 170.
7    Jonathan Hearn, *Rethinking Nationalism: A Critical Introduction* (Basingstoke: Palgrave, 2006), 166.
8    Hearn, *Rethinking Nationalism*, 167.

Thus if we understand nationalism as a political ideology that plays a key role in the legitimization of sovereignty in the modern era whilst at the same time politicizing 'culture', then we can understand how national narratives provide an ideational means by which the state is linked with its citizens.[9] This political task, however, has been given extra urgency in the last thirty years. During the era of neo-liberal globalization, governments in western democracies were keen to draw voters' attention to large areas of previous state activity in which they perceived themselves no longer qualified to govern.[10] As Helen Thompson puts it, 'the political corollary of the practical diminution of the state by the reality of globalization and of the contingent eclipse of the state by the narrative of globalization was the state as the suppressor of the expectations of its citizens'.[11] This 'hollowing out' of the state had an impact on the relationship between the nation-state and its citizens. Thus the accelerated change associated with globalization required new (or renewed) integrating myths to bind the citizen to the *self-weakened state*.

In this historical context, memory and collective remembrance became a link that helped bind the state and citizen and at the same time helped legitimize novel political projects of the elite. Linking nation and memory helped ease the shock of the accelerated change and sense of dislocation associated with neo-liberal globalization. This perspective can help explain the concomitant official emphasis on 'identity' and the so-called 'second memory boom', both of which correlated to the latest round of globalization. Rod Kedward described the development of this public memory in France in the 1980s, but it also applied throughout developed countries:

> In the last third of the [twentieth] century an active national memory was acknowledged to be a necessity. It was neither neutral nor innocent. It could carry exculpation

---

9    Ben Wellings, *English Nationalism and Euroscepticism: Losing the Peace* (Oxford: Peter Lang, 2012), ch. 1.

10   Colin Hay, *Why We Hate Politics* (Cambridge: Polity Press, 2007).

11   Helen Thompson, 'The Character of the State' in Colin Hay, ed., *New Directions in Political Science: Responding to the Challenges of an Interdependent World* (Basingstoke: Palgrave, 2010), 133.

or recrimination [...] From psychoanalysts to historians, the process of memory was linked to recovery of the repressed, to facing trauma at a personal or national level, to therapeutic and cathartic outcomes.[12]

But to therapeutic and cathartic we might also add 'soporific'. History, in its political guises, can act as both a stimulant and a depressant. By the term 'history', I do not mean the method of inquiry into events and phenomena that have taken place previously, but rather the past as a source of political mobilization (history as a stimulant) or as a source of political quietude (history as a depressant). In either case, the political function of a collective and widespread understanding of the past is to induce some sort of action or inaction as part of a legitimizing narrative or in pursuit of a particular political goal. This function operates by weakening potential counter-arguments or framing the national world-view to such an extent that questions are not asked in the first place. As John Brueilly argues, a view of the past associated with a naturalized view of the nation 'does not take the form of explicit historical argument. Indeed, *argument* is the last thing such a view needs'.[13]

In sum, nationalism was and is the product of 'global' forces that are commonly understood as knowing no national borders. Although a specific nationalism manifests itself in particular forms, each one is part of a global system, in which memory of the past is drawn upon to ease the community through the travails of the present. This leads us to a consideration of Australian nationalism in a global era and the relationship between nationalism and globalization to Great War remembrance in contemporary Australia.

---

12    Rod Kedward, *La Vie en Bleu: France and the French since 1900* (London: Penguin Books, 2004), 622.
13    John Brueilly, 'Introduction' in Susana Carvahlo and François Gemenne, eds, *Nations and Their Histories: Constructions and Representations* (Basingstoke: Palgrave, 2009), 20.

## Nationalism and globalization in Australia

The causal link between nationalism and globalization is just as important in Australia as elsewhere. Unusually for the Anglophone world, the policies designed to advance globalization were first of all adopted by what had been a centre-left party, the Australian Labor Party (ALP). The promotion of these policies within Australia required the ALP to repudiate class as a basis of government and electoral support and to seek votes from a broader constituency. It had a further effect too. As Paul Kelly argued, the promotion of globalization 'saw the demise of the post-Federation "Australian settlement" and the struggle to identify a replacement credo'.[14]

This 'Australian settlement' had existed from the time of the federation of the Australian colonies in 1901. Domestically, it involved state paternalism, wage arbitration allowing for the male working wage to support a wife and children and tariff protection for Australian industry. Internationally, it rested upon imperial benevolence: Australia was federated under the auspices of the British Empire. From the Second World War this imperial bond was augmented and eventually replaced by an alliance with the United States, leading to Australian involvement in the wars in Southeast Asia in the 1960s and 1970s. Sitting between the domestic and the international was the so-called 'White Australia Policy', which until the latter half of the 1960s determined that population inflows to Australia were predominantly either British, Irish or other (white) European.

This latter policy in particular played a crucial part in the way that Australian nationhood was constructed. It was seen at the time as an indispensible foundation for the operation of liberal democracy and the way that Australian nationality and citizenship were related to other nations and nationalities. The erosion of this social and political compact had important effects on the content of nationalism in Australia. The first effect was attempts – official and popular – to find new and alternative narratives to replace the certainties formerly provided by the 'Australian settlement'.

14    Paul Kelly, 'Labor and Globalization' in Robert Manne, ed., *The Australian Century: Political Struggle in the Building of a Nation* (Melbourne: Text Publishing, 2000), 224.

Of these new narratives, three were particularly associated with the Hawke-Keating era of Labor government (1983–96). These were multi-culturalism, republicanism and the process of 'Reconciliation' (including indigenous–settler relations more generally). However, the translation of these political arguments and narratives into policies did not go uncontested. This political contestation had two distinct but related expressions: one popular and the other official, although the two were linked to each other. The outcome of such painful contestation was a retreat into a politics of war memory and commemoration that appeared safe from the political partisanship that became a feature of multiculturalism, republicanism and Reconciliation.

The first of these protests against the identity politics of the Hawke-Keating years was known as 'Hansonism' after the leader of this national-popular political movement. Pauline Hanson's brief foray into formal politics was not as significant as her overall impact on policy direction in Australia in the late 1990s and after. Although best known for her fear that Australia was 'in danger of being swamped by Asians' and that a type of 'reverse racism' applied in Australia to the benefit of Aboriginals, multicul-turalists and other minority interest groups, Hansonism was also a critique of globalization in Australia.[15] 'If this government wants to be fair dinkum', argued Hanson in her Maiden Speech to the Australian Parliament in 1996, 'then it must stop kowtowing to financial markets, international organi-zations, world bankers, investment companies and big business people'.[16] Later, Hanson went even further. Seeking to downplay accusations of racism, she wrote:

> Ordinary Australians do have a common enemy, but it is not Aborigines, Asians or people of any particular colour, race or creed. Our common oppressors are a class of raceless, placeless, cosmopolitan elites who are exercising almost absolute power over us; like black spiders above the wheels of industry they are spinning the webs of our destiny.[17]

---

15    Pauline Hanson, *The Truth: On Immigration, the Aboriginal Question, the Gun Debate and the Future of Australia* (Ipswich, QLD: P. Hanson, 1997), 3–7.

16    Hanson, *The Truth*, 8.

17    Hanson, *The Truth*, 155.

Given that this was a critique of the bipartisan consensus that had taken hold around neo-liberal globalization in Australia and a threat to Liberal-National coalition support in particular, this attack demanded some response from the incoming coalition Prime Minister, John Howard. Winning power in March 1996, Howard quickly moved to end what he portrayed as a 'perpetual seminar' on identity, history and Australia's place in the world.[18] This meant defeating republicanism (achieved at the referendum in November 1999) and pushing Reconciliation into more 'practical' as opposed to symbolic outcomes. This was what Carol Johnson referred to as 'the revenge of the mainstream', allowing Howard to emphasize an overall sense of crisis in order to pursue a politics of reassurance.[19]

Anzac was central to this 'politics of reassurance'. In placing war commemoration at the centre of Australian nationalism from 1996 onwards, Howard was advantaged in three main ways. Firstly, by 2001 the other main contenders for the core of Australian nationalism (multiculturalism, republicanism and Reconciliation) had been defeated or neutralized. Secondly, Paul Keating had already prepared some of the groundwork for the popularization of war commemoration, although the Labor Prime Minister had mobilized such commemoration in support of republicanism and 'Asian engagement'. Lastly this bipartisan approach, when combined with the sacrality of the dead and the mute force of their sacrifice, made it very difficult for a political critique of Anzac nationalism to emerge.[20] This became increasingly apparent once the period in question coincided with increased active deployments of Australian troops overseas noticeably in East Timor, Afghanistan and Iraq, as well as the politics associated with the 'war on terror'. The result of this was that by the first decade of the twenty-first century, Anzac nationalism was the dominant means by which Australians were encouraged to explain their national values to each other and increasingly to present themselves to the rest of the world.

18  Cited in Huynh, *The Culture Wars*, 82.
19  Carol Johnson, *Governing Change: Keating to Howard* (St Lucia, QLD: University of Queensland Press, 2000), 7.
20  Marilyn Lake and Henry Reynolds with Mark McKenna and Joy Damousi, *What's Wrong with Anzac? The Militarisation of Australian History* (Sydney: New South Publishing, 2010).

## Internationalizing Australian nationalism

Anzac nationalism thus appeared to have the capacity to contain potentially conflicting narratives of national belonging as well as being an identity project that politicians of both major parties were comfortable promoting. In this way, Great War commemoration in Australia was part of a wider pattern that Anna Clark has referred to as 'an increasingly strategic use of the past by politicians in recent years'.[21] But again, it is possible to go further in this analysis. These Australian narratives were not formed in isolation but were part of a wider process of remembering the Great War and twentieth-century conflict more generally. Thus not all of the reasons for the rise and eventual dominance of Anzac nationalism were domestic. Structural changes in globalized economies facilitated and encouraged Australian engagement with other parts of the world and so indirectly helped to sustain Anzac nationalism in Australia in two notable ways.

The first way that globalization impacted on Anzac nationalism was via new emphases in knowledge production in regions that were of historical importance to Australia's collective remembrance of the Great War, not least Europe and in particular northern France. Advances in European integration therefore provided an important context for a renewed focus on the history and memory of the Great War, developments that ultimately drew Australia into this new round of knowledge production and collective remembrance. Jay Winter noted:

> Due to the emergence of trans-national networks in many fields in Europe in the 1970s and 1980s, reinforcing economic and political trends expressed in the Maastricht Treaty of 1992 [...] historians' attention turned to the massive shock of European *dis*integration in 1914.[22]

21    Anna Clark, 'Politicians Using History', *Australian Journal of Political Science* 56/1 (2010), 120.
22    Jay Winter, 'On Regarding the Pain of Others' in *The Collections of the Historial of the Great War* (Paris: Somogy, 2008), 34.

At the European level, this renewed emphasis on the Great War – both political and historical – helped reinforce important ideological justifications for European integration whilst permitting and demanding the increased transmission of collective memories of the War. As Jack Lang, the French culture and education minister argued in 1999, there was 'a need to stress unifying events and factors which have put Europe together, as well as the great forming elements – be they happy, such as the fall of the Berlin Wall, or difficult and controversial, such as the First World War'.[23] Admittedly, from the perspective of the beginning of the twenty-first century, the remembrance of the First World War was impossible without simultaneously remembering the Second: the two conflicts having become in collective memory 'a new unit, a kind of second Thirty Years' War', an ideological development increasingly necessary to underpin the deepening project of European integration.[24] In Europe as in Australia, global change was driving the need for new forms of identification linking the citizen and the state. Via official and people-to-people engagement, Australia became increasingly involved in this renewed European memory from the early 1990s.

Another way that change overseas impacted on Australian remembrance of the Great War was the growth of so-called 'trench tourism'. This dimension to the formation of collective memory can be regarded as the second wave of such 'pilgrimage' following from the first in the 1920s.[25] The development of the tourist capacity of the Somme was part of a wider process of Great War commemoration and tourism and was an innovation with its origins in the 1980s. Recalling his time as a teacher in the region in the 1950s, French historian Jean-Jacques Becker noted that he could not recall 'the memory of this war, which had hit the region so hard, being in any way a major concern of its inhabitants, or attracting any great number

---

23  Jack Lang, 'Pro-Europe with Passion' in Haus der Geschichte der Bundesrepublik, *The Culture of European History in the 21st Century* (Berlin: Nicolai, 1999), 48.

24  Peter Stadler, 'War and Peace' in Haus der Geschichte der Bundesrepublik, *The Culture of European History in the 21st Century* (Berlin: Nicolai, 1999), 101.

25  Bruce Scates, *Return to Gallipoli. Walking the Battlefields of the Great War* (Cambridge: Cambridge University Press, 2006).

of visitors'. He concluded: 'If "war tourism" was appropriate in the region, then the trend still had to be created'.[26]

The creation of just such a local tourist industry (helping to create what Jay Winter has referred to as the 'second memory boom')[27] had its origins in the economic change occurring in the Somme region in the 1970s and 1980s. Part of the cause for this was a political initiative to generate new sources of income in a region of relative economic decline. The development of the Historial of the Great War in Péronne (opened in 1992) and its associated Visitors' Centre at Thiepval (opened in 2004) were part of an overall strategy aimed at reasserting the place of the Somme region in the collective remembrance of the Great War in France at a time when Verdun dominated the national imagination. It was also a means of addressing an economic imbalance within the Region whereby the eastern Somme attracted far fewer visitors than its western, coastal half.[28]

Thus tourism was increasingly replacing the previous emphasis on textiles, farming and light industry as the economic bedrock of the department. Gary Hutchinson has written that the present-day 'Western Front is a highly organized and competitive tourist operation in France and Belgium'[29] and one which has an impact on the ways in which the Australian national past is generated and remembered. The Somme region itself boasts the Somme Battlefield Partners, being a network of 175 accommodation providers, *restauranteurs*, tourism offices, guides and taxi drivers who are versed in the history of the battles and the region.[30] This local economic shift drew Australians to this part of the world in increasing numbers,[31] and offered

26    Jean-Jacques Becker, 'The Origins of the Historial' in *The Collections of the Historial of the Great War* (Paris: Somogy, 2008), 31.
27    Jay Winter, *Remembering War: The Great War Between Memory and History in the Twentieth Century* (London: Yale University Press, 2006).
28    Becker, 'The Origins of the Historial'.
29    Gary Hutchinson, *Pilgrimage: A Traveller's Guide to Australia's Battlefields* (Melbourne: Black Inc, 2006), 154.
30    Comité de Tourisme de la Somme, *The Somme Guide* (Amiens: Comité de Tourisme de la Somme, 2012).
31    Caroline Winter, 'Commemoration of the Great War on the Somme: exploring personal connections', *Journal of Tourism and Cultural Change* 10/3 (2012), 248–63.

them ways of reaffirming narratives heard at home in an international context. Attendance at Anzac Day Dawn Services and *son et lumière* shows at Pozières were pre-promoted as 'moments of intense emotion',[32] echoing McKenna and Ward's argument about the scripted sentimentality of attendance and performance at such events.[33] The national importance of the events of 1918 were also emphasized in tourist guides, claiming the region as an important location in the development of Australian nationhood: 'Paradoxically, however, it was Australia's participation in the First World War and her own terrible losses which became a contributing factor in this birth of a nation',[34] thus reflecting Australian narratives back at Australians and other English-speakers visiting the sites.

The growth of such tourism provided governments with an opportunity to create new links between state and citizen. Responding to this growing tourist facilitation and engagement was increased official interest in commemorative activities in northern France and Belgium. Thus these commemorative sites also became the location of significant diplomatic activity. The Anzac Centenary Commission recognized the likelihood that the number of people wishing to attend Anzac Day services at Gallipoli in 2015 would exceed the capacity of the site, and recommended that the Australian government begin planning for improved access with the New Zealand and Turkish governments.[35] Another strategy was to open up and renovate other sites to accommodate the expected interest. Villers-Bretonneux in the Somme was one such site, and the Australian Remembrance Trail extending from France into Belgium was another.[36]

32　Comité de Tourisme de la Somme, *The Somme Guide*, 29.

33　Mark McKenna and Stuart Ward, 'It Was Really Moving, Mate', *Australian Historical Studies* 38/129 (2007), 141–51. See also Shanti Sumartojo in this volume.

34　Comité de Tourisme de la Somme, *Visitor's Guide to the Battlefield* (Amiens: Comité de Tourisme de la Somme, 2012).

35　National Commission on the Commemoration of the Anzac Centenary, *How Australia May Commemorate the Anzac Centenary* (Canberra: Department of Veterans' Affairs, 2011), 15.

36　See chapters by Romain Fathi and Shanti Sumartojo, respectively, in this volume for detailed analyses of these sites.

The recent history of Australian engagement at these sites shows the second way that Anzac nationalism was influenced and reinforced by global change. Other examples of commemorative diplomacy such as the statue building of the 1990s in France, the opening of the Australian War Memorial in Hyde Park Corner in 2003 and the dedication of a new Commonwealth War Grave at Fromelles in 2010 illustrated the way that commemorative diplomacy could act as sympathetic 'mood music' for wider diplomatic initiatives. On Anzac Day in 2011, Australian Foreign Minister Kevin Rudd attended the Dawn Service at Villers-Bretonneux and a subsequent wreath-laying ceremony at the Australian Memorial Park in Bullecourt. The content of these commemorations illustrated how Anzac-inspired narratives could be used to further diplomatic ends, much as Billy Hughes had done at Versailles in 1919, using the memory of Australia's war dead in aid of diplomatic goals. This diplomatic use of Anzac also contributed to its internationalization, exposing it further to the forces of globalization and bending the Anzac narrative to its needs. Rudd's attendance at these ceremonies was book ended with participation at the NATO foreign ministers' meeting in Berlin the week before and culminated in official business in Paris ahead of the Cannes G20 summit scheduled for October 2011.[37] On 27 April he gave a speech on the G20 at the Europe American Press Club in Paris. Noting the role of international relations scholars in highlighting 'the merging of the historically discreet domains of the "national" and the "international"; the "internal" and the "external"; the "local" and the "global"', Rudd argued that:

> What this means for all of us, therefore, whether we are French or Australian, whether we are in Europe or whether we are in Asia, is that the challenges of global governance, multilateral governance, or what is sometimes called mini-lateral governance, are now more acute than ever before in human history.[38]

---

37    Australia was permitted to attend these meetings given the deployment of Australian troops alongside NATO in Afghanistan.
38    Kevin Rudd, 'The Future of the G20', Speech at the European American Press Club, Paris, 27 April 2011.

In this context, the value of commemorative diplomacy was enhanced as it facilitated relations between countries that had been bound up in the conflicts of the twentieth century. During his speech at Bullecourt on Anzac Day, Rudd stressed Australia's contribution to forums of global governance (seen as the best means of enhancing Australia's middle-power status) and explicitly linked current Australian military and diplomatic activity around the globe to the Anzac narrative, emphasizing that such activity was fundamentally about nothing less than 'our continued national meaning and national purpose as Australia.'[39]

## Conclusions

Nationalism must be seen fundamentally as a response to change. However it is a response that emphasizes continuity in order to legitimize novel political projects associated with the dislocations caused by accelerated change. The dismantling of the 'Australian settlement' exposed Australia to just such dislocations. Domestically, Anzac was well placed to provide a sense of continuity with the past and to cohere a sense of nationality where other projects, namely multiculturalism, republicanism and Reconciliation, proved politically divisive. Externally, Anzac became a useful supplement to Australia's middle power diplomacy as increasing numbers of Australians were drawn to sites in Western Europe by structural changes taking place within and outside Australia's borders. In the thirty years since the latest round of globalization arrived on Australian shores, Anzac has served to soften its impact. It has also served to remind foreigners of Australia's historical and contemporary contributions to international society and world history: lest you forget.

39   Rudd, 'The Future of the G20'.

ROGER HILLMAN

# From No Man's Land to Transnational Spaces: The Representation of Great War Memory in Film

## Introduction

The films chosen for this chapter are all set during or in close proximity to the Great War and were all made some ninety years or more after its outbreak. That timeframe ensures that they embody questions of historical memory, and its filmic representation. For such an analysis, a transdisciplinary approach seems essential, rather than a purist approach to the logocentrism of written history. Cultural historian Jan Assmann writes: 'In the context of cultural memory, the distinction between myth and history vanishes. Not the past as such [...] counts for the cultural memory, but only the past as it is remembered'.[1] This is an enterprise not to be confused with a twenty-first-century historian's account of the unfolding of the Great War. It signals the focus of this chapter, namely what representations of the Great War, at this historical distance, can tell us about our current vantage point. Seeking to interweave filmic representations with history 'itself' (Assmann's 'the past as such') is an approach exemplified by the work of historian Robert Rosenstone, but also by scholars such as Marita Sturken, Vivian Sobchack and others.[2] It shares Sturken's objective to explore how histories are told through popular culture and how memory engages with

1    Jan Assmann, 'Communicative and Cultural Memory' in Astrid Erll and Ansgar Nünning, eds, *A Companion to Cultural Memory Studies* (Berlin: de Gruyter, 2010), 113.
2    See Robert Rosenstone, *Revisioning History: Film and the Construction of a New Past* (Princeton, NJ: Princeton University Press, 1995); *Visions of the Past: The Challenge*

history in the public sphere.[3] The task is timely in light of the 'memory boom'. Sobchack argues that 'We are in a moment marked by a peculiarly novel "readiness" for history among the general population'.[4] Even the most recent – at the time of writing – history of Germany completes its elaboration of 'German History in Modern Times' with an extensive filmography of 'historically illuminating films'.[5]

Just as all history of the past is a reception history of that past up till the present, the films encountered here are primarily viewed as vehicles for positioning the present vis-a-vis the Great War, in other words for exploring our ongoing investment in understanding this turning point in world history. The films under analysis do not exemplify what Ricœur calls 'repetition-memory', featuring a 'compulsion to repeat', a critique of tradition which, drawing on Freud, eclipses 'the true recollection by which the present would be reconciled with the past'. Instead Ricœur opposes to 'repetition-memory' what he calls 'recollection-memory',[6] a category capable of 'the work of remembering' in a critical vein. In the labour that is memory, the films risk enlisting 'not enough memory [...] hence an abuse of forgetting'.[7] In this light film's greater capacity to render and/or forge myth – for example Peter Weir's *Gallipoli* – then becomes not a suspect quality in relation to written history, but rather a telling document of cultural memory.

Alongside more general issues relating to filmic representations of history, three different focal points of interest to First World War historians will emerge: first, Turkish director Tolga Örnek's *Gelibolu* [*Gallipoli:*

---

*of Film to our Idea of History* (Cambridge: Harvard University Press, 1995); and *History on Film/Film on History* (New York: Longman/Pearson, 2006).

3    Marita Sturken, *Tangled Memories: The Vietnam War, the AIDS Epidemic, and the Politics of Remembering* (Berkeley: University of California Press, 1997), 5.

4    Vivian Sobchack, ed., *The Persistence of History: Cinema, Television, and the Modern Event* (New York: Routledge, 1996), 4.

5    William W. Hagen, *German History in Modern Times: Four Lives of the Nation* (Cambridge: Cambridge University Press, 2012), 449.

6    Paul Ricœur, *Memory, History, Forgetting*, K. Blamey and D. Pellauer, trans (Chicago and London: University of Chicago Press, 2004), 79.

7    Ricœur, *Memory, History, Forgetting*, 81.

*the Front Line Experience*] (2005) attempts a transnational documentary take rather than the myth-making of Peter Weir's iconic film. With its reliance on letters and diaries conveyed in voice over, it is closest to written historical accounts in its presentation, and yet ultimately very different. Second, Michael Haneke's *Das Weisse Band* [*The White Ribbon*] (2009) is set largely in the period immediately prior to the Great War. Towards the end, news of Sarajevo reaches the world of the film's figures. The challenge posed to interpretation is the degree to which this fiction is a premonition of the Great War alone, or whether it inevitably evokes both world wars, the Second with possibly greater prominence. Third, two French titles viewed as European heritage films complete the picture. Jeunet's *Un Long Dimanche de Fiançailles* [*A Very Long Engagement*] (2004), based on a successful novel of the early 1990s, features compelling re-enactments of trench warfare. Hence it comes from a long tradition within film history that includes titles like Milestone's *All Quiet on the Western Front* (1930), Losey's *For King and Country* (1964), Kubrick's *Paths of Glory* (1957) or Weir's *Gallipoli* (1981). A second French film, Christian Carion's *Joyeux Noël* [*Merry Christmas*] (2005), is factually based and the most mainstream example. Yet its implied timeframe of the 'new Europe', postdating the fall of the Berlin Wall, projects what Mark McKenna has called the 'sentimental nationalism'[8] of Anzac observance into what we might call a 'sentimental supranationalism'. The 'home' envisioned at the film's conclusion is that vindicated by the award of the Nobel Peace Prize to the European Union in 2012: it has far more to do with the strivings of the 'new Europe', than with the events of Christmas 1914.

---

8   Mark McKenna, 'Patriot Act', *The Australian Literary Review* (6 June 2007), 15.

## Gelibolu [*Gallipoli: The Frontline Experience*] (2005)

Tolga Örnek offers a transnational perspective on the Gallipoli campaign
by portraying soldiers from four combatant nations, the United Kingdom,
Australia, New Zealand, and his native Turkey.[9] But neither in focus nor
in tone do the 'national' portraits dominate, a feature admired beyond
Turkey but contentious within his homeland. The film features documentary footage, photos, interviews with military historians and re-enactments.
The combinations of 'fact' and fiction, and above all of then and now,
reflect the positioning of the spectator, as colour shots of pristine beaches
alternate with black and white photos of boatloads of troops landing on
the same beaches in 1915.

Typical of the film's narrative and style are the opening five minutes
or so of the (Roadshow Entertainment) DVD, Chapter Seven. The photos
are of people we know to be absent, their documented thoughts (drawn
from diaries and letters) rendered as voiceover, by a voice we know is not
theirs – a ghostly oral history. Talking heads in colour (including author
Les Carlyon and military historian Christopher Pugsley) provide a further channel of information, functioning in this context like animated
witnesses or experts. This mix of past and present voices, a technique that
embodies the memory aspects of Gallipoli then and now, contrasts with
palpable re-enactments of figures largely filmed from behind and hence
faceless. They stand out from the way we viewers are addressed by photos
that look straight out at us. The mismatch between photographic image
and a voiceover that emanates from the photo, but not from the person
himself, combined with re-enactments that conceal faces and hence identities, signals the viewer's imaginary. The whole is unified by elegiac music,
which does not differentiate between nationalities. As employed by Örnek,
montage itself functions to suggest a transnational point of view.

9    This section draws on a section of the author's 'A Transnational Gallipoli?' *Australian
     Humanities Review* 51 (November 2011), 25–42.

In places, the film is irritatingly self-reflexive (in a technical, not a nationalistic sense). While camera movement towards or away from photos is generally gradual, there is (at the beginning) a swish-pan effect across the entourage of Ataturk, to focus on the great man himself. Extravagant fast-forwards ensure that waves lapping the shores of Gallipoli are far from *National Geographic*-type footage. The occasional 'rush' of the camera also seems to substitute for actual charges of soldiers. This in turn contrasts starkly with the slow motion rendition of soldiers' movements in the re-enactments. These sequences are a world apart from the conventional dramatic weighting of body movements elongated in time (for example, in a film such as *Chariots of Fire*). With Örnek their pace links photo stills and re-enactment sequences that are shot more naturalistically. A third representational medium is painting, and at the end of this sequence we see details of a canvas by George Lambert, therefore encouraging the Australian rather than the Turkish imaginary. These details are book ended by (more conventional, documentary) shots of the same terrain, devoid of human life. Örnek's film is the converse of an action movie, and what emerges is a different, elegiac kind of aestheticization.

The processes and processing of memory are central to the film. Above all, the narrative kaleidoscopically combines different national viewpoints with profiles of a handful of participants from four nations. But the palpable enactment that is at play, the combination of voiceover and photo rather than direct recording of sound or image, continually implies the limitations of oral history as a privileged perspective. The viewer, (re)animating the freeze frames of history, is positioned beyond any one national perspective.

The work of synthesis required of this viewer is very different to the more straightforward battlelines of national identity drawn by Peter Weir. Jay Winter claims that the historical film genre has 'power in projecting national stereotypes and narratives'.[10] Örnek combines cinematic devices to avoid such a projection and to ensure an interaction of points of view. His montage of case studies, and the narrative voice linking them all, assembles

10    Marnie Hughes-Warrington, *History Goes to the Movies: Studying History on Film* (London: Routledge, 2007), 80.

a transnational perspective. Unlike Weir's focus on the battle of the Nek, Örnek's film gives a strong sense of the whole campaign, focussing on the carnage of the first landings, especially those of the British forces. Beyond the ninetieth anniversary of the Dardanelles campaign, its own historic moment was a more favourable constellation than today's for Turkey's quest for EU membership, as pendant to Mustafa Kemal's mission to take his Turkey into Europe. In the following year, 2006, Clint Eastwood's challenging duo appeared, *Flags of Our Fathers* and *Letters from Iwo Jima*, two films depicting the one battle from an American, and then a Japanese perspective. Örnek's film presents an even greater challenge to nationalism, with its montage of national representatives across a uniformity of tone, and without strong moral differentiation by nationality.

## Das Weisse Band: eine deutsche Kindergeschichte [*The White Ribbon*] (2009)

Michael Haneke's *Caché* [*Hidden*] (2005) and *Das Weisse Band: eine deutsche Kindergeschichte* [*The White Ribbon*] (2009), set respectively in contemporary Paris and in rural Germany just before the outbreak of the Great War, embody those settings but also raise issues not confined to them.[11] In de Gaulle's France, the Algerian War had been a taboo topic, while the myth of the Resistance, rather than Vichy submission, had been strenuously upheld as the grand narrative of the Second World War. Postcolonial ghosts were not confined to France; they of course extended across Western Europe and its former colonies, but at least on this one score, Germany could never be the bogey of Europe. Haneke's figures in *Hidden* are haunted by a return of the national repressed, a collective guilt incurred by an earlier generation, being paid for and worked through in the present.

11   This analysis draws on a section of the author's 'German Studies and Film Studies in Oz', in Franz-Josef Deiters et al., eds, *Groteske Moderne – Moderne Groteske: Festschrift for Philip Thomson* (St Ingbert: Röhrig, 2011), 199–203.

*The White Ribbon* is a rare attempt in film to approach the psychopathology of the advent of fascism and its inroads in the case of one nation. An equally stylish, but differently styled film, Bertolucci's *Il Conformista* [*The Conformist*] (1970), brilliantly dissected the Italian variant of that theme, and now Haneke's tells the German, but far from just the German story, starting with the rare narrative prominence of Sarajevo. The pillars of society, the pastor, the baron and the doctor, remain apolitical outside their local functions, till the war brews at the end. Not least through this balance between local issues and a worldview, the film serves almost as a prequel to Edgar Reitz's *Heimat* series (1984–2013), while implying a very different course of German history to that suggested by Reitz.

Reitz and others encountered critics who claimed they had elided the Holocaust (a point convincingly refuted by Thomas Elsaesser).[12] Haneke here creates a different entry point, namely eugenics rather than Nazi racial policies. The mentally disabled child is met with cruelty, but such treatment is not confined to him. Typical of the film's dark hues is the contextualization of his conception, the misalliance between the doctor and his housekeeper. In Günter Grass's novel *Die Blechtrommel* [*The Tin Drum*] (1959), it is suggested that as a 'subnormal' human, Oskar's life would have been endangered under the Nazis. With our knowing hindsight, it is all too tempting to read *The White Ribbon* primarily as anticipation of the Third Reich. The narrative and the script continually invite such a reading, while at the same time transcending it. The opening words of 'dialogue', 'Kannst du nicht grüßen?' [Can't you say hello [properly]?] evoke both a mandatory 'Hitlergruss' of a slightly later era, and the authoritarian, hectoring atmosphere of a societal hierarchy that radiates out from the schoolroom. 'Kannst du nicht [...]' pre-empts any reply; there is no dialogue across the generations. When much later in the film a child's vision of an impending disaster is wilfully misconstrued as complicity with the perpetrators, she is intimidated with the words: 'Ich hab' auch andere Mittel, Euch zum Reden zu bringen' [I have other ways of getting you to speak]. As viewers we are situated in a dilemma of the inexorable historical weight of materials in a

---

12  Thomas Elsaesser, 'New German Cinema and History: the Case of Alexander Kluge', in Tim Bergfelder et al., eds, *The German Cinema Book* (London: bfi, 2002), 182–91.

German context and the ever-present danger of over-interpretation. Reitz's central figure Maria was born in 1900, at the dawn of what Eberhard Jäckel called the 'German century'.[13] In Haneke's film that dawn is embodied by the children's confirmation class immediately ahead of the outbreak of the First World War, meaning that they were born on the threshold of the new century. They form the hinge between the nineteenth and the twentieth centuries, and the latter is under intense scrutiny in this film.

However, *The White Ribbon* is neither a documentary concealing its true purpose, nor a film essay on fascism in the purely political sense. It is as if Ingmar Bergman had been assigned the project of Reitz's *Heimat*, combined with Henry James's *Turn of the Screw* (1898) being recast as social realism. Luminous cinematography complements a lack of ambient sound in some interior shots to create a sense of still life, objects drained of life, embodied in the teacher's choice of Schubert's *Tote Blumen* [Dead Flowers] as a fitting piece to play in this salon. In combination with black and white images, the neutral quality of the voice over evokes Fassbinder's *Effi Briest* (1994) and the end of the Wilhelmine era, rather than 'just' a foreshadowing of the 1930s.

Altogether the strain of realism is strong, with this being the first film by this director set in an age preceding media images and hence without the self-reflexive mediatization that dominates his previous films. What remains is what tempered nineteenth century Realism: allegory. In a fade out at the end, a curtain of darkness and conspiracy is drawn on the tableau of the villagers, similar in effect to the pastor drawing the curtains and closing windows in his own home to contain the schoolteacher's accusations. In a further turn of the screw on Haneke's part, the pastor is prepared to humiliate his own children for their 'sins', but not, in this scene, to accept the (enlightened) truth of a genuine threat. By the time of those final frames, the angelic tones of the children's choir have taken on demonic significance, and Bach has become Gothic in a different sense. The enveloping gloom enacts the lamps going out all over Europe. And indeed they

---

13    Eberhard Jäckel, *Das deutsche Jahrhundert: Eine historische Bilanz* (Stuttgart: Deutsche Verlags-Anstalt, 1996).

shall not reappear in our (the film world's) time, to complete the famous quote, because we (the contemporary film viewers) know that the Great War was not the end of European struggle.

The film has its own operatic mad scene when an edit mercilessly cross-cuts from the doctor's daughter being molested by her father, to the pastor's daughter who in crazed reaction to her subjection and humiliation strides to the one weak point she can find in her father's armoury, his caged bird. The arresting aspect of this sequence is the uncanny outward calm with which the first daughter meets the uncomprehending gaze of her young brother as he enters the room. But what follows, even though related to the plight of another daughter, shows the underbelly of such self-control, the crushing of teenage femininity and the further fanning of impotent rage. In the adult world, opposition remains either suppressed, or else largely at the level of pitiful protest, as when a villager, his mother having died after falling through a rotten floorboard, beheads the baron's cabbages. Functioning like a David Lynch soundtrack – a ubiquitous threat – these undercurrents fester until they flicker more effectively with a fire in a barn. The sole reckoning with the rotten foundations of society comes late in the film. The baron's wife voices a historic commentary on what we have witnessed across the three families holding power in this rural community, with a string of abstract nouns in the manner of Thomas Mann: 'Böswilligkeit, Neid, Stumpfsinn, Brutalität' [malevolence, envy, stupidity, brutality]. She alone, with the children, completes a Thomas Mann constellation by leaving the claustrophobia of this society and travelling to Italy, where she also finds an alternative to the village's gendered repression.

Almost immediately news breaks of Sarajevo, which then emerges as neither a single anarchistic act nor a powder keg of international machinations, but yet more devastatingly as a kind of extended 'Decline of a Family' (the subtitle of Thomas Mann's novel *Buddenbrooks* from 1901), as the end-point of a viable European social fabric. But it is also as if a child of the Habsburg Empire has been driven to a comparable act of despairing revenge, the final instance of a historically suggestive psychopathology sustained throughout the film. Above all, the darkness in this film emanates not from a psychotic individual (nor from a somewhat 'normalized' one, as in the depiction of Hitler's final days in *Der Untergang* [*Downfall*]

(2004), but from the *Volk* as a group phenomenon. This is explicit in the note accompanying Karli's torture, an Old Testament sense of justice being visited upon the sins of the fathers. And that is what the baron in his address in the church effectively recognizes, when he threatens a loss of communal peace. Haneke's film strikes new tones in what had seemed very familiar territory.

## Un Long Dimanche de Fiançailles [*A Very Long Engagement*] (2004)

Based on Sébastien Japrisot's 1991 novel of the same title, Jeunet's *A Very Long Engagement* traces the dogged pursuit of a young French soldier, believed dead, by his fiancée. He and four comrades had been forced into the crossfire of No Man's Land as their official disgracing for self-mutilation. This charge itself, ahead of its legal justification or otherwise as a death penalty, is thrown into ambiguity, as at least one injury is an accident. The film features vivid trench scenes, interspersed with whimsical characters and a celebration of the French countryside almost as a dreamscape, as idealized imaginary. 'But paradoxically', as Elizabeth Ezra notes, 'it is in its emphasis on sites of "Frenchness" that the film is at its most transnational: these touristic sites act as screen memories to divert our gaze from the border zones of contested national identity'.[14] Only males people the opening scenes of mud, rain and trenches in that contested territory. An arresting touch, therefore, is for the background story, including its historical basis, to be narrated by a female voiceover. The cultural stereotypes that are engagingly perpetuated throughout the film point to the flipside of No Man's Land, namely nowhere, utopia. What assails the Spirit of France is not the enemy occupier Germany – the sole German soldier seen at close

---

14    See Elizabeth Ezra, *Jean-Pierre Jeunet* (Urbana and Chicago: University of Illinois Press, 2008), 110.

quarters is heinously bayonetted in what in a non-war situation would be cold blood. Instead, responsibility lies with those domestic authorities that are prepared to push five men into supposedly certain death.

There were historical precedents for the film's perspective of restitution – in 1998 Prime Minister Lionel Jospin had called for the 'reintegration into collective memory' of the soldiers who were 'shot for the sake of example' in 1914–15 and those who mutinied in 1917.[15] Such a rescripting is underpinned by the film's style, full of the sepia tonings of memory, like an animated gallery of photos and postcards, or as Annabelle Doherty aptly puts it, a 'digital tableaux'.[16] Mathilde's search for her swain, her physical mobility restricted by childhood polio, pieces together fragmented leads. But finally she finds him, a survivor thanks to an exchange of identity with a dead soldier that made physical escape possible. He is also granted mental escape through amnesia, almost an incarnation of that change of identity.

Although the single mindedness of Mathilde's actions is vindicated, how they are positioned as lovers is a question left dangling at the end. He does, it is true, ask her whether it hurts when she walks, repeating his solicitous enquiry from their childhood days, and simply contemplating him in the final frames seems to fill her with contentment. But for him, the escape from memory seems the only escape from the history of shellshock. While the figure in the film fiction suffers, the film's audience *may* be compensated by a gain in cultural memory: 'Spectators are able, potentially, to acquire a cultural memory of history by experiencing Jeunet's digital reconstitution of the Belle Époque, the First World War, and 1920s Paris'.[17] To be more convincing however, this line of argument which draws on Alison Landsberg's not unproblematic notion of 'prosthetic memory', really needs to engage with more general issues of viewer identification and immersion.

---

15  Pierre Purseigle, 'A very French debate: the 1914–1918 "war culture"', *Journal of War and Culture Studies* 1/1 (2008), 9.

16  Annabelle Doherty, 'Digital Tableaux of Cinematic Cultural Memory in the French Heritage Film: *Un long dimanche de fiançailles*', *Australian Journal of French Studies* 49/2 (2012), 196–207.

17  Doherty, 'Digital Tableaux', 200.

The only other survivor of those days lives on a farm called 'End of the World', and apart from a brief audience with Mathilde towards the end, remains hermetically sealed from the outside world. So no link that might (re)integrate the battered survivors into society seems possible. In this sense a question mark lingers against the enlightenment of changed historical perspectives leading to reassessments such as those championed by Jospin in the quote above. As with the next film to which this chapter turns, Jospin's pronouncement is strongly driven by the desires of the new Europe, a sentimental supranationalism, rather than a real chance to rewrite history. On this score, the melancholy magic of Jeunet's film is the more honest reappraisal, harbouring fewer illusions.


## *Joyeux Noël* [*Merry Christmas*] 2005


*Joyeux Noël* embellishes the outbreak of peace, as Brecht's Mother Courage would have put it, on Christmas Eve 1914, across enemy lines on the Western Front. The instrument for transforming No Man's Land into utopia is music, with a range of carols whose melodies were familiar to both sides (Fassbinder's *Lili Marleen* (1981), with its staged truces each night at three minutes to ten as that song is played on European airwaves, is a parody of the vision). Here, as in the 'new Europe' that financed the film, the German tenor (based on Walter Kirchhoff, brought to the front lines by *Kronprinz* Wilhelm) is foregrounded. He is complemented by his Danish partner's soprano voice, as they sing Latin versions of Christmas carols; the conceit of Kieślowski's *Three Colours: Blue* (1993), a European anthem to be performed but once in twelve European cities, was based on an ancient Greek text, rendering the legitimacy of a pan-European tradition pre-dating Romantic nationalism. Latin, the great leveller of language as national identity, simultaneously recalls a European identity from the past that might, shifted from the terrain of language, serve Europe in the future. The historic moment of this film, corresponding to a ceasefire at a number of points along the Western Front, is a transnational Christmas. This historic moment is styled less as a historically missed opportunity for pacifism, than as European bonding via cultures.

Dramatically the film's mix is very effective, not least the long silences of the differently uniformed cohorts of soldiers as they tentatively approach each other, still not quite believing what is eventuating. Like Weir's *Gallipoli*, it is historically based myth, and where Weir's film witnessed the willing loss of historical innocence in a rite of national passage, *Joyeux Noël* marks in retrospect the final innocence of the west, the lull before the storm of the rest of this war, and all of the next, their scars permeating the remainder of the century. It investigates an unexpected turn within a turning point for European civilization. Film is better suited than written history to honing symbolic history. Film can keep implying connections that written history, less inclined to operate that way in the first place, has to spell out. As a surviving, triumphant tradition, German music is embodied by a Danish woman and a German male who ultimately becomes a 'deserter'. By the time of the film's production, music has long ceased to be 'the most German art' as proclaimed by the Nazis. Instead the *Ode to Joy*, once a Nazi cultural flagship, has become the supranational European anthem and its score, added to the UNESCO Memory of the World programme in 2003, is now a protected cultural treasure.

Beyond the truism that all history of the past relates to the present, *Joyeux Noël* embodies film's capacity to suggest the hindsight of historical perspectives. Thus the German leader in the trenches is Jewish. This does not change everything, but it does change a lot. It is a crucial detail, the poignant reminder of a time before the German-Jewish combination became officially impossible. Such historical knowledge is mandatory for a viewer, and it rules out the following equation: 'the German combatants are presented straightforwardly as honourable soldiers, no different from their British or French counterparts.'[18]

---

18  Paul Cooke, *Contemporary German Cinema* (Manchester and New York: Manchester University Press, 2012), 255.

The final images show this (Jewish-German) leader and his men confined to a cattle car dispatched to the Eastern Front, as punishment for their lapse into non-hostilities. There is an inbuilt historical irony here beyond the anticipatory function discussed below. This irony can be seen in the example of the following written record recently uncovered by Jens Flemming. In September 1914 a Berlin rabbi issued a rallying call for Jewish support of the Fatherland in a sermon appealing to the liberation of coreligionists in the east. 'In the east millions of our brothers are languishing under the yoke of humiliating servitude. In the east lurks the greatest danger for European culture [... and we] hope that Israel's human rights will be restored by the hand of the victor'.[19] Similarly the reflections of a Jewish volunteer shortly before the unique Christmas on which the film focuses are a surprise to us in light of subsequent history. Robert Ziegel wrote home on 1 December 1914 that 'I believe that this time my celebration of *Chanukka* will be a purely private one, but for the rest I shall observe Christmas with my comrades, not as a Christian festival, but as a German one'.[20] Likewise in *Joyeux Noël* the German commander acknowledges his distance from the religious core of Christmas, again emphasizing the national solidarity of Jewish-Germans beyond diverging faiths. He is humiliated when his superior, a mix of fanaticism, dementedness and infantilism, fingers the medal round his neck and says: 'they hand it out to anybody' (the German original, 'Hinz und Kunz', is completely dismissive). Not least via film history, these final images evoke in turn the Second World War rather than a miraculous moment during the First. The cattle truck itself even bears the name 'Tannenberg', and here what would be outright anachronism in a written historical account can only be read for its symbolic value. As Belén Vidal argues, 'This charged gesture towards the retrospective historical knowledge of the audience facilitates a direct transhistorical reflection on the cyclical processes of destruction and violence, and enhances the

19   Cited in Jens Flemming et al., eds, *Lebenswelten im Ausnahmezustand: Die Deutschen, der Alltag und der Krieg, 1914–1918* (Frankfurt am Main: Peter Lang, 2011), 187–8 [author's translation].
20   Cited in Flemming et al., *Lebenswelten*, 188 [author's translation].

pacifist message of the film and its commemorative function'.[21] The Battle of Tannenberg, a resounding German victory in September 1914, preceded the Christmas Eve truces. But of course we read, are meant to read it via the very different outcome to the Battle of Stalingrad in 1942–3 and beyond.

In their confinement, the German soldiers do not sing martially, but hum the theme melody of the film's soundtrack, the *Hymne des Fraternises*, by Philippe Rombi, and then over the final frames a voice with a non-English accent breaks into the lyrics 'I feel so alone, I'm dreaming of home'. But the Fatherland as home is discredited, and these symbolic figures, who would be outright preposterous in written history, long for the end of those traditions that seal their cattle car, and the future of their children. Their longing evokes a homecoming at the end of the historical tunnel, with progress towards the 'normalization' of Germany in the 'new Europe' of the post 1990s. And in the representation of that Europe, the supranational anthem of the *Ode to Joy*, with its embrace of millions sealing the brotherhood of mankind, is paralleled here by a hymn to fraternity commissioned by a European co-production. Indeed, 'I'm dreaming of home' is mostly rendered by a girls' choir, neutralizing the military aspect of the soldiers, but more importantly neutralizing an opening sequence in which, in schoolroom settings, children of three European nations spout inculcated slogans of chauvinism.

The historic event of the Christmas Truce showed an alternative to entrenched European nationalisms. *Joyeux Noël* synthesizes many incidents from that truce, as documented by a popular historical account such as Stanley Weintraub's.[22] But whereas Weintraub's account, in its final chapter ('What if?'), projects a Niall Ferguson-type rewriting of the twentieth century proceeding from an enduring truce, Christian Carion's film almost reinstates the 'old Europe' as the 'new'. It thus elaborates on the 'old'/'new' Europe as 'mythscape', a concept defined by Duncan Bell as 'the temporally

21    Belén Vidal, *Heritage Film: Nation, Genre and Representation* (London and New York: Wallflower, 2012), 88.
22    Stanley Weintraub, *Silent Night: The Story of the World War I Christmas Truce* (New York: The Free Press, 2001).

and spatially extended discursive realm in which the myths of the nation are forged, transmitted, negotiated, and reconstructed constantly'.[23] Probably the most distinctive aspect of that mythscape is the no longer paradoxical combination of Jewish and German identities, yet to be sundered in the timeframe of the film's setting, and yet to be more fully restored in the timeframe of the film's production. The Jewish-German lieutenant also lends the film a degree of complexity, amidst its stereotypes. The French bring champagne and coffee to the truce table, the Scots play bagpipes, etc. But far less predictably, the Jewish-German commander does not want artists among his troops, while his key role, weighted as his very presence is by the history of the immediate future, confounds any comfortable stereotyping of 'the Germans'. This is less the territory of No Man's Land, than of utopia, nowhere. Or alternately, in a Europe of open borders, No Man's Land has become the transnational space of everyman's land. *Joyeux Noël* does indeed contain a 'visual and aural pastiche [which] sets a tone of diffused nostalgia for an idealised, pre-First World War past where focus is not on national specificity, but on the commonality of memory'.[24] Vidal's criticism is fair in relation to the contemporary dimension of the film: '*Joyeux Noël*'s celebration of a pan-European past solely through the symbols of white, Christian Europe, as represented by the main western colonial powers, is especially problematic in a film whose politically neutral stance and humanist universalism can be regarded as simplistic and highly ideological'.[25] *Joyeux Noël*'s Janus-face also focuses on a still crystallizing European present and diffused prospects for the future.

23    See Duncan Bell, 'Mythscapes: Memory, Mythology, and National Identity', *British Journal of Sociology* 54/1(2003), 63 (although he also reminds us that 'myth is not […] an antonym of history', 75).

24    Vidal, *Heritage Film*, 80.

25    Vidal, *Heritage Film*, 84.

## Conclusion

Such cultivation of memory work as the two French films particularly exhibit risks eclipsing the past not through evading it, but through submerging it in the discourse of today. Ricœur's notion of 'recollection memory' may therefore be the most accurate, if melancholic, way to read the motif of amnesia at the end of *A Very Long Engagement.* The whole arc of this film implies that to progress, however uncertainly, we need to return to the pre-Great War roots of the tale that is spun. Yet it leaves us with the bodily shell of a man without recall of the immediate past, a pristine museum relic for our processing as twenty-first century viewers. *Joyeux Noël* projects the wishful thinking of post-memory Europe onto a glitch of pacifism crossing the screen of national warfare. *Gallipoli: The Frontline Experience* finds transnational sense in a campaign that for the Allies at least was absurd in military terms. In a vertiginous pincer movement, *The White Ribbon* combines everyday history from below with the most abstract history from above, seeking the roots of supranational fascist mentalities. Collectively these films shed light on those aspects of the written histories of the Great War which go beyond, and in some cases defy, more conventional history.

# PART II

# Commemoration and the Politics of National Belonging

FRANK BONGIORNO

# Anzac and the Politics of Inclusion[1]

## Introduction

The eminent historian Henry Reynolds recently commented that 'Australia must now have more days of military remembrance than there were saints' days in the medieval calendar'.[2] The centrepiece of the commemorative culture to which Reynolds pays this back-handed compliment is Anzac Day, 25 April, which is the anniversary of the first landing of Australian and New Zealand Army Corps (Anzac) forces at Gallipoli in 1915. With ceremonies being held all over the world each year – a pattern that emerged as early as April 1916 – it might well also be described as the ceremony on which the sun never sets.

But the term 'Anzac' is more than 25 April; it refers to an entire culture of military commemoration and war remembrance that links Australian national identity to military endeavour. The argument developed in this chapter is that while the cultural authority of Anzac has been achieved by developing its inclusiveness – it gestures powerfully towards both a multi-cultural and an Aboriginal Australia – the result has been a declining toleration in public culture of critique of Anzac. Anzac's inclusiveness has been achieved at the price of a dangerous chauvinism that increasingly equates national history with military history, and national belonging with a willingness to accept the Anzac legend as Australian patriotism's very essence.

1   This chapter comes out of an Australian Research Council Linkage Project (LP110100264), 'Anzac Day at Home and Abroad: A Centenary History of Australia's National Day', led by Professor Bruce Scates of Monash University. The author gratefully acknowledges this support.
2   Henry Reynolds, *Forgotten War* (Sydney: New South, 2013), 232.

## Anzac ascendancy

When Brendan Nelson, the newly elected Leader of the Opposition in
the Australian Parliament, replied to Labor Prime Minister Kevin Rudd's
speech accompanying the motion for an apology to the Stolen Generations
of Aboriginal children, he did not take long to mention the war. 'Let no
one forget', said Nelson, that Australians who lived during the era of child
removal had 'sent their sons to war, shaping our identity and place in the
world. One hundred thousand in two world wars alone gave their lives
in our name and our uniform, lying forever in distant lands; silent witnesses to the future they have given us [...]. Aboriginal and non-Aboriginal
Australians', he added, 'lie alongside one another'.[3]

Nelson's seemingly anomalous reference to war makes sense once you
know something of recent Australian cultural politics. In the last twenty
years Australia's military tradition has displaced all other versions or understandings of national identity, except possibly sporting achievement – which
is arguably warfare by other means.[4] In the years between the end of
empire in the 1960s and the 1990s, Anzac and Australian military tradition were unquestionably prominent in debates about national identity
but they had never overwhelmed all else. The late 1960s and 1970s saw
the rise of a nationalism that connected Australian identity with creative
achievement. In the mid-1970s through to the mid-1990s, multiculturalism was promoted with varying levels of enthusiasm by governments and
the intelligentsia as a way of celebrating unity in diversity. The republic

---

3    *Sydney Morning Herald* (13 February, 2008) <http://www.smh.com.au/news/
     national/brendan-nelsons-sorry-speech/2008/02/13/1202760366050.html> accessed
     2 February 2013.
4    See Jim Davidson, 'Sport with Guns', *Meanjin* 67/4 (Summer 2008), 10–13; Marilyn
     Lake and Henry Reynolds with Mark McKenna and Joy Damousi, *What's Wrong
     with Anzac?: The Militarisation of Australian History* (Sydney: New South, 2010);
     Peter Stanley, 'Monumental Mistake: Is War the Most Important Thing in Australian
     History?', in Craig Stockings, ed., *Anzac's Dirty Dozen: 12 Myths of Australian Military
     History* (Sydney: New South, 2012), 260–86.

briefly flourished as a vehicle for an Australian national identity in the 1990s. And from the 1970s, there was the notion that an accommodation between Indigenous and non-Indigenous Australia – whether by treaty, reconciliation or apology – could provide the foundation for a modern Australian nation at ease with itself.[5]

Especially during the long prime ministership of conservative Liberal Party leader John Howard (1996–2007), all of these alternative national identities received short shrift, often at the hands of the Prime Minister himself, assisted by a sympathetic coterie of supporters in the media. They ridiculed any alternative to the government's authorized nationalism as a product of the 'chattering classes'. Howard, when he came to office, derided the 'perpetual seminar' on national identity that he claimed had been carried on by these 'elites';[6] and when he made a final appeal to voters in 2007, he claimed having ended this 'seminar' as one of his major achievements.[7] Yet it would be hard to imagine a politician *more* obsessed with national identity than Howard. Although the process certainly began earlier, probably under the Labor Government of Bob Hawke, under Howard Anzac and Australian military heritage came to occupy centre stage in prime ministerial efforts to tell Australians who they really were. The reasons were complex, but they were partly a reflection of Howard's own family history and political preferences. His father and grandfather were both First World War veterans, but the emphasis on Australia's role in that conflict also allowed Howard to distance himself from his predecessor Labor Prime Minister Paul Keating's efforts to promote an alternative military legend centred on 1942, one that claimed Australia was betrayed by Britain over the

5    Some of these debates and understandings are examined in James Curran and Stuart Ward, *The Unknown Nation: Australia After Empire* (Carlton: Melbourne University Press, 2010).

6    John Howard, 'The Liberal Tradition: The Beliefs and Values Which Guide the Federal Government', Sir Robert Menzies Lecture, 18 November 1996 <http://menzieslecture.org/1996.html> accessed 2 February 2013.

7    'Howard Makes Final Pitch to Voters', 22 November 2007, 'Australia Votes 2007', ABC Elections, <http://www.abc.net.au/news/stories/2007/11/22/2098077.htm?site=elections/federal/2007> accessed 2 February 2013.

defence of Singapore, and saved by Australians at Kokoda in New Guinea. Howard's stress on the First World War underlined Australia's debts to its British heritage and European roots, in contrast with Keating's emphasis on Asia and republicanism.[8]

Moreover, as Mark McKenna has suggested, the new stress on Anzac Day allowed political leaders to avoid the difficulties raised by its major competitor on the national commemorative calendar – Australia Day, 26 January, the anniversary of the arrival of the First Fleet in 1788 – which necessarily drew attention the original settler dispossession of Indigenous people. Especially in the wake of the divisions between 'Indigenous' and 'Settler' histories exposed by the Bicentenary of European settlement in 1988, Australia Day's deficiencies as a day for fostering a sense of unity could hardly be overlooked. Anzac Day had the virtue of bypassing this 'vexed account of Australia's nationhood'.[9] Meanwhile, as Bruce Scates has shown, Anzac was also rewritten so that there was a premium on personal, emotional and familial connections.[10]

For Howard, Gallipoli was 'where our nation's spirit was born',[11] the product of an era in which Australia celebrated its racial homogeneity under the proud banner of a White Australia, and sought to preserve it by sending an expeditionary force to the other side of the world to defend the British Empire. Howard did not say as much; that was the genius of a rhetoric that allowed for the depreciation of later contributions to national identity, such as those provided by post-Second World War migration, without actually saying so. The core of Australian identity was the product of an

---

8    James Curran, *The Power of Speech: Australian Prime Ministers Defining the National Image* (Carlton: Melbourne University Press, 2004), 242–3.

9    Anne Brennan, 'Lest We Forget: Military Myths, Memory, and Canberra's Aboriginal and Torres Strait Islander Memorial', *Memory Connection* 1/1 (December 2011), 37; Mark McKenna, 'Anzac Day: How did it become Australia's national day?' in Lake and Reynolds with McKenna and Damousi, *What's Wrong with Anzac?*, 116.

10   Bruce Scates, *Return to Gallipoli: Walking the Battlefields of the Great War* (Cambridge: Cambridge University Press, 2006), 108–9, 115, 163–5.

11   Judith Brett, *Australian Liberals and the Moral Middle Class: From Alfred Deakin to John Howard* (Cambridge: Cambridge University Press, 2003), 204.

Anglo-Celtic identity; later contributions were colourful window-dressing. Anthony Smith has argued that successful territorial nationalisms need to contain an ethnic core and embody a shared mythology, usually based on a particular sense of the past and its relationship with a present national community.[12] Dirk Moses has argued the case for applying Smith's ideas to modern Australia:

> [...] the majority of non-Indigenous Australians has come to understand that authentic 'Australian-ness' inheres in those descended from Anglo-Celtic settlers and those who have shed blood defending the country. [...] they have died in their tens of thousands in its name. The incessant invocation of Australian military history and the reiteration of the sacred lexicon of sacrifice in our public life are designed to reaffirm that core Australian ethnic memory and definition. The cultural dominance of the core ethnicity is what makes a nation a nation.[13]

Moses's application of Smith's ideas helps explain how it can be that we have Aboriginal Anzacs, Irish Anzacs, German Anzacs and Russian Anzacs without any fundamental alteration of the Anzac legend's emphasis on blood sacrifice in the making of nationhood. What I do in this brief chapter is to examine in outline the manner in which both Aboriginality and ethnicity feature in Australia's sense of its military past as a means of exploring Anzac as both an inclusive and exclusive tradition. In the 1960s critics of the Anzac legend and Anzac Day identified them, pejoratively, with a rough Anglo-Celtic masculinity that they represented as increasingly irrelevant to Australia's imagined post-imperial future. The revival of Anzac since then has been achieved through a radical redefinition of its historical and cultural meanings, and a recasting of its commemorative rituals.[14] The result has unquestionably been a greater inclusiveness. But Anzac today is neither a multicultural festival, nor a celebration of Aboriginal culture. Under the sway of liberal multiculturalism, it is so tempting to treat inclusiveness as

---

12   Anthony D. Smith, 'The Origins of Nations', *Ethnic and Racial Studies* 12/3 (July 1989), 340–67.

13   Dirk Moses, 'Pogrom Talk', *On Line Opinion*, 11 January 2006, <http://www.onlineopinion.com.au/view.asp?article=4038&page=0> accessed 2 February 2013.

14   McKenna, 'Anzac Day', 34.

desirable in itself that the complex results of this transformation can be easily misunderstood.[15] When Anzac was a less inclusive tradition, those who were most responsible for policing its boundaries and regulating its rituals essentially courted – and often received – criticism from other citizens and groups. There is a long and rich history of contention over the significance and meaning of the Anzac legend.[16] But once a tradition is defined in more inclusive terms, those who refuse to participate can readily be represented as beyond the pale. To question, to criticize – even to analyse – can become un-Australian.


## Indigenous diggers


'Aboriginal and non-Aboriginal Australians lie along side one another'. Nelson's words evoke a sense of equality and shared sacrifice in defence of nation. It is, at best, a part-truth. Thanks in large part to Robert Hall's pioneering 1989 study *The Black Diggers*, we know much more about the Aboriginal experience of war, and especially the Second World War, than we did a generation ago. This knowledge has, in turn, come to form the basis of a quest for proper recognition. Hall believed that perhaps 300 or 400 Aboriginal people served in the Great War and about ten times that number in the Second World War.[17] His book was mainly devoted

---

15    Ghassan Hage, *White Nation: Fantasies of White Supremacy in a Multicultural Society* (Sydney: Pluto Press, 1998).

16    Bruce Scates, *A Place to Remember: A History of the Shrine of Remembrance* (Cambridge: Cambridge University Press, 2009), 44–7; and Carina Donaldson and Marilyn Lake, 'Whatever happened to the anti-war movement?', in Lake and Reynolds with McKenna and Damousi, *What's Wrong with Anzac?*, 71–93.

17    Recent research on Aboriginal and Torres Strait soldiers of the First World War suggests that at least 800 Aboriginal men volunteered to fight, although this number includes those rejected. See Philippa Scarlett, *Aboriginal and Torres Strait Islander Volunteers for the AIF: The Indigenous Response to World War One* (Macquarie, Australian Capital Territory: Indigenous Histories, 2012), 9.

to the latter conflict, and Hall meticulously outlined the varieties of service in which Aboriginal and Torres Strait Islander men and women were involved. He produced a positive interpretation of the effects of the war on Aboriginal people: Hall argued that Aboriginal people's experience of the war taught many of them important skills, instilled a sense of confidence, and laid the foundations for the wider advances in civil rights of later years.[18] All the same, Hall was not shy about examining the ways in which racial discrimination disfigured the Indigenous experience of war. Aboriginal people who joined the armed forces had to run the gauntlet of regulations that, for the most part, officially barred them. Later, governments resisted the efforts of Aboriginal organizations to claim citizenship rights on the basis of war service. But in the armed forces, Aboriginal men often experienced an easy fellowship with white men that was less common in civilian life.[19]

Hall's effort was one of historical recovery. The Aboriginal contribution to the defence of Australia was, in his view, little appreciated – he pointed out that in 1989 it had not at all registered in the Australian War Memorial (AWM) – and he wished to make it known. In 1994, when the New South Wales parliament passed a motion noting 'as a matter of public importance its acknowledgment and tribute to the courageous and dedicated service of Aboriginal and Torres Strait Islanders during the second world war', Hall's book was quoted in the short debate.[20]

Other books have appeared on Aboriginal Anzacs since Hall's *Black Diggers* – including histories published by Aboriginal people themselves[21]

---

18    Robert A. Hall, *The Black Diggers: Aborigines and Torres Strait Islanders in the Second World War* (Sydney: Allen & Unwin, 1989).

19    *Ibid.*, p. 186.

20    'Aboriginal And Torres Strait Islander Servicemen, Matter of Public Importance, Parliament of New South Wales, Legislative Assembly, *Hansard*, 21 April 1994 <http://www.parliament.nsw.gov.au/prod/parlment/hansart.nsf/V3Key/LA19940421027> accessed 2 February 2013.

21    Doreen Kartinyeri, *Ngarrindjeri Anzacs* (Adelaide: Aboriginal Family History Project, South Australian Museum and Raukkan Council, 1996); George Bray, Kenny Laughton and Pat Forster, *Aboriginal Ex-Servicemen of Central Australia* (Alice Springs: IAD Press, 1995).

– and we now know much more about Aboriginal people's contribution to Australia's defence. When Ken Inglis published his great study of war memorials, *Sacred Places*, in 1998, he noted that '[m]emorials to Aboriginal participation in Australia's wars are few, modest and late'. But they were beginning to appear by the 1980s. Aboriginal servicemen in Melbourne conducted their own march on Anzac Day 1987. The men were criticized for their separatism by Victorian Returned and Services League (RSL) President Bruce Ruxton, and they erected a wooden cross as a memorial after they had been refused Australian Bicentennial Authority funding for a larger memorial.[22] Reading accounts of this episode in the press, a (white) Canberra resident, Honor Thwaites, paid for and erected a plaque on Mount Ainslie in 1988, near the AWM but outside its precinct, 'Remembering the Aboriginal people who served in the Australian armed forces'. While this private venture was mainly ignored in the early years, its recent acquisition of a 'quasi-official' status is testament to the growing stature of Anzac commemoration in civic culture. The AWM itself has promoted this higher profile, and the little memorial is now the site of ceremonies on Anzac Day and during National Aboriginal and Islander Day of Observance Committee (NAIDOC) Week. Anne Brennan has revealed how a 2007 Anzac Day ceremony (conducted by a retired Indigenous naval officer and an Aboriginal army chaplain) represented the site as commemorating not only Indigenous people in the armed forces but *all* Aboriginal warriors, including those who were 'freedom fighters for their own country'.[23] In 2012 Garth O'Connell, who led the ceremony on behalf of the Aboriginal and Torres Strait Islander Veterans' and Services' Association of Australia of which he was secretary, expressed his pride in being both a fourth generation soldier and 'an Aboriginal warrior'.[24] There is a quiet claim here to a tradition extending much further back into the Australian past than 1788 or 1915.

22    K. S. Inglis assisted by Jan Brazier, *Sacred Places: War Memorials in the Australian Landscape* (Carlton South: The Miegunyah Press, 1999), 445–51.
23    Brennan, 'Lest We Forget', 35–44.
24    Personal observation by author, Anzac Day Indigenous Commemoration Ceremony, Mount Ainslie, Canberra, 25 April 2012.

In the 1990s the AWM began to register the Aboriginal contribution in its displays, thereby responding to the kinds of criticisms that had been made by Hall at the beginning of the decade. The issue of whether the AWM should commemorate the war on the Australian frontier, however, including the thousands of Aboriginal people who died in defence of their country, has proven more controversial than honouring Aboriginal people who served in the armed forces.[25] Especially between the 1890s and the 1970s, Australians emphasized, exaggerated and both celebrated and regretted the peacefulness of their past. Writing early in the twentieth century, the historian Henry Gyles Turner remarked, 'War, in one shape or another, forms so preponderating an item in the history of any country whose records exist, that it almost justifies the superficial observer in saying that since we have no warfare to chronicle, we can have no properly called history'.[26] As recently as 1965, the left-wing historian, Russel Ward, noted that the absence from Australia of a 'warlike native race' meant that 'men seldom had to go armed on the Australian frontier'. The Aborigines, said Ward, 'were among the most primitive and peaceable peoples known to history'.[27]

Within a few years, these claims would lie in tatters at the hands of younger historians, both black and white. Since the 1980s, there has been a growing tendency to refer to Australia as having been 'invaded' by Europeans, rather than 'settled'. In the new histories of the 1970s and 1980s, Aboriginal resistance to European invasion was sometimes framed as a form of guerrilla warfare, a view strenuously contested in the first volume of Keith Windschuttle's revisionist *The Fabrication of Aboriginal History* (2002). Tasmanian Aboriginal people, he said, desired consumer goods and 'their murders were incidental accompaniments to robbery' of the British population.[28] Windschuttle even likened Aboriginal attacks

---

25  Reynolds, *Forgotten War*, 32–3.
26  Henry Gyles Turner, *Our Own Little Rebellion: The Story of the Eureka Stockade* (Melbourne: Whitcombe & Tombs, n.d. [1913]), 15.
27  Russel Ward, *Australia* (Englewood Cliffs, New Jersey: Prentice-Hall, 1965), 21–2.
28  Keith Windschuttle, *The Fabrication of Aboriginal History, Volume One, Van Diemen's Land 1803–1847* (Paddington, NSW: Macleay Press, 2002), 128.

on British settlers not to warfare, but to 'modern-day junkies raiding service stations for money'.[29] He insisted on the essentially peaceful nature of the British settlement of Australia, and thereby sought to return the historiography to its pre-1970s emphasis on Australia as a quiet continent.

Meanwhile, Anzac Day has recently been an occasion on which some Aboriginal activists have protested the killing of Aboriginal people on Australian soil or, as Michael Anderson, who led a 2012 protest in Canberra, put it, the continuing 'war of attrition against Aboriginal people'. The choice of Anzac Day for this purpose was a controversial one within and beyond the Aboriginal community. Derek Robson, the RSL National Secretary, was quoted in the press condemning the idea of a separate march for Aboriginal ex-servicemen. He added: 'It wasn't that many years ago that WAR [Women Against Rape] were protesting and they got chased out of town'. Uncle David Williams, an Indigenous man and retired submariner who spoke at the Canberra Indigenous Anzac Day ceremony in 2012, clearly had Anderson in his sights when he declared: 'Leave Anzac Day alone'. Yet despite Williams' apparent lack of sympathy for the protests planned for later in the day, the latter still clearly saw a role for separate Aboriginal commemoration. 'We belong to the land', Williams said at the Indigenous service held in bushland at the foot of Mount Ainslie, a short walk from the site of the recently concluded National Anzac Day Dawn Service. 'I feel really comfortable here. It's not the same if we held it down there'.[30]

---

29   Quoted in Lyndall Ryan, 'Who is the Fabricator?', in Robert Manne, ed., *Whitewash: On Keith Windschuttle's Fabrication of Aboriginal History* (Melbourne: Black Inc., 2003), 233.

30   *Canberra Times* (11 April 2012), 1; Personal observation by author, Anzac Day Indigenous Commemoration Ceremony, Mount Ainslie, Canberra, 25 April 2012.

## Multicultural Anzac

In recent years, there have been attempts to recover a kind of multicultural history of Anzac. We now have studies of German Anzacs, Russian Anzacs, Irish Anzacs and Chinese Anzacs.[31] More recently, Tim Soutphommasane, in an eloquent defence of multiculturalism, has called on Australians to view the Anzac tradition not primarily in the context of 'an ethnic or genealogical understanding of the nation' but as a 'civic touchstone [...] that reflects – if only in fragments – Australia's pluralism'. An awareness of the role played by men such as Billy Sing, the great Gallipoli sniper and the Queensland-born son of migrants – his father from China and mother from England – means that 'even the Anzac tradition involves a certain pluralism'.[32]

This mode of argument might be seen as an example of what John Hirst has called 'contribution history':

> In its continuing search for legitimacy multiculturalism has declared itself ancient. Australia, it is claimed, has always been multicultural. Its population has always been diverse. It has always been composed of migrants and the children of migrants. Its society is the summation of the 'contributions' made by the various ethnic groups which have constituted its population.[33]

31 John F. Williams, *German Anzacs and the First World War* (Sydney: University of New South Wales Press, 2003); Jeff Kildea, *Anzacs and Ireland* (Sydney: University of New South Wales Press, 2007); Morag Loh, *Dinky-Di: The Contributions of Chinese Immigrants and Australians of Chinese Descent to Australia's Defence Forces and War Efforts 1899–1988* (Canberra: Australian Government Publishing Service, for the Office of Multicultural Affairs, Canberra, 1989); John Fitzgerald, *Big White Lie: Chinese Australians in White Australia* (Sydney: University of New South Wales Press, 2007), 156–8. For Russian Anzacs, see below.

32 Tim Soutphommasane, *Don't Go Back to Where You Came From: Why Multiculturalism Works* (Sydney: NewSouth, 2012), 105–6. For Sing, see John Hamilton, *Gallipoli Sniper: The Life of Billy Sing* (Sydney: Pan Macmillan, 2009 [2008]).

33 John Hirst, 'Australian History and European Civilisation', in his *Sense & Nonsense in Australian History* (Melbourne: Black Inc., 2006), 68, originally published in *Quadrant* 296 (1993), 28–40.

Whereas for Hirst the problem with this form of thinking is that it misrepresents the formative role played by British and European civilization in shaping Australian history, Hsu-Ming Teo argues that its problem is that in 'accepting the nation-building paradigm of grand national history', the contributions of non-British and non-Irish Australians might gain 'fleeting acknowledgement' in mainstream Australian history – 'women and ethnic groups were there and did their bit too' – but such additions 'hardly de-centred or transformed the focus [...] on "white" people of British/Irish descent'. While such histories were often conceived with the political purpose of challenging an older unitary identity, their capacity to do so was limited by a nationalist framework and discourse of 'cultural enrichment' that left the idea of a white and Anglo-Celtic mainstream intact.[34]

A vivid example in the field under consideration in this chapter is a 1989 study of Chinese-Australians in the armed forces, the evocatively titled *Dinky-Di*. It was conceived in the Australian Government's Office of Multicultural Affairs out of a concern 'that in some sections of the community there was a perception that Australians of non-British descent would not willingly defend their country in time of conflict'. The 1980s had seen the development of a conservative critique of multiculturalism for its supposed promotion of social fragmentation, along with periodic criticism by conservative public figures such as the historian Geoffrey Blainey of Asian migration as a threat to Australia's traditional British heritage, social cohesion and national unity. In 1988, the year of the Bicentenary, a government enquiry led by Stephen FitzGerald, Australia's former Ambassador to China, reported considerable public hostility to multiculturalism which was said to be eroding support for the country's immigration programme.[35] *Dinky-Di*'s story of Chinese-Australian contributions to Australia's military history needs to be seen against this background. Yet neither the book's

---

34    Hsu-Ming Teo, 'Multiculturalism and the Problem of Multicultural Histories: An Overview of Ethnic Historiography', in Hsu-Ming Teo and Richard White, eds, *Cultural History in Australia* (Sydney: University of New South Wales Press, 2003), 147. For the notion of 'cultural enrichment', Teo draws on Hage, *White Nation*, 117–18.

35    Soutphommasane, *Don't Go Back to Where You Came From*, 23–7.

historical commentary nor its oral histories frame its enterprise of historical recovery as a story of 'Anzac'. Rather, as in Hall's account of the black
diggers, Chinese-Australians were there, they did their duty and they did
it well, despite the environment of discrimination imposed by a White
Australia. But as the cultural ascendancy of Anzac has grown since 1989
– the seventy-fifth anniversary of Gallipoli in 1990 appears in retrospect a
turning point – 'ethnic' histories of Australians at war have become more
insistent on the status of their group as true 'Anzacs', who evince a spirit
associated with the 'Anzac' tradition.

Elena Govor's *Russian Anzacs* is especially romantic in its Australian
nationalism. Her book begins with an epigraph from a Mary Gilmore
poem: 'The nation was –/Because of me'. Although Govor doesn't say so,
Gilmore's verse is about convicts, not Anzacs. Govor, herself a migrant
from Russia, makes it clear from the outset that this is no debunking history. Rather, she wishes to find a place in the Anzac legend of the 'forging
of our nation' for Russian-born men. Such a history will be therapeutic
for their descendants, who 'are a stolen generation' on account of their
separation from 'the native language, history and culture of their fathers'.
She found about 1,000 of these people's 'heroic forefathers', surely evidence
of her technical virtuosity as a historical researcher. For Govor, these men
comprise 'a virtual battalion [...] of Russians that never served together in
a single unit, the battalion that never was' but 'might have been'.[36]

Govor adds a layer of ethnic complexity to the Anzac story, but also
writes *within* the Anzac legend. Anzac is arguably so powerful in contemporary Australia that to find a place in it for each ethnic group becomes
an important claim to inclusion in the national story, and therefore in the
national community. If Gallipoli was where the nation was born, and if
the Anzacs were responsible, then national inclusion implies a place in
Australian military tradition. The easiest way in for any ethnic group is
to find your own in the First Australian Imperial Force (AIF), preferably
at Gallipoli.

36   Elena Govor, *Russian Anzacs in Australian History* (Sydney: University of New
     South Wales Press in association with the National Archives of Australia, 2005), 13,
     20, 1–2, 82.

'Ethnic' histories of Anzac are not necessarily uncritical in their treatment of the Australian past, nor is their discussion of ethnicity without its
nuances. Govor recognizes the diversity obscured by the use of a catch-all
term such as 'Russian' (her book includes Finns, Poles, Latvians, Ukrainians,
Jews and ethnic Russians, among others), and she unpicks this complexity
in her story. Govor also points to the discrimination often suffered by the
Russian Anzacs on account of their foreignness, especially after the revolution and Russia's withdrawal from the war. Yet she suggests that such men
were admitted to the mateship of Anzac, that their sufferings were more
often the result of official action than uncomradely behaviour.[37] In this way,
the essential components of an Anzac legend are retained, for it has long
been capable of accommodating official neglect of the ordinary digger.

John Williams's *German Anzacs* is more securely in the tradition of
critical social history. While a large part of his purpose is to challenge the
traditional understanding of the AIF as 'the pure expression of an ethnically
distinct British Australia', he suggests that many German-Australians might
have joined up in the hope that their families in Australia would therefore
receive better treatment at a time when they were extremely vulnerable.
Many German-Australians, he says, despite their pro-British sentiments,
were not welcomed into the AIF's 'community of mates'. Even having a son
in the army did not prove a safeguard against allegations of disloyalty for
family left behind. Williams's book depicts a morally ambiguous wartime
experience which by reminding readers that the Great War 'was the darkest
chapter in the history of Germans in Australia', unsettles Anzac as a focus
of national identity, even as it claims a place for the German-Australian
community in that very legend.[38] Jeff Kildea's revelation in *Anzacs and
Ireland* of the role played by Australians in the suppression of the Easter
1916 uprising in Dublin similarly unsettles the notion of Australians as
natural defenders of the underdog, at the same time as it claims a place
for the Irish 'in building that most enduring edifice of Australian national
identity, the Anzac tradition'.[39]

37    Govor, *Russian Anzacs*, 10–12, 44, 103–4, 150–1, 163–6, 169.
38    Williams, *German Anzacs*, 64, 103, 293.
39    Kildea, *Anzacs and Ireland*, ch. 2 and 120.

The Anzac Day march itself has taken on 'multicultural' dimensions. Ken Inglis pointed out that Italians were marching as early as the 1930s.[40] In 2005 a memorial depicting an Australian and South Vietnamese soldier standing side-by-side under a helicopter donated by the United States Army was unveiled in Dandenong, an outer-Melbourne suburb, outside the local RSL. Although it received retrospective Commonwealth funding, much of the money for the venture came from the Melbourne Vietnamese community, an endeavour led by Andy Nguyen, a Melbourne man formerly of the South Vietnamese army. The memorial's evocation of comradeship between the Australian digger and his South Vietnamese counterpart, as well as its location in an area of Melbourne with a large concentration of Vietnamese migrants, translated into a celebration of common national belonging in an ethnically diverse society.[41]

The extent of ethnic minority identification with Anzac should not be exaggerated. A report recently commissioned by the Department of Veterans' Affairs found little evidence of engagement with the upcoming centenary of Gallipoli among such groups: it was Turks, for obvious historical reasons, and Sudanese, as a vulnerable recent migrant group, who were most interested in participation although the latter, in particular, had 'concerns about racism and being made to feel unwelcome'.[42] Indeed, for all its supposed inclusiveness, contemporary Anzac culture often has a deeply authoritarian tone. When in 2002 there was some polite questioning of whether sending into primary schools posters of the celebrated Gallipoli figures of Simpson and his Donkey was an effective way of promoting a sense of civic responsibility, Brendan Nelson, then Education Minister, now Director of the Australian War Memorial, declared: '[I]f people don't want to be Australians and they don't want to live by Australian values and

40   K. S. Inglis, 'ANZAC and the Australian Military Tradition', *Current Affairs Bulletin* 64/11 (1988), 15.

41   *Dandenong Star* (4 January 2007) <http://www.starnewsgroup.com.au/star/dandenong/73/story/32721.html> accessed 2 February 2013; Inglis, *Sacred Places*, 478.

42   Department of Veterans' Affairs, '*A Century of Service' Community Research Phase* II (Canberra: Colmar Brunton, August 2011), 2 <www.anzaccentenary.gov.au/documents/colmar_brunton.pdf> accessed 2 September 2013.

understand them, well then they can basically clear off'.[43] Conservative op-ed columnists and even academic historians have also been known to descend to abuse of real or imagined opponents when they feel the country's civil religion under attack.[44] Dissident academics who appear in the media to question Anzac pieties receive hate-mail.

## Conclusion

Authoritarianism and intolerance, however, might paradoxically be a function of Anzac's post-Vietnam War *inclusiveness*. If everyone is invited to participate in a national ritual – even if the terms of that inclusion remain unequal – it becomes easier to criticize as ungrateful those who remain aloof, and as disloyal or even dangerous those sufficiently bold to offer critique. In a commemorative culture of this kind, to criticize the civil religion is to compromise one's claims to full membership of the national community. To question whether every Anzac was a paragon of courage, virtue and fair play is potentially to dishonour a cherished family member, as well as the embodiment of national identity. Even to suggest the Anzac tradition might be analysed in the classroom, rather than merely being transmitted as a received body of lore, is to poison the minds of the young with the treachery or nihilism of sixties radicalism.

In a very real sense, multiculturalism has still had too *little* influence on the way in which we understand the Australian experience of war, not too much. The stories of Holocaust survivors and of the war criminals who made them suffer might have a place in Australian history, but they are

43    'Teach Australian values or "clear off", says Nelson', ABC PM, Transcript, 24 August 2005 <http://www.abc.net.au/pm/content/2005/s1445262.htm> accessed 2 February 2013.
44    Frank Bongiorno and Grant Mansfield, 'Whose War Was It Anyway? Some Australian Historians and the Great War', *History Compass* 6/1 (2008), 62–90.

seen as part of the history of post-war immigration, not usually an integral aspect of the experience of Australians in war. The same still mainly applies to the Indo-Chinese migrants who came to Australia from the late 1970s; they, too, usually feature in the history of Australian migration, settlement and multiculturalism rather than in war history. The history of war-related trauma has for some time extended to Australian war widows, but is only just beginning in the historical study of those who came to Australia after 1945, migrant families whose trauma had its roots in wars fought elsewhere.[45]

Multiculturalism in the historical writing on Australians at war often means staking a claim to the Anzac tradition. While there is some room for critical history in this body of work, wider public understandings of Anzac remain difficult to challenge from the angle of ethnic contribution history. To this extent, an ostensible historical pluralism might have been complicit in a conservative cultural politics that has progressively closed off possibilities both for interpreting Australian pasts, and imagining Australian futures. By contrast, the cultivated ambiguity of Indigenous war remembrance may offer a more radical challenge to Anzac, through an expansive understanding of the identity of Aboriginal warrior, and an inclusive notion of what has constituted the defence of country.

45   But see Joy Damousi, 'Legacies of war and migration: Memories of war trauma, dislocation and second generation Greek-Australians', in Niklaus Steiner, Robert Mason and Anna Hayes, eds, *Migration and Insecurity: Citizenship and Social Inclusion in a Transnational Era* (Abingdon: Routledge, 2013), 31–47.

ANDREW MYCOCK

# The Politics of the Great War Centenary in the United Kingdom

## Introduction

In October 2012, UK Prime Minister David Cameron unveiled government plans to mark the centenary of the First World War in a speech at the Imperial War Museum in London. Cameron argued it was crucial to commemorate the 'Great War' as the scale of sacrifice and its considerable impact on Britain and the world meant a durable emotional connection to British national consciousness had been established. He announced the commitment of £50 million from Government and National Lottery funds to support a programme of commemorative events including the refurbishment of the First World War galleries at the Imperial War Museum in London and a number of educational and heritage initiatives. Cameron also noted that a 'Centenary secretariat' and an unpaid centenary advisory board, drawn from a range of military, political and cultural backgrounds, had been established under the chair of his own 'special representative', Andrew Murrison MP, and were to meet regularly to ensure 'we really do this properly as a country'.[1]

Cameron was at pains to stress that 'remembrance must be the hallmark of our commemorations', thus rejecting the notion that the centenary should embrace celebratory elements. His speech was notable for his stated ambition that the centenary would be 'a truly national commemoration' whilst

---

1    David Cameron, 'Speech at Imperial War Museum on First World War centenary plans', 11 October 2012 <http://www.number10.gov.uk/news/speech-at-imperial-war-museum-on-wwi/> accessed 12 January 2013.

also seeking to acknowledge the sacrifice of 'friends in the Commonwealth' and from across all of Ireland. Cameron's announcement was broadly welcomed, particularly by those sections of the UK media who had previously claimed the UK had been 'left behind' by other countries, such as Belgium, France and Australia, in the development of plans for marking the centenary.[2] This chapter seeks to explore the extent to which the UK government's plans to mark the First World War centenary can be realized within the terms outlined. It will first explore the politics of war commemoration, assessing the historical and contemporary challenges in establishing inclusive narratives and memory cultures to mark the Great War in an appropriate manner. It will then examine the implications of the national, multi-national and transnational contexts of the commemorations. Overall it will assess whether the UK government's centenary plans can, as Cameron asserted, capture 'our national spirit'.

## Commemorating the 'Great War'

As noted in the introductory chapter of this volume, the complexities relating to history, memory and war commemoration raise significant questions with regards to the stated aims of the UK government centenary plans. One of the most pressing questions relates to what is actually being commemorated during the centenary events and why. Commemoration of the First World War has proven neither static nor universal in its motivations and meaning. Popular participation has been motivated by diverse narratives emphasizing an (appropriately respectful) patriotic acknowledgement of the positive contribution of militarism, a futile and terrible warning of the dangers of war, or even a call for world peace. Mosse notes concerted

---

2    See for example Bernard Carlin, 'Will we remember them? Anger as Britain lags behind France – and Belgium – in plans to mark the centenary of the First World War', *Daily Mail* (30 October 2011).

efforts undertaken by the British state after the war that sought to justify the fighting and sacrifice through the promotion of patriotic national myths and commemorative acts and rituals 'to make an inherently unpalatable past acceptable'.[3] This was driven by a need to justify the scale of losses in the war in the name of the British nation *and* Empire, not least so that others might risk their lives in future wars.

Levels of participation in commemoration, however, have proven variable. High levels of public engagement were maintained during the inter-war and immediate post-Second World War periods. As in Australia, by the end of the 1980s, popular participation in war commemoration across the UK had reduced considerably, largely due to declines in the membership and influence of key sponsors such as the Church of England and veterans' associations. This combined with shifts in social attitudes and practices that meant more people were unwilling or unable to participate in official acts of war commemoration.[4]

There has, however, been a rekindling of interest in war commemoration in the UK, particularly since the early 1990s. This, in part, has been a response to the gradual dying out of the First World War generation. Although surviving veterans were increasingly peripheralized in comparison to their dead comrades during war commemorations in the inter-war period,[5] after 1945 they arguably became the most influential representation of official war commemoration.[6] Growing public recognition of social or ethnic groups whose experiences were often largely overlooked within mainstream 'official' forms and practices of war commemoration have also proven influential, stimulating participation. Moreover, annual

---

3    George L. Mosse, *Fallen Soldiers: Reshaping the Memory of the World Wars* (Oxford: Oxford University Press, 1990), 6.

4    Tony Walter, 'From cathedral to supermarket: mourning, silence and solidarity', *The Sociological Review* 49/4 (2001), 494–511.

5    Adrian Gregory, *The Silence of Memory: Armistice Day 1919–1946* (Oxford: Berghahn Books, 1994).

6    Martin Shaw, 'Past wars and present conflicts: From the Second World War to the Gulf', in Martin Evans and Kenneth Lunn, eds, *War and Memory in the Twentieth Century* (Oxford: Berghahn Books, 1997), 191–205.

cycles of commemoration have been more frequently punctuated by major anniversaries (typically marking the beginning, end and key events of the First and Second World Wars), have gone beyond established traditions and have encouraged extraordinary acts of remembrance. Finally, the UK has engaged in a series of conflicts since the late 1990s which have raised the profile of the military and seen veterans' associations, the media and politicians encourage greater public recognition of and participation in war commemoration.

Todman argues that certain aspects of how the war has been officially and unofficially commemorated in the UK have proven durable, particularly the sense of shock in response to the scale of loss of life.[7] Such revulsion has been mediated through narratives that stress notions of sacrifice, though the precise nature of the cause for which people died has proven less clear. More positive conceptions of the First World War that celebrated victory and the defeat of militaristic threats to the nation, which were also prominent in the inter-war period, have largely dissipated. This in part is due to the widespread denouncement of the notion that it was the 'war to end war' in the wake of the Second World War. More recently, many Britons have been strongly influenced by historical revisionism that since the 1960s propagated the view that the First World War was largely futile and the huge loss of life was the result of political and military elite incompetence. This revisionist narrative was vividly analogized as 'lions led by donkeys', a phrase that has proven extremely powerful in permeating popular memory cultures but whose origin was fictitiously attributed by the late Alan Clark MP to a conversation between German generals Erich Ludendorff and Max Hoffmann.[8]

Shifts in popular understandings of the First World War, including how it is remembered, raise pertinent questions as to the content and purpose of the UK government's centenary plans. Andrew Murrison has stated the commemorations would focus on remembrance, thus 'making

7    Daniel Todman, *The Great War: Myth and Memory* (London: Hambledon Continuum, 2005).
8    Alan Clark, *The Donkeys* (New York: William Morrow, 1962).

no judgment about fault, right or wrong, or indulging in any jingoistic sentiment'. Although he acknowledged 'there are bound to be differences of opinion about how the Great War is remembered', Murrison quickly sought to distance the UK government from such disputes. He instead argued academics and historians had the responsibility to undertake the 'heavy lifting in terms of debating the background to the war', concluding 'it would be wrong for the government to insist on a particular narrative'. This noted, he indicated some appreciation of the extent that popular perceptions of the war might be somewhat skewed in terms of perspective, and encouraged historians to adopt 'counter-intuitive' approaches to challenge 'some of the mythology' such as the 'lions led by donkeys' thesis.[9]

This 'call to arms', suggested Murrison, lacked an of appreciation the considerable work already undertaken by historians over the past thirty years to provide more nuanced and critically objective analyses of British military leadership during the conflict, as well as wider issues concerning the causes, conduct and legacies of the war.[10] It is clear, however, that many of those involved in planning the centenary are sympathetic to depictions of the First World War as a futile conflict. Murrison has stated the war was 'a cataclysmic failure on the part of rulers and governments sustained by rhetoric and jingoism'.[11] Lord Guthrie, a member of the centenary advisory committee, declared 'it was a totally unnecessary war [...] there were horrifying casualties. It was not the soldiers' fault, it was the politicians'.[12] Historian and Labour MP, Tristram Hunt, highlighted cross-party

9   Nick Hopkins and Richard Norton-Taylor, 'First World War commemorations "will be like Titanic anniversary"', *The Guardian* (8 February 2013).

10  See for example Todman, *The Great War*; Gary Sheffield, *Forgotten Victory: The First World War, Myths and Realities* (London: Headline, 2001); Adrian Gregory, *The Last Great War: British Society and the First World War* (Cambridge: Cambridge University Press, 2008); Catriona Pennell, *A Kingdom United: Popular Responses to the Outbreak of the First World War in Britain and Ireland* (Oxford: Oxford University Press, 2012).

11  Andrew Murrison, 'A great tribute to the Great War', *Daily Telegraph* (4 November 2011).

12  Nick Hopkins and Richard Norton-Taylor, 'Kickabout that captured the futility of First World War to be replayed for the centenary', *The Guardian* (8 February 2013).

support for the government plans, arguing 'the tone should be of solemn remembrance – there is little to celebrate in what can only be described as a human catastrophe'.[13]

Debate regarding the morality of the Great War has failed to extend beyond the need to remember those who served and died to 'ensure that the lessons learnt live with us forever'.[14] Cameron has suggested that, in remembering those who fought and died, 'we will continue to fight for the values they fought for'.[15] He failed, however, to identify what those values were, beyond banal personal qualities such as 'friendship, loyalty, what the Australians would call "mateship"'. A leading member of the centenary advisory committee, Brigadier Sir Hew Strachan, has suggested that those fighting 'were mostly citizen soldiers, whose values reflected the society from which they were recruited'.[16] Many of those who fought therefore sought to defend the patriotic values of a 'strongly religious society' which was deeply hierarchical and whose 'collective loyalties' were shaped by monarchy, Empire, and nation.[17]

Although it is questionable whether such values continue to resonate with many British citizens in the twenty-first century, alternative narratives that link the causes which motivated those who fought in the First World War to the present lack widespread acceptance. The argument offered by some that the war should be understood as an ideological struggle between British (and French) democracy and German (and Ottoman

---

13   Tristram Hunt, 'We must strike a solemn tone to mark centenary of catastrophe', *The Sentinel* (12 November 2012).

14   Cameron, 'Speech at Imperial War Musuem'.

15   Tim Montgomerie, 'We Shall Remember Them', *Conservative Home* (25 July 2009). <http://conservativehome.blogs.com/thetorydiary/2009/07/we-shall-remember-them.html> accessed 12 February 2013.

16   Hew Strachan, 'Why we should celebrate the First World War as well as commemorate it', 4 September 2012 <http://www.historyextra.com/blog/why-we-should-celebrate-first-world-war-well-commemorate-it> accessed 12 February 2013.

17   Andrew Frayn, 'Armistice Day and a mythologised distant version of the First World War', *The Guardian* (12 November 2011).

and Austro-Hungarian) autocracy has some merit.[18] It is, however, highly contestable in light of the reactive, partial and reluctant post-war reform of the British political system after 1918.[19] As one commentator has countered, 'the idea that the war was some kind of crusade for democracy when most of Britain's population – including many men – were still denied the vote, and democracy and dissent were savagely crushed among most of those Britain ruled, is laughable'.[20]

Concerns about the limitations of reworking 'familiar themes of remembrance', particularly now there are no living combatants, has led to some public questioning of how it is possible to honour those who fought if the cause for which they did so is peripheralized or rejected outright. The Great War was, according to historian Gary Sheffield, 'a war of national survival'.[21] This was, Hew Strachan argues, because 'Germany was a militarist and imperialist regime which had to be defeated and from that point of view, the victory is a serious victory'. There was, he concluded, 'intent in government not to upset the Germans'.[22] This view has been supported by some sections of the British media who suggest the UK government policy would appear to be 'don't mention we won the war'. In an editorial, *The Times* argued the war was 'essentially just', being 'a necessary military response that stopped aggression by an expansionist power' which was 'xenophobic and anti-democratic'.[23] One commentator even made a case for 'why we SHOULD upset the Germans', arguing there was a 'politically correct' notion that it was 'somehow insulting to the millions who died to suggest that it wasn't all a monstrous waste of blood'. He railed against

18   Gary Sheffield, 'The Origins of World War One', BBC (8 March 2011) <http://www.bbc.co.uk/history/worldwars/wwone/origins_01.shtml> accessed 12 February 2013.

19   See John Garrard, *Democratisation in Britain: Elites, Civil Society and Reform since 1800* (Basingstoke: Palgrave, 2002).

20   Seumas Milne, 'The First World War: the real lessons of this savage imperial bloodbath', *The Guardian* (16 October 2012).

21   Gary Sheffield, 'The Great War was a just war', *History Today* 63/8 (2013).

22   Nicholas Hellen and Richard Brooks, 'Don't Mention that we won the First World War', *The Sunday Times* (13 January 2013).

23   'Remembrance Aright', *The Times* (12 October 2012).

the 'historical inaccuracy' to 'suit contemporary sympathies' which meant there would be no discussion about who started the war, German 'massacres' in Belgium and its empire, or its use of gas in 1915 and the policy of sinking civilian ships, concluding 'give it long enough and we may find that we actually lost the Great War after all'.[24]

Contention regarding the centenary commemorations has also extended to what events during the war should be marked. The UK government has announced three 'national commemorative events' – the anniversary of the start of the war in 2014, the first day of the Battle of the Somme (2016) and Armistice Day (2018) – as well as recognizing the battles of Jutland and Passchendaele and the Gallipoli landings. The UK government has argued the commemoration of the beginning of the war afforded 'the opportunity for reflection, enlightenment and community'.[25] This led the author and centenary advisory committee member, Sebastian Faulks, to caution that 'a degree of humility is needed, initially particularly, as this was an avoidable calamity'. Plaid Cymru MP Jonathan Edwards went further, tabling a UK Parliamentary Early Day Motion (EDM) in October 2012 which stated 'this House should recognise the loss and pain suffered by the victims of the war and that it would be more appropriate to commemorate the end of the war rather than its beginning'.[26]

Others have questioned the 'blinkered' focus of the centenary commemorations on the frontline and the lack of appropriate recognition of the domestic situation within the UK, particularly the impact of the First World War on working class representation in political and union terms during the war. Historian Martin Pugh suggested that the emphasis on military events is the product of 'a selected bunch of conservative historians and generals'. He noted that 'several generations of scholars have recognised the war as a major social, political, economic and cultural phenomenon'.[27]

24   Robert Hardman, 'Why we SHOULD upset the Germans – by reminding them of their Great War atrocities', *Daily Mail* (14 January 2013).
25   Murrison, 'A great tribute to the Great War'.
26   The EDM only gained seventeen signatures. See <http://www.parliament.uk/edm/2012-13/614>.
27   'Blinkered view of the First World War', *The Guardian* (13 February 2013).

Tristram Hunt concurred, arguing the liberation of women and the growth of trade unions and the Labour party meant the war 'wreaked enormous change on the shape of society'.[28]

Some of those debating the plans for the centenary have questioned whether the 'honourable and equally brave role' of contentious objectors should also be commemorated.[29] In September 2013, the 'No Glory' campaign was launched by anti-war activists and high-profile supporters. It challenged the narrative of the official programme that marked the centenary of the First World War with an alternative range of activities.[30] But plans by the Heritage Lottery Fund (HLF) to give money for commemorations of the Peace Pledge Union have been publicly questioned, with one MP, Julian Brazier, stating 'the HLF is throwing money on celebrating the role of those who refused to fight, but cannot reach into its pockets to find a little more to remember those who died'.[31]

## Capturing 'our national spirit'

As we have already noted, British war commemoration has typically drawn on what are perceived to be shared experiences and memories of past conflicts. This has been based on widespread political and popular subscription to mutually inclusive narratives, rituals and symbols of remembrance involving all of the nations of the UK.[32] However the explicitly

28 Hunt, 'We must strike a solemn tone'.

29 Hansard, Column 1358 (4 March 2013) <http://www.publications.parliament.uk/pa/ld201213/ldhansrd/text/130304-0002.htm>, accessed 25 March 2013.

30 For further details, see <http://noglory.org/>.

31 Jasper Copping, 'Poppies? No, but we can fund a show about migrants', *Daily Telegraph* (11 September 2013).

32 See for example Alex King, *Memorials of the Great War in Britain: Symbolism and Politics of Remembrance* (London: Berg, 1998); Daniel Todman, 'Representing the First World War in Britain: The 90th Anniversary of the Somme' in Michael Keren

pluri-national structure of the UK state raises pertinent questions on the degree that ethno-national hierarchies impact on common patterns of war commemoration. The UK has, to a certain extent, always functioned as a nation-state, with central government establishing a common framework of social, economic and political citizenship and directing foreign affairs including warfare. British national identity has similarly drawn on a shared attachment and identification with common political and cultural institutions, symbols, values and rituals, suggesting the UK state possesses 'national' forms of sovereignty and identity. But the UK is not a nation-state in the sense that its multiple nations only exist within the sovereign boundaries of a unitary state. Nationhood has thus been realized at both state and sub-state national levels, highlighting that constructions of 'national' history, identity and memory that inform war commemoration are layered and interdependent but not necessarily universal.

Generalizations about the universal nature of the 'British' experience of the First World War conceal pluri-national asymmetries, particularly the conflation of British and English narratives informing state war commemoration and marginalization of non-English national interpretations. Anglocentric bias has thus often overlooked distinctive and sometimes contradictory national constructions of official and unofficial history and memory. As Jim McAuley discusses in this volume, commemoration of the First World War in Northern Ireland has persistently highlighted its politically contentious and culturally divisive legacies. Scholars have also explored the distinctive impact and legacy of the First World War in Scottish and Welsh national terms, drawing attention to distinctive frontline and domestic experiences and, in the case of Scotland, the disproportionate human cost.[33]

---

and Holger Herwig, eds, *War Memory and Popular Culture* (Ottawa: McFarland, 2009).

33   See for example Trevor Royle, *The Flowers of the Forest: Scotland and the First World War* (Edinburgh: Birlinn Publishers, 2006); Derek Young, *Scottish Voices from the Great War* (Stroud: Tempus Publishing, 2006); Chris Williams, 'Taffs in the Trenches: Welsh National Identity and Military Service, 1914–1918', in Matthew

Although Cameron has claimed the commemorations will draw on 'our national spirit in every corner of the country', plans originating from Westminster for the centenary have proven distinctly Anglocentric, focusing solely or predominantly on England rather the UK more widely. For example, the vast majority of UK government funding for 'national' events will be spent in England, with most being spent on the Imperial War Museum in London. Another programme involving battlefront visits for school children was claimed by one Government minister to have the potential to 'bind us together as a nation'.[34] However UK government funding was only made available to English schools.

In Scotland, the election of the Scottish National Party (SNP) in 2011 to take sole control of the Scottish Parliament has marked a seismic change in debates about future constitutional arrangements with the UK. A referendum on whether Scotland should become independent will be held in September 2014. There is evidence that the nationalist-led devolved Scottish government has sought to develop distinctive centenary commemorations emphasizing the Scottish nation rather than the UK more widely. In March 2013, they announced the formation of a Scottish advisory panel under the leadership of Norman Drummond who noted that 'it is important that Scotland remembers the sacrifice of those who served during the First World War and the wider impact that the war has had on our country and upon Scots across the world'.[35] In announcing the Scottish Government's own plans for the centenary, First Minister Alex Salmond focused entirely on the impact of the Great War on Scotland, making no reference to the wider British context. This noted, the Scottish government has drawn on a similar centenary narrative as the UK government, declaring it was in

Cragoe and Chris Williams, eds, *Wales and War: Religion, Society and Politics in the Nineteenth and Twentieth Centuries* (Cardiff, 2007), 126–64.

34   Eric Pickles, 'We all have a duty to remember the millions who lost their lives during the First World War', *Daily Telegraph* (10 June 2013).

35   Scottish Government, 'Former military chaplain to lead WW1 commemorations', 24 January 2013 <http://www.scotland.gov.uk/News/Releases/2013/01/WW1> accessed 12 February 2013.

'no sense a celebration of the centenary of this devastating conflict'.[36] The Scottish Government's plans have also come under attack from groups who argue that the causes and domestic political and social consequences of the Great War have been overlooked in favour of the frontline.[37]

But although both pro- and anti-independence campaigns have formally signalled a 'political armistice' with regards to the First World War commemorations,[38] there is evidence that the political dynamics of the Scottish independence referendum have influenced debates about the centenary. Supporters of Scottish independence have raised concerns that the UK government plans for the Great War centenary could become part of a wider unionist 'Britannia fetishism'[39] or politicized 'Britfest' which they argue began with the Diamond Jubilee and Olympics celebrations in 2012.[40] One prominent independence supporter, drawing attention to the greater ratio of Scots' mortality rates on the Western Front when compared to other parts of the UK, suggested 'British military commanders have always viewed Scottish forces as expendable'. A vote for independence, he argued, would ensure future generations of Scots could not be 'sent like lambs to the slaughter for a monarch or a crusading Westminster zealot'.[41]

Conversely, Unionists argue the centenary will provide 'ample opportunity to remind the Scottish people how they stood together with the English, Welsh and Northern Irish'.[42] Unionist politicians in both the

---

36   Scottish Government, 'WWI commemorations in Scotland', 25 May 2013 <http://www.scotland.gov.uk/News/Releases/2013/05/ww1-commemorations-in-scotland23052013> accessed 14 August 2013.

37   Scott MacNab, 'Scottish WWI tribute accused of whitewash', *The Scotsman* (27 May 2013).

38   David Maddox, 'Political armistice promised as Britain marks WWI centenary', *The Scotsman* (12 October 2012).

39   Richard Seymour, 'The First World War centenary and the Britannia fetish', *The Guardian* (12 October 2012).

40   Michael Fry, 'Time to reflect, not celebrate', *The Scotsman* (19 October 2012).

41   Mark MacLachlan, 'Why Ypres matters more than Bannockburn in the independence vote', *Caledonian Mercury* (16 April 2012). The loss ratio of Scots was 26.4 per cent compared with an average death rate of 11.8 per cent for the rest of the British Army.

42   Simon Johnson, 'Why war anniversaries will influence the battle over Scottish independence', *Daily Telegraph* (8 November 2011).

Scottish and UK parliaments have accused the Scottish government of investing more funding in marking the 700th anniversary of the Battle of Bannockburn, where the Scots defeated the English, whilst deliberately overlooking the centenary.[43] Such an approach has been interpreted by one commentator as an attempt by the Scottish Government to appeal to the 'inner nationalist' of Scots rather than their 'outer Brit'.[44] This noted, one study suggested Scots participants viewed the centenary as a vehicle for British rather than Scottish interests and was thus less relevant to them. Moreover the study suggested that sectarian divisions in cities such as Glasgow strongly influenced views on the centenary.[45]

The sub-state nationalization of the UK-wide centenary commemorations is also evident in Wales. Welsh First Minister, Carwyn Jones, has noted that in planning for the centenary, 'it is extremely important that we remember those who died and reflect on how it changed Wales'.[46] Welsh initiatives for the centenary have focused on the need to establish a memorial in Flanders to 'all Welsh men and women who served during the war',[47] and the digitization of war archives and artefacts to 'to reveal the hidden history of World War One as it affected all aspects of Welsh life, language and culture'.[48] Welsh nationalists, Plaid Cymru, have however countered

43    David Maddox, 'Clash between WWI and Bannockburn memorials feared', *The Scotsman* (28 April 2013).

44    Alan Cochrane, 'What we should unite behind in 2014 – inner nat or not', *Daily Telegraph* (11 October 2012).

45    British Future, *Do Mention the War: will 1914 matter in 2014?* (London: British Future, 2013).

46    'Expert advisor appointed to help Wales remember the First World War', National Library for Wales, 2 March 2012. <http://www.llgc.org.uk/index.php?id=1514&no_cache=1&tx_ttnews%5Btt_news%5D=4740&cHash=4a62c31367489957c9e6f65d c6ad970a> accessed 12 February 2013.

47    'Wales Flanders memorial: Carwyn Jones announces £25,000 grant', BBC, 18 September 2013 <http://www.bbc.co.uk/news/uk-wales-24131181> accessed 3 October 2013.

48    'Collecting and sharing the Welsh experience of World War One', National Library for Wales, 25 January 2013. <http://www.llgc.org.uk/index.php?id=1514&no_cache=1&tx_ttnews%5Btt_news%5D=5208&cHash=9e94de7ba3e51a6ed743699 2b7dad5aa> accessed 12 February 2013.

that the commemorations for the Great War centenary are 'reminiscent of the jingoistic nonsense we saw from the British state elite to drum up support for the war in the first place'.[49] One leading Plaid Cymru member has claimed that the origins of the Welsh independence movement can be located in the First World War as a response to 'British imperialism' within the UK.[50]

The situation regarding the centenary of the First World War and its aftermath is more complex still in Northern Ireland. Between 2012 and 2021, a number of high-profile commemorations will mark the centenary of the Home Rule disputes, the Battle of Somme, the Easter Rising, and the Irish civil war. Such events will once again draw attention to the contemporary resonance of historical events surrounding Ireland's partition and divided past. It also highlights the extent to which the UK government's plans for a 'national' commemoration myopically simplifies the transnational and inter-state dimensions of the centenary. For example, Theresa Villiers, the Secretary of State for Northern Ireland, has stated, 'World War One profoundly affected the whole community across Northern Ireland and involved terrible sacrifice [...] it is important that a century on, this generation recognises and pays tribute to those who gave so much for our country'.[51] Villiers thus sought to overlook the division within the 'community' or contentions as to which was 'our country'. Indeed whilst the UK government appears to believe that the First World War offers further opportunities for reconciliation with the Republic of Ireland, it remains somewhat insensitive to enduring divisions within the UK that the centenary will undoubtedly encourage some of its citizens to revisit.

49    Jonathan Edwards, 'Why we shouldn't commemorate the start of WWI', *Morning Star* (31 October 2012).

50    Alex Stevenson 'MPs fight back against WW1 commemoration', 24 October 2012 <http://www.politics.co.uk/news/2012/10/24/mps-fight-back-against-ww1-com-memoration> accessed 12 February 2012.

51    Anna Maguire, 'Northern Ireland schools will play a part in WWI centenary', *Belfast Telegraph* (15 October 2012).

## Beyond the nation? War commemoration after Empire

In announcing the UK plans for a 'truly national commemoration', Cameron also noted that the 'extraordinary sacrifice' and 'catastrophic' death toll of 'our friends in the Commonwealth'.[52] Murrison has subsequently suggested that the centenary offers opportunities to reflect on why 'Britain and her family' went to war.[53] Such sentiment appears to acknowledge the enduring multinational and transnational dynamics of British Great War commemorations and highlights the power of British commemorative projects established after the First World War to fortify a range of national identities founded in an imperial age. By establishing redemptive narratives that extended beyond the imperial metropole to include parts of the colonial periphery, Jay Winter suggests the 'shadow of empire mattered' in encouraging a sense of shared loss and trauma underpinning transnational networks of memory. These were particularly resonant for the large numbers of settlers who served in the Australian, Canadian, South African and New Zealand (the so-called 'White Dominions') armies who were British-born or who had British ancestry, thus indicating that war commemoration was strongly defined by shared bonds which were racially determined.[54]

Conversely, First World War commemorations in the 'White Dominions' indicated that the common bonds of imperial kinship were also beginning to fragment as many increasingly saw their sacrifice in national rather than imperial terms. Emergent historical narratives and memory cultures drew on postcolonial interpretations of the perceived British military incompetence and scepticism about the British political leaders who took the Empire to war. The First World War was therefore understood as a foundational moment of national birth that diluted the emotional power of the imagined imperial community. The imperial framing of national

---

52   Cameron, 'Speech at the Imperial War Museum'.

53   Murrison, 'First World War commemorations "will be like Titanic anniversary"'.

54   Jay Winter, *Remembering War: The Great War between Memory and History in the Twentieth Century* (New Haven: Yale University Press, 2006), 170.

war commemoration was further compromised in the wake of the Second World War by the diverse experiences across the Empire of the conflict. Winter argues that transnational imperial or post colonial networks as acts of commemoration were increasingly recast within discrete British national contexts that predominantly focused on European theatres of conflict in both world wars.[55]

Although shared transnational modes of war commemoration across the 'White Dominions' continue to reflect shared sentiments, the proposition that the UK government will bring the British 'family' together to commemorate the centenary of the Great War overlooks differences in how the conflict has been remembered. Revisionist narratives that stress the futile but necessary nature of the conflict provide some common ground. However such sacrifice is also understood in terms of post-imperial nation-building and progress towards national self-determination. For example, Australian narratives of the First World War have been typically founded on the 'legend' or 'myths' of the Australian and New Zealand Army Corps (ANZAC) which are strongly associated with those troops involved in the Gallipoli landings of 1915. These emphasize the perceived shared robust physical attributes, personal and group characteristics, such as courage, humour and ingenuity, and egalitarian values associated with ANZAC soldiers when compared to their British commanding officers. Though such mythology has been strongly exposed to critical analyses by academics and others,[56] they have emerged as postcolonial tropes underpinning distinctive 'national characteristics' that dilute shared war narratives informing a common Britishness.

The arrival of 'new Commonwealth' migrants since the late 1940s has also raised new challenges to the inclusivity of transnational elements of war commemoration. Many post-colonial migrants from former colonies who came to the UK after 1945 were initially considered to have not shared in transnational 'collective memories' informing the content of British war

55   Winter, *Remembering War*, 171.
56   Some historians have been prepared to challenge the 'myths' of British-led incompetence and deliberate sacrifice of ANZAC forces. See for example Graham Wilson, *Bully Beef and Balderdash* (Newport, NSW: Big Sky Publishing, 2012).

commemoration (unlike their 'White Dominion' counterparts). More recently, increased representation of migrant communities has encouraged some redress of those groups who had been peripherialized or excluded. Acknowledgement of the contribution of troops from the Indian sub-continent, Africa and the Caribbean is now a growing dimension of war commemoration and the wider historiography of the First World War.[57]

The UK government has outlined its intention to ensure minority groups will be recognized during the centenary commemorations. Speaking during a visit to the battlefields of France and Belgium in April 2013, UK Faith and Communities Minister, Baroness Sayeeda Warsi, stated 'I will make it my mission to ensure that the centenary is a chance for everyone to learn about the contribution of the Commonwealth soldiers'. She claimed that the First World War offered opportunities to acknowledge that 'so many men from so far away came to Europe to fight for the freedoms we enjoy today. Their legacy is our liberty, and every single one of us owes them a debt of gratitude'. She concluded by noting 'our boys weren't just Tommies; they were Tariqs and Tajinders too', meaning that 'our shared future is based on our shared past'.[58]

The notion that subjects from across the Empire sought to defend British domestic liberties is questionable, particularly in the context of the exploitative and hierarchical nature of colonialism. Many troops did enlist voluntarily, their actions underpinned by a confluence of domestic and broader imperial motives.[59] However a considerable number were

---

57  See for example Santanu Das, ed., *Race, Empire and First World War Writing* (Cambridge: Cambridge University Press, 2011).

58  Department for Communities and Local Government, 'Baroness Warsi kick-starts campaign to remember Commonwealth Servicemen of the First World War', 16 April 2013 <https://www.gov.uk/government/news/baroness-warsi-kick-starts-campaign-to-remember-commonwealth-servicemen-of-the-first-world-war> accessed 18 April 2013.

59  See for example John Connor, 'The "superior", all-volunteer AIF', in Craig Stockings, ed., *Anzac's Dirty Dozen: 12 myths of Australian military history* (Sydney: University of New South Wales Press, 2012), 35–50; David Omissi, 'Through Indian Eyes: Indian Soldiers Encounter England and France, 1914–1918', *English Historical Review* 122/496 (2007), 371–96.

conscripted and many lacked a comprehensive understanding of the cause for which they were expected to fight.[60] Moreover, such a perspective focuses the contribution of the British Empire solely in terms of the sacrifices at the front line, thus overlooking the extent to which resources and commodities were appropriated to support of the war effort. Similarly, claims by Prime Minister Cameron that the First World War marked 'the beginnings of ethnic minorities getting the recognition, respect and equality they deserve' overlook the documented experiences of Commonwealth forces that reveal the pervasive influence of racial hierarchies. For example, West Indian troops serving on the Western Front were not entrusted to fight and were instead allocated dangerous but menial manual labour and their service went unrecognized at the end of the war.[61] Furthermore there is evidence that the sacrifices of troops from the colonies were not recognized equally in remembrance on war memorials after the war.[62] A plan announced by the British government to lay commemorative stones in towns of those awarded the Victoria Cross in the war suggest such attitudes still exist, as the scheme applied only to soldiers born in the UK, thus excluding recipients born overseas.[63]

The UK government's focus on the Commonwealth, particularly its Anglospheric elements, potentially relegates the contribution of its European allies during the Great War, such as Italy, whilst also furthering anti-German sentiment in the UK. This in part reflects the extent to

60    See for example, Albert Grundlingh, *Fighting Their Own War: South African Blacks and the First World War* (Johannesburg: Ravan Press, 1987); Glenford D. Howe, *Race, War and Nationalism: A social history of West Indians in the First World War* (Kingston: Ian Randle Publishers, 2002); David Omissi, *The Sepoy and the Raj: The Indian Army, 1860–1940* (Basingstoke: Palgrave MacMillan, 1994).

61    Arthur Torrington, 'West Indian soldiers in the First World War', 11 March 2013 <http://blogs.iwm.org.uk/research/2013/03/west-indian-soldiers-in-the-first-world-war/> accessed 15 April 2013.

62    Michèle Barrett, 'Death and the afterlife: Britain's colonies and dominions' in Santanu Das, ed., *Race, Empire and First World War Writing* (Cambridge: Cambridge University Press), 301–20.

63    Kounteya Sinha, 'Indian heroes forgotten in UK WW1 tribute?', *The Times of India* (5 August 2013).

which the centenary commemorations in many European countries will be underpinned by distinctive themes and memory cultures. In France and Germany, for example, the war is being presented as a vital lesson in why there is need for global peace and stability, particularly in terms of post-Second World War European integration.[64] This has encouraged some Eurosceptic politicians and commentators to link German imperial militarism to recent German interventions to support the Eurozone.[65] Simon Heffer, an influential right-wing commentator, has even argued that the British should commemorate the 'terrible consequences' of failing to adopt a strategy of isolationism in 1914.[66]

## Conclusion

The UK government has claimed its role in the First World War centenary is one that provides leadership and encouragement for the organization of commemorative acts whilst not dictating the themes of commemoration itself. This suggests the UK government is keen to be seen to be acting appropriately but reveals deep insecurities as to the exact purpose of the centenary beyond the commemoration of sacrifice during the war. This reticence in establishing clear themes to define centenary commemoration highlights the tensions between popular collective memories of the First World War, which are pessimistic and view the war in largely negative terms, and more critical and objective analyses of it which are more balanced in their conclusions.

64   See for example Matthias Strohn, 'First World War centenary: let's remember a world, rather than a British, conflict', *The Guardian* (23 July 2013).

65   Tim Shipman, 'Don't Mention the War: German Embassy calls for Britons not to celebrate First World War victory', *Daily Mail* (18 August 2013).

66   Simon Heffer, 'Honour the dead yes but don't celebrate a futile conflict that blights us to this day', *Daily Mail* (4 August 2013).

It is apparent that some sections of the right-wing press and political classes remain wedded to jingoistic frames of historical reference that seek to sustain a common British identity. But by framing the First World War centenary commemorations in British national terms, the UK government has also overlooked the extent to which the pluri-national foundations of the UK state have been further enhanced by devolution since 1998. Moreover it appears unwilling to engage with the complex legacies of Empire that the centenary highlights, particularly in terms of the role of the Commonwealth. The adoption of a multidimensional approach that acknowledges the interconnected and entangled histories of the citizens and nations of the UK and its former Empire during the First World War, and the pluralities and complex configurations that result from it, are as such largely absent from the UK government's plans.

JAMES W. MCAULEY

# Divergent Memories: Remembering and Forgetting the Great War in Loyalist and Nationalist Ireland

## Introduction

It has become commonplace at football matches to conduct an act of remembrance in any game taking place over the Armistice Sunday weekend. In November 2012, for example, I travelled to watch my own local heroes, Huddersfield Town, play at Barnsley. The hosts had produced not only a special commemorative programme, but before the observation of a minute's silence by players, officials and the crowd, the match ball was delivered by members of the British Army abseiling from the top of the main grandstand. In recent years it has also become usual for those playing in the English Premier League to wear specially commissioned shirts with an embroidered poppy, which are then usually auctioned for charity. This year however, amidst much controversy, one footballer, Sunderland's James McClean, who was raised in the strongly Irish nationalist Creggan Estate in Londonderry, refused to wear such a shirt. On the same weekend, in Belfast, when Linfield (overwhelmingly Protestant and unionist in support) played away at Cliftonville (with a large Catholic and nationalist following) the pre-match minute's silence was loudly disrupted by many of the home fans. Both incidents offer a clear reminder that in Ireland, and within the Irish diaspora, involvement in the commemoration of the Great War has been, and remains, inseparable from broader political divisions.

The aim of this chapter, then, is to trace the origins of these divergent memories of the Great War, the reasons for which the nationalist and loyalist communities fought and the political influences that have shaped subsequent collective memories, official and popular. I argue that

the conflict over the Partition of Ireland from 1916–23 powerfully shaped
the way that the Great War was remembered and forgotten in Ireland,
both north and south. This initial divergence was then compounded by
the Troubles from the 1960s and has softened somewhat since the Belfast
Agreement. Despite this change in the political context, commemoration
and memorialization by Loyalist paramilitaries has led to a vast number
of highly localized and populist Great War memorials appearing over the
past three decades, in contrast to the more officially controlled and managed commemorations in other parts of the United Kingdom and further
afield in places such as Australia.[1]

## The social memory of Ireland at war

Although the outbreak of the war saw support for Great Britain from
both Nationalist and Unionist political leaders, and both Catholics and
Protestants joined the British Army in sizable numbers, Protestant and
Catholic experiences at the war's end differed vastly.[2] The number of
Irish soldiers involved in the Great War was considerable. Around 200,000
Irishmen served during the First World War, about 140,000 of whom
were volunteers.[3] Enlistment patterns reflected intensifying divisions

1    See David Officer, '"For God and For Ulster": The Ulsterman on the Somme', in
     Ian McBride, ed., *History and Memory in Modern Ireland* (Cambridge: Cambridge
     University Press, 2001) and David Officer and Graham Walker, 'Protestant Ulster:
     Ethno-history, Memory and Contemporary Prospects', *National Identities* 2/3 (2000),
     293–307.
2    See Keith Jeffery, *Ireland and the Great War* (Cambridge: Cambridge University Press,
     2000) and Terence Denman, *Ireland's Unknown Soldiers: the 16th (Irish) Division in
     the Great War* (Dublin: Irish Academic Press, 1992) and Myles Dungan, *They Shall
     Not Grow Old: Irish Soldiers in the Great War* (Dublin: Four Courts Press, 1997).
3    Keith Jeffery, 'Ireland and World War One', 2011 <http://www.bbc.co.uk/history/
     british/britain_wwone/ireland_wwone_01.shtml> accessed 12 June 2012.

between Nationalist and Unionist political groups that had sharpened since the debates over Home Rule in 1912 and the approach of armed conflict that followed subsequently. Concentrated in the industrialized province of Ulster, Protestant Unionists had recruited and organized the Ulster Volunteer Force (UVF) as a paramilitary force created to oppose Home Rule for Ireland. An idiosyncrasy of the Ulster Protestants was that although they were 'willing to resist Parliament [...] these men were passionately loyal to the British Crown'.[4] Having so openly displayed their Unionism, large numbers of the UVF joined up for 'King and Country' to form the core of the 36th (Ulster) Division.

However, while not recruited en masse like their UVF counterparts, many Irish Nationalists, who had also organized and armed through the Irish Volunteers to enforce Home Rule, enlisted. This made the 10th and 16th Divisions distinctively (nationalist) Irish in their composition. In August 1914 Home Rule, the over-riding goal of Irish nationalists, had seemed imminent with the third Irish Home Rule Bill becoming law on 18 September. The legislation, however, was suspended for the duration of the conflict. Thus many nationalists concluded that their interests were now directly aligned with the speedy victory of 'England', following which Home Rule could (and would) be fully implemented. Thus, albeit in very differing ways, both Irish nationalists and Ulster unionists felt they were expressing patriotism by enlisting in the British Army.

The majority of Irishmen who enlisted served in three divisions: the 10th (Irish) Division, the 16th (Irish) Division and the 36th (Ulster) Division. Both the 16th and 36th divisions served on the Western Front, perhaps most famously at the Battle of the Somme, where the Ulster Division suffered appallingly heavy casualties particularly on 1 July. By September 1916 the 16th Division was also embroiled in the Somme campaign, while some eight months later the 16th and 36th Divisions fought together at the Battle of Messines. Importantly, the first day of the Somme coincided with a major anniversary in the Orange calendar; being also the original

---

4    Richard Grayson, *Belfast Boys: How Unionists and Nationalists Fought and Died Together in the First World War* (London: Continuum, 2010), 24.

date of the Battle of the Boyne in 1690, it created a powerful connection within Loyalist popular culture. As such, memory of the fighting on the river Somme became conflated with that on the river Boyne, elevating and integrating it directly into the existing symbolism of the Orange Order.[5] This conflation became a core part of unionist and Orange collective identity, forming a reference point within Protestant Unionism.

But even as the Ulster and Irish Divisions were fighting on the Somme, events in Ireland had moved in a direction that would shape the memory of the Great War in decades to come. During Easter 1916, around 1,800 members of the Irish Volunteers, which had been founded as a direct response to the threat posed by the UVF, seized by force several of the main buildings in Dublin (most famously the General Post Office) and proclaimed an Irish Republic. They held out for a week before surrendering to the 16,000 British troops that had been deployed to suppress the armed rising. The strength of the British response was no doubt in part, at least, due to the widespread belief that the rebels had acted with active German support. The engagement saw the death of sixty-two rebels, 132 British Army and Police officers and 270 civilians, alongside another 2,000 civilians wounded. The executions of fifteen rebel leaders in the aftermath of the fighting drew widespread revulsion from across every strata of the Irish public. It motivated a growing sense of populist separation from the British administration. This found expression in Sinn Féin's republican politics and a clear outlet in the December 1918 general election, in which a Sinn Féin landslide swept away the Redmondite nationalists and transformed Irish politics.

5    Dominic Bryan, *Orange Parades: The Politics of Ritual, Tradition and Control* (London: Pluto, 2000), 56.

# At war's end: Post-war experiences and a divided Ireland

Hence, when around 100,000 veterans of the Irish Divisions returned home following demobilization, it was to a more definitively nationalist Ireland than the one they had left. Many who had marched off amidst much pomp and public celebration returned to what was a sharply contrasting atmosphere. When the Irish War of Independence broke out in 1919 and the new Free State emerged through overt conflict and violence, most Irish Great War veterans found themselves as a marginalized and unwelcome group.[6]

In this situation, some veterans aligned with the Irish Republican Army (IRA), while others supported the new Irish Free State and joined those forces directly opposing them, but most appear to have taken little or no part in the conflict. That is not to say, however, that many were not subject to intimidation, including beating, punishment shootings, forced expulsion and even murder.[7] In the years between 1919 and 1924 an estimated 120 veterans were killed by the IRA and anti-Treaty forces.[8] While some were targeted as alleged informants to British forces, 'the vast majority appear to have been killed simply as a retrospective punishment for their service in the Great War'.[9]

In the North the legislation for a new parliament was provided under the *Government of Ireland Act* (1920) and although strong reservations were expressed even within their own circles, most unionists reluctantly accepted that the arrangement was the best they could hope for.[10] Following

6    Jane Leonard, '"Facing the Finger of Scorn": Veterans' Memories of Ireland and the Great War', in Martin Evans and Kenneth Lunn, eds, *War and Memory in the Twentieth Century* (Oxford: Berg, 1997), 59–72.

7    See Peter Hart, *The IRA and its Enemies: Violence and Community in Cork, 1916–1923* (Oxford: Clarendon Press, 1998) and Jane Leonard, 'Getting them at last: The IRA and ex-servicemen', in David Fitzpatrick, ed., *Revolution? Ireland 1917–1923* (Dublin: Trinity History Publications, 1990).

8    Leonard, 'Facing the finger of scorn', 62–3.

9    Ibid., 63.

10   Patrick Buckland, *Irish Unionism, 1885–1922* (London: Historical Association, 1973).

partition, anxieties concerning the structure and validity of the Northern Ireland state were exaggerated into an obsession with differences between the two Irelands.[11] With partition came the institutionalization of sectarian, political, social and economic relations. Narratives of mutual exclusion were reinforced through the production of divergent collective memories.[12]

The new Northern Ireland Unionist government set about establishing and reinforcing what it saw as the inherent Britishness of Northern Ireland, marking out how clearly it differed from the Free State, particularly in key aspects of living standards and economic life. Unionist concerns in government revolved around the perceived need to protect the very existence of Northern Ireland from Catholic nationalists both within and outside its borders. The belief that the continued existence of the new state of Northern Ireland rested on 'Protestant unity' underpinned by a majority Unionist government determined much of the direction taken by the state. It structured the state apparatus and was displayed clearly in unionism's determination to hold power over domestic security forces, particularly the Royal Ulster Constabulary (RUC).[13]

Following the settlement of the boundary in 1925 and the formal dissolving of the Council of Ireland in 1926, a growing gap developed in relations between Dublin and Belfast as each set about constructing 'competing narratives of cultural identity'.[14] Indeed, Kennedy-Pipe suggests that throughout the 1930s 'the triangular relationship between North and South, between Dublin and London and between the two communities in the North appeared to grow more strained'.[15] Within Northern Ireland, politics

11    Dennis Kennedy, *The Widening Gulf: Northern Attitudes to the Independent Irish State, 1919–1949* (Belfast: Blackstaff, 1988).

12    Brian Walker, *A Political History of the Two Irelands: From Partition to Peace* (Basingstoke: Palgrave Macmillan, 2012).

13    James W. McAuley, *Ulster's Last Stand? Reconstructing Unionism after the Peace Process* (Dublin: Irish Academic Press, 2010).

14    Nuala Johnson, *Ireland, the Great War and the Geography of Remembrance* (Cambridge: Cambridge University Press, 2003), 2.

15    Caroline Kennedy-Pipe, *The Origins of the Present Troubles in Northern Ireland* (London: Longman, 1997), 25.

was dominated and structured by a triumvirate of the Ulster Unionist Party, the Orange Order and the Royal Ulster Constabulary (RUC), including its part-time paramilitary wing the Ulster Special Constabulary, which at its formation in October 1920 included over 30,000 veterans of the Great War, almost entirely from the 36th Division. Such broad social and political relationships framed the processes of commemoration and political memory within both states.

The hostility expressed by many nationalists towards the British Army since 1916 similarly found expression in and by the new Irish state. Subsequently those Irishmen who fought and died in the Great War found little acknowledgement.[16] Between 1919 and 1925, a Remembrance Day ceremony was held each November in central Dublin, but it was consistently embroiled in conflict, and sometimes even open violence, between nationalists, unionists and ex-servicemen. Even after the event was moved from the city centre to Phoenix Park, disruption of public Remembrance Day events continued throughout the 1920s and 1930s. Violence towards poppy sellers grew as 'Armistice Day became a rallying point for republican street fighters',[17] and the poppy itself, which in the 1920s had higher sales in Dublin than in Belfast, became a symbol of 'imperialist ascendancy recalcitrance, rather than ex-servicemen's welfare'.[18]

As this symbolic shift occurred, war memorials were often vandalized but usually allowed to fall into disrepair. Although in 1927 the Irish government donated the then considerable sum of £50,000 to help construct a Great War Memorial in Dublin, which eventually opened in 1948, it was not until 2006 that the Irish state held an official commemoration there, marking the 90th anniversary of the Battle of the Somme. In what many saw as a stark contrast, the state sponsored a large scale nationwide commemoration of the 50th anniversary of the 1916 Easter Rising, culminating

---

16   John Morrissey, 'Ireland's Great War: Representation, Public Space and the Place of Dissonant Heritages', *Journal of Galway Archaeological and Historical Society* 58 (2006), 98–113.

17   See Leonard 'The Finger of Scorn', and Donal Lowry, 'Review of Keith Jeffrey's "Ireland and the Great War"', *History Today* 51/7 (2001), 57.

18   Lowry, 'Review', 11.

in a huge public event in Dublin. Those ceremonies highlighted how far the role of the Catholic nationalist Irishmen who had served in the British Army had been erased from Ireland's official memory.

When the 'Troubles' erupted in Northern Ireland there was a further distancing from those who had served Britain, leading to the abandoning of public commemoration (on police advice), the suspension of poppy sales on the streets and the halting of Catholic masses in memory of the War dead.[19] It was not until the 80th anniversary of the armistice in 1998, when the peace process had established a tentative hold in Northern Ireland, that Anglo-Irish relations thawed to the point where the two states could jointly mark the Great War. The then President of Ireland, Mary McAleese, and Queen Elizabeth II jointly inaugurated the Island of Ireland Peace Park and dedicated a memorial at Messines, where in June 1917 the 36th Ulster Division fought alongside the 16th Irish Division for the only time, to all of the Irish fallen in the Great War.

## Ulster Loyalism, commemoration and popular cultures

If the history and experiences of the veterans did not fit with the Irish republican legacy within the Irish Republic, neither did they directly dovetail with the unionist tradition of the north. The development and form of remembrance in Northern Ireland was set in the early 1920s, when parades began to be staged to mark the Somme anniversary, alongside Ulster Division memorial services, on 1 July and 11 November.[20] The commemoration of the Great War in general and the Somme in particular quickly became associated directly with the Protestant unionist community, rather

19    Leonard, 'Finger of Scorn'.
20    Gillian McIntosh, *The Force of Culture: Unionist Identities in Twentieth-Century Ireland* (Cork: Cork University Press, 1999).

than the Catholic nationalist one.[21] Thus, by the end of the 1920s, both northern and southern states had seriously set about constructing narratives of divergent and conflicting memories 'embodying rival ideologies and representing two hostile peoples'.[22] Both memories rested on a blood sacrifice: if the Irish Free State looked increasingly to Easter 1916 as its founding moment, so too could Northern Ireland summon up a blood-soaked foundational moment from 1916 – albeit one that had its setting in France, far from its Ulster homeland.[23]

These similarities aside, commemoration in Northern Ireland existed to express the 'Britishness' of the new state. In the 1920s the symbolism of Loyalism became engrained. Orange Lodges and streets were regularly named after the battles fought by the 36th Division and 'Somme Day' began to be celebrated across the Province.[24] All this was seen to confirm Ulster's continuing loyalty to the United Kingdom and (while it still existed) the British Empire. Although as Grayson points out, during the Great War northern Catholics had enlisted just as often as Protestants, they too – like their fellow veterans in the Republic – became marginal to commemoration, which became focused on the sacrifices of the Ulster Division on the Somme.[25] Overwhelmingly, however, it was the Protestant and unionist community in Northern Ireland that saw their commitment during the war in general, and events at the Somme particular, as an overt example of patriotism and blood sacrifice for the Union and in many ways the pinnacle of masculinity for Ulster Protestantism.[26] Overtly public statements

---

21 Catherine Switzer, *Unionists and Great War Commemoration in the North of Ireland 1914–1939* (Dublin: Irish Academic Press, 2007).

22 David Fitzpatrick, *The Two Irelands, 1912–1939* (Oxford: Oxford University Press, 1998), vii. See also Thomas Hennessey, *A History of Northern Ireland 1920–1996* (Dublin: Gill and Macmillan, 1997), and Kennedy, *Widening Gulf.*

23 Philip Orr, 'Remember 1916', *Lion and Lamb* 41 (2006).

24 Orr, 'Remember 1916'.

25 Grayson, *Belfast Boys.* See also Brian Graham and Peter Shirlow, 'The Battle of the Somme in Ulster memory and identity', *Political Geography* 21/7 (2002), 881–904.

26 Keith Jeffrey, '"Writing out of opinions": Irish experience and the theatre of the First World War', in Santanu Das, ed., *Race, Empire and First World War Writing* (Cambridge: Cambridge University Press, 2011) and Jane McGaughey, *Ulster's Men:*

of loyalty to the British Crown were a feature of these commemorations. Many Catholics, already feeling apprehensive in the new state, were simply excluded or chose not to be involved in the public rituals of the Province.

For contemporary unionists the actions of the 36th Ulster Division have reached an almost sacred status in popular memory.[27] A significant part of that popular memory was formed through Remembrance Sunday or Armistice Day commemorations, observed in Northern Ireland on 11 November in broadly the same way as in the rest of the UK. However, in Northern Ireland active participation in the day, and indeed the wearing of poppies, was an overtly political act. Poppy wearing tended to symbolize direct association with the unionist community, while such displays were opposed, or at best ignored, by Irish nationalists and republicans. Thus when the Provisional IRA exploded a bomb just before a Remembrance Sunday ceremony in Enniskillen in 1987 killing eleven people, its significance registered far beyond that of simply another action in the IRA's ongoing military campaign. The bombing was widely condemned. There is some evidence to suggest that as a response attendance at Remembrance events, by both nationalists and unionists, rose in the following years.[28] Walker notes that over the subsequent decade the nature and attitude towards commemoration 'changed markedly',[29] while Leonard suggests that in the Irish Republic public revulsion provided the momentum to remember anew those who had served in both world wars.[30]

Since the outbreak of the Troubles, Ulster loyalists have expressed overlapping senses of identity, which at the macro level emphasized a distinct

---

    *Protestant Unionist Masculinities and Militarization in the North of Ireland, 1912–1923* (Montreal: McGill-Queen's University Press, 2012).

27   See Neil Jarman, *Material Conflicts: Parades and Visual Displays in Northern Ireland* (Oxford: Berg, 1997) and Catherine Switzer, *Ulster, Ireland and the Somme: War Memorials and Battlefield Pilgrimages* (London: The History Press, 2013).

28   Helen Robinson, 'Remembering War in the Midst of Conflict: First World War Commemorations in the Northern Irish Troubles', *Twentieth Century British History* 21/1 (2010), 80–101.

29   Walker, *Two Irelands*, 159.

30   Leonard, 'Finger of Scorn', 9.

sense of Britishness, while at the micro level often rested on a very localized sense of belonging, drawing on collective memory that at times overlapped with, but which at other times was distinct from, unionism.[31] This can be seen in those parts of the Protestant unionist community that formed paramilitary groups as a largely working class response to a perceived threat to their constitutional position in the 1960s and after. One important ideological aspect of these paramilitary groups has been their need to seek legitimacy within their own communities. For the grouping set around the contemporary UVF (that is the organization that came into existence in 1966) a key strategy in seeking legitimacy has been to construct linkages with the UVF of 1912. This has taken several forms, including the well known murals depicting a continuity of resistance.

Significant for the purposes of this volume, the UVF was also involved in organizing Somme anniversary parades, which commemorated not just Great War UVF volunteers, but also promoted the memory of paramilitaries who died in the contemporary Troubles from 1969 onwards. Loyalist commemoration linked to the 90th anniversary of the formation of the UVF in 2002 was marked by very large organized events, numbering thousands of participants and spectators. Commenting on these and other developments, Brown noted that '[t]he creation of spectacle has been a key feature of larger memorial events, with street theatre, tableaux, motorized floats', noting that 'the wearing of the period costume of earlier [...] Loyalist groupings in parades [is now] commonplace'.[32]

This growth in loyalist spectacle is ironic as in many ways the post-Belfast Agreement period has seen the politics of those identifying as loyalist marginalized in orthodox narratives of the 'Troubles' and pragmatically by more mainstream unionist positions. One way loyalists have sought to resist this is through the reinforcement of their 'own' culture through popular culture. For example, contrast the anti-British sentiment of the nationalist song *Gallipoli* written and performed by The Fureys:

---

31   McAuley, *Ulster's Last Stand?*
32   Kris Brown, '"Ancestry of Resistance": The Political Use of Commemoration by Ulster Loyalists and Irish Republicans in a Post-War Setting' (Transitional Justice Institute, University of Ulster, Working Paper, 2009), 4.

You fought for the wrong country, you fought for the wrong cause,
And your ma often said it was Ireland's great loss,
All those fine young men who marched to foreign shores to fight the wars,
When the greatest war of all was at home.

with the song *Billy McFadzean* sung in Loyalist pubs and clubs across Northern Ireland:

Let me tell you a story of honour and glory,
Of a young Belfast soldier Billy McFadzean by name,
For King and for Country young Billy died bravely,
And won the VC on the fields of the Somme.

Gone like the snowflake that melts on the river,
Gone like the first rays of days early dawn,
Like the foam from the fountain,
Like the mist from the mountain,
Young Billy McFadzean's dear life has gone.

Now Billy lies only where the red Flanders poppy,
In wildest profusion paints the field of the brave,
No piper recalling his deeds all forgotten,
For Billy McFadzean has no known grave.

So let us remember that brave Ulster soldier,
The VC he won, the young life that he gave,
For duty demanding his courage outstanding,
Private Billy McFadzean of the UVF.

Such songs draw on collective memories that drive a social dialogue in the development of popular cultures and individual and collective memories. These coalesce into a collectivity where they are distilled and refined to reconstruct the remembered occurrences of the social group. In 2001 in East Belfast, for example, a wall mural was painted showing four UVF volunteers, two from the 1912 period, and two who had been killed in the recent conflict. Despite the many years, and very different political circumstances separating the men, the UVF orator made clear at its unveiling that he saw the link between them as seamless, claiming that all 'were volunteers without whom Ulster would have been lost'.[33]

Thus, Great War commemoration in Northern Ireland merges remembrance into a grand unionist/loyalist narrative that rolls together 'the Siege of Derry', the 'Battle of the Boyne' and the sacrifice of 'the Great War' to mark a continuity of events, thought and politics across Orangeism and unionism.[34] Unionists' selective memory of the Great War as one reference point in this grand narrative has erased the history of Catholic and nationalist participation in the War, just as, although for very different reasons, the nationalist memory of the past in the Republic marginalized the role of Irish veterans of the British Army in the Great War.

## Conclusion

Since the end of the First World War, the dominant collective memories and official commemorations have been constructed in ways to all but eliminate the predominately Catholic 10th and 16th Divisions from the popular memory of the Great War in the south. Because of their perceived 'Britishness' and commitment to Empire, they have been subject to what some have called 'the Great Oblivion' or a 'national amnesia'. In the north, Catholics in general, and memories of the 10th and 16th Divisions in particular, were marginalized by the majority population because of their 'Irishness', while during the same period the 36th Division was lauded to form a core pillar of Northern Irish Protestant unionist identity following partition. Since the outbreak of the Troubles in the late 1960s, collective memory of the Great War in loyalist communities served a double purpose:

33    Ulster Murals, 'UVF Heroes of East Belfast', 2013 <http://www.ulstermurals.20m.com/custom.html> accessed 12 June 2012.
34    James W. McAuley, Jonathan Tonge and Andrew Mycock, *Loyal to the Core? Orangeism and Britishness in Northern Ireland* (Dublin: Irish Academic Press, 2011).

to legitimize continuing British rule and Protestant unionist ascendency in Northern Ireland and at the same time to legitimize paramilitary organizations and operations within the loyalist community itself. Thus in both the Republic and Northern Ireland over the past century, the memory of the past has been enlisted in the cause of contemporary politics, a role that it serves to this day.

LAURENCE VAN YPERSELE

# The Great War in Belgian Memories: From Unanimity to Divergence

## Introduction

This chapter examines the gradual *de*construction of Belgian national identity since 1918. Two broad questions have guided this inquiry. Firstly, is it possible to speak of a de facto differentiation or even 'federalization' of the so-called 'national past' in Belgium; and secondly, how do Belgians choose to remember *and* forget this past? To contribute to an understanding of these issues, the paper takes the Great War as its starting point for consideration, because the memory of this devastating event appears to provide the template for subsequent memory conflicts in Belgium and thus informs the memory of other conflicts like the Second World War. Likewise, the politics of nationalism and international diplomacy reflects, reinforces and repositions memory of the Great War in contemporary Belgium. Overall, the historical and political contexts of commemoration over the past century have seen the Great War shift from being a focus of Belgian unanimity to being a point of sharp divergence in collective memory.

The limited scope of this paper does not allow for a thorough historiographical study. Instead, it focuses on the ways in which the past has been represented, and how these portrayals have evolved, often becoming fragmented over time. This research is based on a corpus of official speeches, parliamentary documents, news articles and commemorative monuments. The study of how memories are transmitted is essential if we are to understand what makes collective national memory, despite how little such a concept may still apply in Belgium. The 'official memory' – understood here as the collection of official representations of the past – has a number of characteristics, of which two are key. Firstly, it is an *authorized* version of the past, conveyed by the legitimate spokesperson of a particular group. As such, it tells us something about the identity of the group, however fragile. Secondly, such speeches are a way of presenting events to the world, of showcasing the country for a domestic and external audience. As such, they do not represent a systematic bringing together of the recollections of group members. It is, therefore, interesting to identify any inconsistencies between the official version and remembered versions, between public and individual representations of the national past.[1] One of the main questions that arises throughout the study concerns the degree of compatibility of these representations. Do the various accounts of the past result from a series of different viewpoints – a set of historical ripples or tensions generated by certain key events – or do they reveal fundamental contradictions in which one version of events is systematically denied by another? An examination of the memory of the Great War in Belgium over the past one hundred years suggests that divergent representations of the past are both symptomatic of and contribute to political divisions in the present.

## The Great War: From heroism to injustice

The triumphal return of King Albert to Brussels on 22 November 1918 at the head of his troops symbolized the end of the First World War for Belgians. Belgian and Allied forces were welcomed by joyful crowds, and the royal family received a massive welcome on its way to Parliament. There, the King pronounced his famous 'Discours du Trône',[2] in which he first paid tribute to his army and to the soldiers killed in action but also

---

1    Marie-Claire Lavabre, *Le fil rouge: sociologie de la mémoire communiste* (Paris: Presses de Sciences Po, 1994), 18.

2    *Annales parlementaires. Chambre* (22 november 1918), 1-sv; Georges Rency, *Albert, roi des Belges* (Brussels: Henri Bertels, 1934), 107–17.

spoke of the civilians who had been executed by death squads, deported, or fallen victim to the massacres of August 1914. The result of this speech was that the highest authority in the land solemnly recognized the heroism shown and martyrdom suffered by Belgium and its citizens, acknowledging the many personal losses and ruins left behind whilst proclaiming his faith in the future of the Belgian nation through a programme of social and political reforms.

Yet Belgium, in particular, had been severely hit by the war. Located at the very heart of the conflict, it had experienced not only the horrors of the trenches, but also the human shields and civilian massacres of August 1914, the destruction of several of its major towns and cities, the deportation of workers in 1916, grinding poverty, starvation and the systematic plunder of its occupied territories. Almost 44,000 Belgian soldiers died on the battlefields as well as an estimated 20,000 civilians.[3] The Belgian reaction to the end of the Great War was thus a mixture of patriotic joy and sadness.[4] Not since 1839 had the nation seemed so united in its feelings. Never before had Belgian national identity seemed so strong. However, as we shall see later, as soon as the early 1920s, it became apparent that this outburst of unitary national fervour would not last.

## 'Our Dead Heroes': A unified set of memories

At the end of the Great War, in Belgium as elsewhere, the prevailing version of recent events was the direct result of the 'war culture' that had been generated since 1914.[5] In order to enable people to cope with their losses

---

3    Luc De Vos, *La Première Guerre Mondiale* (Bruxelles: JM Collet, 1997), 163.
4    Laurence van Ypersele and Axel Tixhon, 'Célébrations de Novembre 1918 au Royaume de Belgique', *Vingtième Siècle. Revue d'Histoire*, 67 (2000), 61–78.
5    Stéphane Audoin-Rouzeau and Annette Becker, *Retrouver la guerre, 1914–1918* (Paris: Gallimard, 2000).

and accumulated suffering, logic had to be applied to the war: heroes had fallen on the battlefield, dying for their nation, but they would remain forever alive in people's memories. Concomitant to the notion that they had fought on the side of civilization against the barbarians, was the idea that the hated enemy would pay for all the evil deeds committed and that traitors would be punished. The dead had thus earned their permanent place in history. This commitment to preserving memories was not just orchestrated by those responsible for developing an official version of the past but was shared by all members of the societies involved in the establishment of such a collective memory. Across the country, for the national funeral of the Unknown Soldier or around monuments to the fallen, the national authorities, former soldiers and local people came together with equal fervour. During this time of mourning, then, official and personal memories coincided and reinforced each other.

Although the Belgian reaction followed a general trend, it also had certain specific characteristics, notably the relatively weak record of the Belgian state in forming a collective memory, and above all, the place given to civilians in these accounts of the war. With the exception of the king and his 'Discours du Trône' (the structure of which closely reflected the collective memory of the Belgian people as a whole), the national authorities found it difficult to impose their version of the past. In 1919, for instance, Parliament chose 4 August, rather than 11 November, as a national date to commemorate the Great War. The August date was supposed to recall the great wave of patriotism that had engulfed the entire Belgian population at the time of the German invasion. Five years later, however, this date had come to symbolize the beginning of a long period of trial, extreme poverty, suffering and mourning, rather than the victorious patriotism it was hoped people would recall. In 1922, Parliament reversed its decision and acquiesced to the general wish to see 11 November – already given special status by the Allies – named as a public holiday in Belgium. At the same time the Belgian authorities discouraged the construction of war memorials throughout the country to commemorate local people who had been killed and also failed to erect one large, national monument to the fallen soldiers, civilians and Allied forces.

In 1922, the Belgian government conformed to the practices inaugurated in 1920 by Britain and France. Under pressure from veterans' groups and public opinion, a funeral for the Unknown Soldier took place under the Column of Congress in Brussels.[6] Clearly, the national authorities were trying, if rather clumsily, to promote a unified collective memory to reinforce the national identity which had emerged from the war and one that focused on heroes and martyrs, soldiers and civilians. School textbooks, for example, immediately took these ideas on board, glorifying the Soldier-King, the Nurse-Queen, General Leman the heroic defender of Liège in August 1914, the 'patriots' such as Gabrielle Petit and Edith Cavell shot by the occupiers, and many others. As of June 1919, a memo from the Minister of Science and Arts recommended that governors, mayors and school inspectors encourage the reverence of such figures from the recent past throughout Belgian schools. A few months later, national and local authorities, high-ranking church officials, a wide range of associations and the public at large came together at the national funerals of patriots executed by the occupying forces, in a common wish to commemorate their sacrifice.[7]

As a result of this commemorative activity, the idea of the victorious Belgian nation was established. In this official memory, victory was achieved by both civilians and soldiers; this was a contrast to many other countries involved in the Great War, for whom only soldiers participated in the fighting. Thus, although the figure of the Belgian soldier was used as the symbol of national heroism on monuments to the dead, in commemorative speeches or heroic narratives, civilians were commemorated, too. Memorials or speeches often featured a civilian massacred in August 1914, a patriot executed by the enemy or a deportee. Across the country, stories of heroes and martyrs were used to shore up the greatness of the nation for which they had given their lives. Yet, this concept of the Belgian

6   Stéphanie Claisse, *Ils ont bien mérité de la Patrie! Monuments aux Soldats et aux Civils Belges de la Grande Guerre* (Unpublished doctoral thesis, Université Catholique de Louvain, Louvain-la-Neuve, 2006).

7   Laurence van Ypersele and Emmanuel Debruyne, *De la Guerre de l'ombre aux ombres de la Guerre: l'espionnage en Belgique durant la Guerre 1914–1918. Histoire et mémoire* (Bruxelles: Labor, 2004).

nation was never straightforward, but rather had many layers: national identity remained rooted in local or provincial identities. National symbols such as the female allegorical figure of the 'Motherland', the Belgian lion or the royal family coexisted easily with local saints, as at the village of Mormont with the village's coat of arms, and as at La Louvière with the *perron* (the symbol of the Province of Liège), or sometimes, in Flanders, with the nationalist 'AVV-VVK' logo (*Alles Voor Vlaanderen-Vlaanderen voor Kristus*). Similarly, school textbooks published in the provinces figured so-called 'national' heroes (since they died for the nation of Belgium) who were revered solely in their local area.

## The fragmentation of collective memory

Belgian identity, in the period just after the war, can be characterized as a Russian doll, but the different layers varied in importance from one region to another. Provincial identity was particularly strong in Liège and also in the province of Luxembourg. In Hainaut, however, national identity and local identity were important, but provincial identity less so. Equally, in the north of the country, the symbols used on monuments did not set Flemish identity against Belgian identity. The 'AVV-VVK' symbol was not just a nationalist symbol but also (and perhaps more importantly during this period of mourning) a religious symbol expressing a need for consolation.[8]

Similarly, the wish to see traitors punished was initially one shared by virtually everyone. The memory of heroes and martyrs was used, moreover, to stir up the desire for vengeance: 'In the name of those who died for the Fatherland, death to the traitors!' There were three categories of people classified as traitors: Flemish and Walloon activists, those who had made

8    Mariette Jacobs, *Zij die vielen als helden... Cultuurhistorische analyse van de oor-logsgedenktekens van de twee wereldoorlogen in West-Vlaanderen* (Bruges: Provincie West-Vlaanderen, 1995).

their fortunes from the war and spies paid by the occupying authorities.[9] The latter, though fewer in number than the activists and profiteers, were particularly hated by the population at large. It was commonly believed that they had betrayed Belgian heroes to the occupiers and therefore deserved to be executed. Those made wealthy, by contrast, were more numerous and became an obsession of the general population, who feared they would escape justice. Finally, for the majority of public opinion, the activists obviously deserved to be condemned, although unlike spies, no one sought the death penalty for them.

The crackdown itself lasted a relatively short time from 1919 to 1922 and it was not excessively severe. Of the tens of thousands of cases examined, only 3,900 were brought to court. Moreover, only a few dozen death sentences were pronounced, none of which were ever carried out. The strong feelings generated by the idea of punishing traitors rapidly faded. The nationalist wing of the Flemish movement (*Vlaamse Beweging*) would, however, during the interwar period and even beyond, preserve the memory of Flemish activists and portray it as an injustice committed by the Belgian state against the Flemish cause. In January 1921, two Flemish Socialists put a question to the Belgian government concerning the severity of the judicial measures taken against certain activists who 'committed a political error in good faith', and asked whether it might not be appropriate to extend clemency to them. The French-speaking press in Flanders reacted at once, violently, and equated the whole Flemish Movement with the shameful memory of a few activists. The stereotypical portrayal of a pro-German Flanders spread rapidly throughout the Francophone press and continued to strengthen throughout the inter-war period. This pro-German stereotype was used to fight Flemish demands, in particular, against subsequent proposals for amnesty.[10]

---

9    Xavier Rousseaux and Laurence van Ypersele, eds, *La Patrie crie vengeance! La Répression des 'inciviques' belges au sortir de la Guerre 1914–1918* (Bruxelles: Le Cri, 2008).

10   Rousseaux and van Ypersele, *La Patrie crie vengeance!*, 215–17.

In 1925, the signing of the Locarno Pact began an international détente that favoured a transformation of the memory of war.[11] From this point, previous emphasis on sacrifices made for their country and hatred of the enemy disappeared in the face of a narrative that stressed the common suffering incurred to put an end to all wars. The soldier was no longer portrayed as the warrior defending a sacred cause against infamy, but a heroic victim who played his part in creating a world without war. Belgian authorities immediately aligned themselves with this international movement, exalting the League of Nations rather than the atrocities of August 1914 or the sufferings of the Belgian people during the occupation and fighting. By 1926 a ministerial circular required that textbooks reflect the spirit of the League. From that point on, the government banned 'institutions managed or controlled by state structures that preach hatred between races and peoples'. It recommended instead, 'books that, for the objective study of facts and ideas, share at the same time the obligation of patriotism and the duties of international morality'.[12] In addition, national authorities no longer participated in the inauguration of monuments recalling the massacres of civilians. This official attitude did not prevent people from maintaining this memory locally, however; and in addition, many Francophone writers took to the pen to fight against such official 'forgetting'. What Horne described as 'cultural demobilization' in this period was undeniably experienced by many as a serious threat.[13] Note however, that publications seeking to extend the memory of the heroic war – as opposed to celebrating the rise of pacifism – were often seen as a denial of memory themselves and, moreover, an exclusively Francophone phenomenon. For example, the memoir of Flemish patriot Martha Cnockaert, written and published in English in 1933, was immediately translated into French and

11    John Horne, 'Locarno et la Politique de démobilisation culturelle: 1925–1930', *14–18*, *Aujourd'hui, Today, Heute*, 5 (Paris: Noêsis, 2002), 72–87.

12    Louis Bauwens, *Code de l'enseignement moyen et de l'enseignement normal Moyen* (Bruxelles: A Dewit, 1929), 141–3.

13    van Ypersele and Debruyne, *De la guerre de l'ombre aux ombres de la guerre*, 151–66.

even brought to the screen, but was not translated into Dutch until 2000.[14] On the other hand, the spirit of Locarno suited Flemish nationalists well. Pilgrimages to the Yser Tower (or *Ijsertor*, a memorial erected in 1928–30 along the river Yser in Diksmuide) were becoming increasingly dominated by the nationalist militants known as *flamingants*, a subject to which I will return below.[15]

In contrast to the *flamingants*, veterans' associations were much less militant in Flanders and Wallonia, although the legend that eighty per cent of Flemish soldiers died in the trenches for a cause that was not theirs continued to grow. Additionally, little by little, the 'traitor' activists of 1914–18 were transformed into 'martyrs' for the Flemish cause as their treason to the Belgian state became overshadowed by their nationalist idealism, although such motivations were not obvious at the time.[16] At the same time, however, many Walloon newspapers continued to wield the memory of the heroic war against the Flemish movement and its political demands that scared them. Cartoons published in the French-speaking press vividly illustrate this trend. During the interwar period, the 'Flemish threat' – as seen by Walloon illustrators – increased in step with the actual progress of the Flemish Movement. This trend continued throughout the 1930s: Flemish citizens were often shown in association with Germany but were also depicted as being able to act independently (notably in order to colonize Wallonia).[17] Conversely, within the French-speaking community, the memory of the 1914–18 war was increasingly used to argue in

14 Marthe McKenna, *Souvenirs d'une espionne* (Paris: Payot, 1933); R. Quaghebeur, *Ik was een spionne. Het mysterieuze spionageverhaal van Martha Cnockaert uit Westrozebeke* (Koksijde: De Klaproos, 2000).

15 Frans Seberecht, 'Slechts de Graven Maken Een Land Tot Vaderland', in Frans Seberechts, ed., *Duurzamer Dan Graniet. Over Monumenten en Vlaamse Beweging* (Tielt: Lannoo-Perspectief uitgaven, 2003), 123–54.

16 Sophie de Schaepdrijver, 'Les dangers de l'idéalisme. Souvenirs contestés de l'occupation allemande en Belgique', in *14–18, Aujourd'hui, Today, Heute*, 5 (Paris: Noêsis, 2002), 115–27.

17 Luc Courtois and Jean Pirotte, *Images de la Wallonie dans le dessin de presse (1900–1961). Une enquête dans la presse d'action wallonne* (Louvain-la-Neuve: Fondation wallonne P. M. and J. F. Humblet, 1993).

favour of Belgian unity, perceived as under threat from Flemish nationalist claims.[18] Flemish nationalists, however, began to argue increasingly that Flemish identity was incompatible with Belgian identity, yet the majority of the Flemish population did not share this view.[19] Nevertheless, in approximately ten years, Belgian memory of the Great War had become fragmented: Flemish and French-speaking versions of the past began to diverge; the official version of history no longer corresponded exactly with local versions. Collective memory had become fragmented memories.

This fragmented memory of the Great War had an ambiguous impact on how people perceived and acted in the Second World War. On the one hand, the collaborationist movements used the memory of an absurd and futile war to justify their positions. Former nationalist activists became zealous collaborators of the Third Reich. Even the policy of accommodation pursued by the Belgian authorities with the German occupiers remained rooted in the experience of the first occupation. On the other hand, many Second World War resistance fighters also claimed the memory of the heroes of the First World War, considering themselves worthy heirs of their predecessors. Observe, for example, the omnipresence of memories of 1914–18 in the Belgian underground press and the commitment to veterans and their children in the clandestine networks of the resistance movement. But, again, the phenomenon was mainly Francophone.[20] After the Liberation, moreover, memories of the Great War were put to the service of another kind of war: the resistance fighters were assimilated into the glorious ranks of the soldiers of 1914–18. Memorials of the Great War were often inscribed with the names of civilians and soldiers who fell

18   *La Patrie belge* (Bruxelles: éd. Illustrée du 'Soir', 1930), 8.
19   For example, in 1930, the Flemish veterans association (the VOS) asked veterans to boycott the main ceremony for the Belgian national centenary, an appeal that was ignored. See Laurence van Ypersele, *Le roi Albert, histoire d'un mythe* (Bruxelles: Labor, 2006), 199–200.
20   Fabrice Maerten, 'L'impact du souvenir de la Grande Guerre sur la Résistance en Belgique durant le second conflit mondial', in Laurence van Ypersele, ed., *Imaginaires de Guerres. L'histoire entre mythe et réalité* (Louvain-la-Neuve: Académia Bruylant, 2003), 303–36.

during the second conflict to defend the homeland. From this time on, the ceremonies before the memorial to the Unknown Soldier were tributes to veterans of both wars.

Thus, in the post-war years, the official memory remained dominated by the image of heroes; of martyrs fighting and suffering for the nation. It would be more than twenty years before the innocent victims of the Second World War in Belgium, mostly Jews, were officially recognized for their specific experiences. Similarly, the harsh treatment of traitors after the Liberation was rooted in memories of the Great War. By 1945, some voices in Flanders again demanded the consideration of 'mitigating circumstances' for Flemish collaborators (once more citing the traitors' 'idealism' to mask their anti-democratic tendencies). Meanwhile, on the Francophone side there was a unanimous demand to strike hard and uncompromisingly against traitors, and any proposal for amnesty was systematically rejected. In short, post-War repression and recrimination crystallized new memory conflicts: Francophone intransigence once more gave the impression that the Belgian state was unduly harsh vis-à-vis the Flemings. However, this impression extended beyond committed nationalist circles to permeate a large segment of Flemish public opinion.[21]

## Contemporary fragmentation and the politics of the past

Two contemporary issues can be used to illustrate the way that memory of the Great War, the Second World War and nationalist politics all serve as a basis for fragmentation of Belgian unity today. These issues are the 'In Flanders Fields Declaration' and innovations to the *IJzertoren* Pilgrimage instigated in 2012.

21    Marnix Beyen, 'Elle est de plus en plus noire, la masse des flamingants. Comment s'est forge l'image de l'occupation et de la repression en Flandre', in José Gotovitch and Chantal Kesteloot, eds, *Collaboration et répression. Un passé qui résiste* (Bruxelles: Labor, 2002), 99–113.

As noted above, the conflicting memories of the First World War were replayed even more virulently after the end of the Second, but the ideological and ideational structures of state, nation, treason, collaboration and resistance remained broadly the same. In fact, the importance of the conflicting memories of the Second World War quickly obscured those of the First. However, today, in a context where the memory of the Holocaust has acquired a central place in European collective remembrance, Flemish historiography has stopped idealizing Flemish collaboration with the Nazi regime. In other words, it has been possible to alter the discourse about the Second World War in a way that has not been possible with the First.

Yet, at the same time, the pacifist memory of Great War has been honoured by the official authorities of Flanders. Thus, the Ypres museum *In Flanders Fields*, financially and politically supported by the province of West Flanders since its opening in 1998, has become the symbol of the pacifist ideal which accounts for the slaughter of 1914–18. In the same vein, the Minister of Tourism, Geert Bourgeois (a nationalist N-VA MP in the Flemish government) argued in 2008 that the commemorations associated with the Great War centenary should be used as an opportunity to promote international peace and international tourism on the battlefields in Flanders. His proposal was immediately accepted unanimously by the Flemish government.[22]

Consequently, the 'In Flanders Fields Draft Declaration' was tabled for discussion by the Flemish government in the summer of 2010. The politics surrounding this Draft Declaration illustrate some of the difficulties in commemorating the Great War in Belgium. Since 1980, Belgium had been divided into three major political and administrative regions: Flanders, Wallonia and Brussels. As a federation organized along consociational, linguistic lines, each of these regions was and is highly autonomous. In this political context it was possible for the Flemish government to draft the Declaration and circulate it for discussion amongst the fifty foreign governments participating in the planning of centenary activities in Belgium. However, the Flemish government sent this Draft Declaration

22   *Vlaams Parlement, zitting 2008–2009*, Resolutie, 27 March 2009 (stuk 2205), 5590.

neither to the Walloon government nor to the federal (Belgian) level of government. Objections were then raised from amongst the representatives of the foreign governments that this was diplomatically inappropriate and that the diplomatic services of those foreign governments would only deal with the federal level of government in Belgium in equal government-to-government discussions.

When the Flemish regional government, under pressure from foreign ambassadors, gave its 'In Flanders Fields' declaration to the federal level of government, thus making it a 'national' declaration, changes to the wording and meaning were proposed. The Walloon government, as well as the Federal government,[23] immediately suggested using the word 'Belgium' in place of 'Flanders' in the text. It also called for recognition of the rights of minorities, explicit recognition of the involvement of soldiers and civilians in the name of freedom and democracy, and mention of the Second World War as well as the First. Eventually, a political compromise was reached on 2 October 2012. After one year of political discussion, the word 'Belgium' was inserted into the text, along with reference to the people who defended democracy, as well as mention of the respect for 'diversity' (in place of the term 'minorities'). All of these suggestions and compromises ultimately served as pointed reminders of historical divisions rather than renewed grounds for Belgian unity, providing another forum where Flemish and Walloon collective memories of the Great War could publicly diverge.[24]

The second event that provided a public outlet for divergent memories of the Great War was the Pilgrimage to the *IJzertoren* [Yser Tower], Dixmuide. This annual ceremony, that remembers and commemorates Flemish sacrifice and loss during the Great War, is organized by a Flemish nationalist committee at the *IJzertoren* at the end of August. It has also

---

23 At the Federal level, the two coordinators for the centenary, Paul Breyne (Flemish-speaking) and Jean-Arthur Régibeau (French-speaking), refused to recognize the Flemish Government's capacity to have its own international relations distinct from the Belgian Government. See Pierre Havaux, 'Peeters rompt les usages diplomatiques', *Le Vif-L'Express* (8–14 March 2013).

24 Nico Wouters, '"Poor Little Belgium?" Flemish- and French-language politics of memory (2014–18)', *Journal of Belgian History*, XLII/4 (2012), 192–9.

been used as an opportunity to express Flemish claims against the Belgian state. Until the 1970s, this ceremony involved participants numbering in the thousands. But after the political reorganization of Belgium into a federal state, fewer and fewer people attended. In order to change this situation an innovation was deployed in 2012. For the first time, the organizing committee invited the family of Amé Fievez and the mayor of the village of Calonne where Fievez lived before the War. Fievez was a Walloon soldier who was killed alongside the van Raemdonck brothers in 1917. These brothers, Frans and Edward, had long been an important symbol of Flemish victimhood, combining an image of fraternal love with the long-standing sense that Walloon officers were indifferent to the casualties in the Flemish ranks.

Of course, the truth is more complicated than employing history this way allows. The graves of the brothers van Raemdonck and of Amé Fievez rest under the Yser Tower. But it was not until the 1960s that the name of the Walloon soldier was inscribed on the grave. Again in 2012, for the first time, some Walloons not associated with government were invited to participate in the Yser Pilgrimage. The French-speaking authorities sent flowers but, like the federal authorities and major Flemish political figures, were not invited to the wreath laying ceremony. As usual, the speeches demanded more autonomy for Flanders and a 'Belgian Confederation' (which in reality meant independence) so that the Flemish could finally live in peace with the Walloon community, represented on this occasion by the family of Amé Fievez and mayor of his village.[25]

Despite this cross-communal innovation, the broader public was not particularly engaged and did not attend in the pilgrimage or ceremony in large numbers. Following the failure of this initiative the President of the Committee announced that the following year, the ceremony would take place on 11 November, billed as a 'return to the origins' of the ceremony. However, as the ceremony had never before taken place on Armistice Day, Flemish historians as well as other Belgians immediately denounced this

25   Christian Laporte, 'Un Wallon à l'honneur au pèlerinage de l'Yser', *La Libre Belgique* (24 August 2012).

decision and the reasons given for it.[26] The reaction to the announcement demonstrated that many Flemish people who profess a love of Flanders do not desire the end of Belgium. The Flemish secessionists are aware of that sentiment too, which is why they now always speak about and argue for confederation rather than full independence. Thus we can clearly link the shift of a commemorative date to an overt nationalist political project. Armistice Day – itself suffering from waning public attendance in Belgium – was being used by Flemish nationalists in an attempt to relegitimize and popularize their political programme.

## Conclusion

The outburst of Belgian unity that accompanied the German invasion of Belgium in August 1914 did not survive long into the inter-War period. Despite a programme of post-War reconstruction that attempted to allay social and national tensions, memories of the Great War diverged by the 1930s. The second period of German occupation in 1940–4 exacerbated this existing conflict over the memory of the Great War, resulting in a deepening of political fragmentation along nationalist lines. In the contemporary period, the politics of nationalism in Belgium have combined with the international preparations for the Great War centenary to provide public forums where communal differences over the past can be aired. Thus in Belgium, memory of the conflict of 1914–18 has provided an avenue for greater fragmentation rather than deeper unity.

26   Beyen, 'Marnix, 'Laat die hele IJzerbedevaart maar achterwege', *De Morgen* (3 Mei 2012). The author, a Professor of the University of Antwerpen in Flanders, reminds us that the pilgrimage was always organized at the end of August and never on 11 November, invalidating the Committee's claim that it wanted to return the event to its original date.

# PART III

# Mobilizing the Great War

MARK MCKENNA

# Keeping in Step: The Anzac 'Resurgence' and 'Military Heritage' in Australia and New Zealand

## Introduction

In light of much of the recent historical scholarship regarding the resurgence of the Anzac myth over the last two decades, it is now commonly accepted that we can only understand the politics and resurgence of Anzac Day in Australia and New Zealand as part of the international surge in the commemoration of war.

Just as it became impossible for scholars to write on nationalism without drawing on Benedict Anderson's concept of 'imagined communities', it is now difficult to write on the contemporary commemoration of war without acknowledging what Jay Winter has described as the 'second memory boom' of the late twentieth century. There exists today, particularly in western nations, a global industry concerned with the commemoration of war. This industry is found in both the public and private sphere, it is funded both by states and private corporations and it has been greatly encouraged by global media corporations and the tourist industry. Commercial and market-driven factors (local, national and international) are therefore crucial to understanding the resurgence of Anzac Day as a source of national communion, particularly because they are closely entwined with political and cultural drivers.[1]

---

1 Jay Winter, *Remembering War: The Great War between Memory and History in the Twentieth Century* (London: Yale University Press, 2006); Benedict Anderson, *Imagined Communities: Reflections on the origin and spread of nationalism* (London: Verso, 1991).

Increasingly, the public remembering of war in liberal democracies is less concerned with the territorial, political, economic or strategic ambitions associated with military engagement. Rather, past wars are remembered through the prism of present-day cultural concerns: the need to provide a binding myth of national sacrifice, purpose and identity, together with the need to mollify anxiety regarding the erosion of liberal 'values', whether threatened by terrorists, immigration, globalization, or generational change. Remembering war, therefore, has become the key instructive parable of our times, one that constitutes the crucible through which political leaders have sought to identify themselves with a noble, honourable and heroic national past. Closely associated with these developments is an overwhelming tendency in the public domain towards *ahistorical remembering*.

In the popular memory of war, the distance from the past prized by professional historians takes second place to being present in the past, to the language of immediacy, spectacle and recreation. The boundaries that once separated history from fiction and myth appear more blurred. Increasingly, the popular embrace of war (often expressed through the choreographed rituals of public commemoration) is an emotional embrace, one that runs counter to the more critical understanding brought to the past by historians. Rather than interrogating the history and politics of war, popular memory closes ranks behind a sanctified past. In the public domain, the history of war is sanitized, sentimentalized and depoliticized. The currency of the phrase 'military heritage' particularly in Australia and New Zealand, demonstrates the manner in which war memory has increasingly been portrayed as something to be protected, an exhibit locked in the precious storehouse of 'national memories'. Consequently, stories of courage and sacrifice on the hills above Anzac Cove in Turkey in 1915 are celebrated and worshipped in the same vein as national architecture, folklore and cuisine. Long before war is perceived as history, it is memorialized as a sacred component of national heritage, a body of lore that occupies the realm of myth and thus lies beyond the bounds of critical inquiry.

Shifting political contexts have also played a key role in determining which particular aspects of a nation's 'military heritage' have been elevated in the public culture. For example, in post-peace process Republic of Ireland, the country's participation in the First World War (a history that was conveniently forgotten after the declaration of the Republic in

1949) has recently been dusted off and publicly aired as a means of establishing a new relationship with the United Kingdom. In Australia and New Zealand, the resurgence of Anzac Day has occurred within the broader context of both nations' ongoing struggle to address the vexed history of frontier conflict, conquest and settlement. Against this history, the Anzac legend has appeared less controversial and divisive, a far more malleable history for the purposes of national communion than competing demands of invasion, settlement and sovereignty.[2]

As public enthusiasm for Anzac commemoration has grown, both conservative and Labor governments in Australia and New Zealand have substantially increased government funding of a wide range of initiatives designed to promote the Anzac legend as the crucible of national identity; this chapter traces the recent politics of Anzac. Particularly in Australia, with the exception of the Keating Labor government (1991–6), which placed greater emphasis on Australia's role in the South Pacific during the Second World War (a stance that was consistent with Keating's republican nationalism which saw the Gallipoli campaign as part of an 'imperial war'), successive administrations under conservative Prime Minister John Howard (1996–2007), Labor prime ministers Kevin Rudd and Julia Gillard (2007–13) and conservative Prime Minister Tony Abbott (2013–) have 'proudly' endorsed Anzac as the nation's inviolable foundational story.

## Anzac Day in Australia

There is little doubt that Anzac Day is now effectively installed as Australia's National Day, one that is far more significant than 26 January (Australia Day), when British settlement commenced at Sydney Cove in 1788. One

---

2   Dominic Bryan and Stuart Ward, 'The "Deficit of Remembrance": the Great War Revival in Australia and Ireland', in Katie Holmes and Stuart Ward, eds, *Exhuming Passions: the Pressure of the Past in Ireland and Australia* (Kildare Irish Academic Press, 2011).

means of gauging the ascendance of the Anzac legend in Australia is to examine the recent surge in popularity of military history, which began in the mid to late 1990s and erupted in the wake of 11 September. Walk into any bookstore and dozens of war histories jostle for attention. The array of titles includes everything from the staple diet of Nazi atrocities to the epic battles of the world wars and the story of Australia's greatest war horse: 'Bill the Bastard'. While the popularity of military history is an international phenomenon, in Australia it takes on a particular inflection – almost every book that deals with the nation's engagement in war, either explicitly or as a point of comparison, refers to one military campaign: the landing of Australian troops on 25 April 1915 at Gallipoli. Over the last decade or more, the 'Anzac legend' has become so ubiquitous, so all-consuming and so sacrosanct that Australians seem unaware of the unique qualities they have bestowed upon it. No other nation has established its founding moment 15,000 kilometers away from its own soil.

In the past decade alone, more than 150 books have been published bearing the words 'Anzac' or 'Gallipoli' in their titles. If other military histories, government publications and community and self-published titles are included, the figure easily climbs to several hundred. Few of these books endure. As the centenary of the Gallipoli Anzac landings and the First World War approaches, each round of new publications will quickly be supplanted by yet another wave of war histories. Keenly aware of the impending deluge, publishers try desperately to stake out a niche for their authors. Invariably, each new book claims to tell the story of 'lost' or 'forgotten' diggers, stories that have 'slipped through the cracks of history'. Despite the publication of so much 'Anzac' history, readers are encouraged to believe that the stories of Gallipoli remain 'untold'. Such is the mythical status of the Anzac sagas: stories so well known and infinite, that Australians are meant to hear them with each telling as if for the first time.

Historian Marilyn Lake has noted how in Australia many military histories have been published courtesy of generous subsidies from the Army History Unit of the Department of Defence, the Australian War Memorial, the Department of Veterans' Affairs and the veterans' association, the Returned Services League (RSL). Concerned that the 'avalanche of military history is suffocating our intellectual life and stultifying the possibilities for knowing the richness of our past', Lake has a succinct explanation for the popularity of Australian military history: 'it is intensely familial, nationalist and internationalist history at once. It connects people with their family and nation at the emotional level, while it also gives them the pleasure of travel overseas to explore foreign, often exotic lands.'[3]

Much of the most successful popular military history is told, unnervingly (at least for this historian) in the present tense. Rewriting the past in the present tense creates the immediacy and intimacy that all good 'storytellers' strive for. The distance between the past and the present is broken down. History reads like a film script. The reader relives the experience, recoiling in horror at yet another tale of barbarity, rising to applaud the many examples of human courage and ingenuity. Emotional impact is everything. The past is felt before it is understood. Past characters speak as if giving testimony, dutifully emerging to play their allotted role on the stage. But history is more than storytelling. Of all its many faces, probably its most crucial quality is the deeply read, critical interpretation of the past in its fullest context. For the historian, the past is past. The danger of repackaging it in the present tense is that we risk creating the past in our own image, judging it not by its own standards but by our present day concerns, as if we have airlifted the Anzacs out of their imperial world and recast them as more naïve incarnations of our contemporary selves – a group of innocent larrikins who sailed off to the Dardanelles to fight the good fight for Australian 'values'.

Addressing the crowd before sunrise at the Anzac dawn service at Gallipoli in 2011, Australia's first woman Commander-in-Chief, Governor-General Quentin Bryce, proclaimed that Anzac Day was, at its heart, about love. 'Love of every kind', Ms Bryce said, 'Love of nation, of service, of family. The love we give and the love we allow ourselves to receive. To use some words that many of us know: it is the love that is patient and kind, not jealous or arrogant. It rejoices in the truth. It bears all things, believes all things, hopes all things, endures all things. And it never fails.'[4]

---

3    Marilyn Lake, email to me, November 2012; more generally, see Marilyn Lake and Henry Reynolds with Mark McKenna and Joy Damousi, *What's Wrong with Anzac?* (Sydney: New South Press, 2010).

4    For Bryce's speech see <http://www.gg.gov.au/speech/anzac-day-gallipoli-dawn-service> accessed 19 February 2014.

Bryce's testament paraphrased a reading from Corinthians 13:4, the most frequently quoted Biblical passage on love, reflecting the fact that Ken Inglis's seminal characterization of Anzac Day as a form of civil religion has never been more accurate. In its 2012 Easter editorial, *The Weekend Australian* compared Anzac Day to major *religious* festivals around the globe, which are increasingly attracting greater numbers of younger people. 'Jerusalem, like Gallipoli', noted the *Australian*, 'is now a popular place of pilgrimage for young Australians who want to see the Church of the Holy Sepulchre. The trends suggest that many young people are [...] more in tune with the enduring power and purpose of sacrifice'. Here, Gallipoli becomes Australia's Jerusalem, while the sagas of Anzac Day become a liturgy of faith for the purpose of national communion.[5]

At the same Gallipoli dawn service last year, a Melbourne retiree, Darrell Hughes, offered a typical example of the sentiments of those who visit Anzac Cove on 25 April. Hughes explained how he had never been so moved as he was by this dawn service: 'It touched my heart in a way that I could never have expected [...] watching the sunrise, thinking of the sacrifice of those brave young men. It made me so proud to be an Australian'. As Stuart Ward and I have argued, the comments of both Bryce and Hughes point to the fact that Anzac Day has become the leading manifestation of a much broader trend in Australian society – the rise of a sentimental and conservative nationalism.[6]

As Australians peer into the faces of the diggers on the Western Front or Gallipoli, they confront a time when warfare was the ultimate gladiatorial conquest. Unlike today, when the enemies of liberal democracies often lurk within our own societies, this was a time when war seemed more

---

5    Ken Inglis, *Sacred Places: War Memorials in the Australian Landscape* (Melbourne: Melbourne University Publishing, 2008); *The Weekend Australian* (7–8 April 2012).

6    Hughes in Jason Koutsoukis, 'A View from Gallipoli', *Sydney Morning Herald* (26 April 2010); Mark McKenna and Stuart Ward, '"It was really moving, mate": The Gallipoli Pilgrimage and Sentimental Nationalism in Australia', *Australian Historical Studies* 129 (2007), 141–51; also Martin Crotty, 'The One Day of the Year and all that: Anzac between History and Memory', *Australian Journal of Politics and History* 58/1 (2012), 123–31.

straightforward. There was a line. There were two sides. They charged at one another, fighting desperately to gain even a few metres of ground. It was a special type of hell; one that George Orwell, growing up in England's militaristic culture, felt he had been prepared for since he was a young boy: 'a war in which the guns rise to a frantic orgasm of sound, and at the appointed moment you clamber out of the trench, breaking your nails on the sandbags, and stumble across mud and wire into the machine gun-barrage'.[7]

Contemplating that moment, Australians stand in awe of their soldiers' courage. The memory of the enormous loss suffered by a generation of Australians is galvanizing. It heightens the intensity of their own existence and the bonds they share with one another. Many Australians want to believe that the soldiers died for their freedom, as if they were defending Australia itself. They return again and again to these stories of sacrifice and loss, hoping that within them they will find the true values of their own society, some essential spirit or quality of character that sets them apart from other nations and makes them truly exceptional in the world. Yet they forget that there was nothing particularly unique about the courage of Australian soldiers. Bill Gammage, the historian who did much to draw attention to the experience of Australian soldiers in the First World War, pointed this out long ago in his 1974 classic account, *The Broken Years*:

> I make no claims about the uniqueness of the Australians I describe, or of any Australian soldier: I believe that much of what is written here might apply to New Zealanders or Canadians, and that some of it would be true of soldiers in every army.[8]

Much like Australia Day, Anzac Day has shifted from a day of commemoration to a day of celebration. The imperial nature of the Gallipoli campaign is airbrushed out or simply overlooked. Far more important is the politically led, emotional embrace of a history of melancholy, loss, honour and pride.

---

7    George Orwell, 'My Country Right or Left', in Bernard Crick, ed., *The Penguin Essays of George Orwell* (London: Penguin, 1994), 135–6.

8    Bill Gammage, *The Broken Years: Australian Soldiers in the Great War* (Melbourne: Melbourne University Publishing, 2010 [1974]), xvi.

The conflicts that Australians remember, like much of the recent wave of popular military history, focus their attention not on the politics or economics of war, but on the character of individual soldiers – on those particular qualities they see as most useful to bind the nation: courage, sacrifice in the course of duty and 'mateship'. Rather than remember the horror of war and confront the Anzacs as killers as well as 'fallen' heroes, Australians prefer to misremember the Anzacs in order to celebrate Australian values and inflate their national pride.

In the 1920s, the 'white bones of unburied soldiers and the rusting guns along the shore' of Gallipoli were still visible. Thirty years later, when Alan Moorehead visited the Turkish peninsula while writing his seminal history, *Gallipoli*, published in 1956, the hills were 'deserted as ever, and packs of wolves still appear[ed] from time to time'. As for the war cemeteries tended by an old Australian soldier, Major Millington, and a handful of Turkish stonemasons and gardeners, Moorehead observed that 'hardly anyone ever visits them'. 'Except for occasional organized tours not more than half a dozen visitors arrive from one year's end to the other. Often for months at a time nothing of any consequence happens, lizards scuttle about the tombstones in the sunshine and time goes by in an endless dream'.[9]

In little over fifty years, Australia has so dramatically transformed its conception of what happened at Anzac Cove on 25 April 1915 that the men who clawed their way up those steep hills would not recognize themselves in the images the nation has created of them. The chasm between what occurred at Gallipoli and what Australia remembers grows ever wider.

9    Alan Moorehead, *Gallipoli* (London: Hamish Hamilton, 1956).

## Anzac Day in New Zealand

Anzac Cove, 25 April 2012: 7,000 Australians and New Zealanders wait for the sun to rise and the dawn service to begin. The scene resembles a rock concert. Enormous video screens and grandstands dwarf the crowd; a light show begins and music plays through large loudspeakers.

> Tour buses line the road for kilometres. There are backpacker tour groups aplenty – Contiki, Top Deck and so forth. All could be easily identified by their matching sloppy joes, specially printed for the occasion. Also here, in bright yellow tops, were the fanatics, the same group of diehards usually seen at sporting events [...]. The Kiwis, ever keen to differentiate themselves, had their silver fern and Steinlager logos prominent. The two nations' flags are too similar for quick differentiation. Even the government was in on the act, handing out showbags, the contents of which included Gallipoli beanies, pins and information booklets.

Phillip Coorey's insightful report of the 2012 Dawn service reveals the manner in which the annual pilgrimage of young Australians and New Zealanders to Anzac Cove in Turkey is driven as much by commercial factors as it is by a grassroots hunger for sacred ritual. The commemoration of the Anzac landings is a major spectacle, a carefully choreographed, tightly scripted, stage-managed production designed to ensure full emotional impact.[10]

The rise of Anzac Day as Australia's national day has undoubtedly been paralleled by the increasing importance of Anzac Day in New Zealand over the last two decades. The pilgrimage of New Zealand's youth to the Gallipoli Peninsula for the Anzac Dawn service began around the same time, in the early 1990s. In both countries there has been a notable enthusiasm for Anzac Day among Generation Y (those born from the mid-1970s to the mid-1990s), while similar explanations have been put forward to explain this phenomenon: the demand for community-binding ritual in an undeniably secular age; the growing fascination with the trench warfare

10   Phillip Coorey, *Sydney Morning Herald* (25 April 2012).

of the First World War, one which has increased as the distance from that same war grows ever greater; and the fruit of decade-long government-funded educational programmes focusing on the Anzac legend. For both Australians and New Zealanders, a visit to Anzac Cove is today seen as a rite of passage, proof of the very depth of one's attachment to the nation. The connection between national identity and the events of 25 April is largely unquestioned. As Philip Burdon, New Zealand Trade Negotiations Minister observed in 1996, Anzac Cove was the 'birthplace of the creation of New Zealand's unique [...] sense of identity'.[11]

From the seventy-fifth anniversary of Anzac in 1990, political leaders and veterans have also visited Anzac Cove in greater numbers. In the same year, Australian Prime Minister Bob Hawke and New Zealand Prime Minister Helen Clark became the first prime ministers of their respective countries to visit Anzac Cove on 25 April. As both countries have entered a period of post colonialism yet remained constitutional monarchies, prime ministers have become more important as *interpreters* of the nation. With the decline of the British connection and the civic personality of the British monarch as Head of State, the role of the prime minister in both countries has become more presidential, ceremonial and priestly, especially in the public theatre and rituals associated with the office. Moreover, the narratives of war recited in prime ministerial speeches have taken on greater prominence in defining national self-image in Australia and New Zealand.

---

11    Philip Burdon in Jason Koutsoukis, 'A View from Gallipoli', *Sydney Morning Herald* (26 April 2010); on New Zealand, Maureen Sharpe, 'Anzac Day in New Zealand 1916–1939', *New Zealand Journal of History* (NZJH) 15/2 (1981), 97–114; also Scott Worthy, 'A Debt of Honour: New Zealanders' First Anzac Days', *NZJH* 36/2 (2002), 185–200; Ian McGibbon, 'Anzac Day' in Ian McGibbon, ed., *The Oxford Companion to New Zealand Military History* (Auckland: Oxford University Press, 2000), 29; Helen Robinson, 'Lest We Forget? The fading of New Zealand War Commemorations, 1946–1966', *NZJH* 44/1 (2010), 76–91; George Frederick Davis, 'Anzac Day meanings and memories: New Zealand, Australian and Turkish Perspectives on a day of commemoration in the twentieth century', PhD, University of Otago, 2008; the recent resurgence of Anzac day in New Zealand is examined by Graham Hucker, 'A Determination to Remember: Helen Clark and New Zealand's Military Heritage', *The Journal of Arts, Management, Law and Society* 40 (2010), 105–18.

This is not only driven by the need to fill the vacuum left by the demise of British race patriotism with new myths of national identity. It is also driven partly by geopolitical anxieties. Governing within an international climate in which wars are being fought on several fronts, the recitation of war narratives has been employed as a means of bolstering national unity and galvanizing political resolve in 'the war against terror'. At a time when liberal democratic values are perceived to be under threat, prime ministerial language extolling the virtues of the Anzac legend in Australia and New Zealand has placed 'values' at the heart of war commemoration. The Anzacs, many Australians and New Zealanders believe, went to war to defend their countries' 'values' and 'lifestyle'. As recently as Anzac Day 2009, New Zealand Prime Minister John Key went so far as to suggest that the Anzacs had fought to maintain the country's economic advantage, miraculously securing New Zealand's wealth for a century to come. The Anzacs, said Key, 'were everyday people who rose to heights of sacrifice and, in doing so, preserved the living standards of all of us, for generations to come'.[12]

Together with a marked increased in media coverage of Anzac Day in both countries and much greater numbers attending Anzac Day services at home and abroad, one of the most notable parallels between Australia and New Zealand is the role of government funding in driving enthusiasm for Anzac heritage. The range of measures is numerous, but includes such initiatives as school based competitions for the best Anzac essay, the promotion of Anzac rituals and observance across the education system as the basis of civic cohesion, substantial government funding of domestic and international 'military heritage' projects such as the erection of war memorials overseas, dutiful observance of military anniversaries, site specific building projects on the Gallipoli Peninsula, including a New Zealand government funded Gallipoli walking track dedicated for the ninetieth anniversary of Anzac in 2005, provision of greater support for military heritage research projects, and the increased funding and prominence of both countries' national war memorials. As the centenary of the First World

12   John Key (25 April 2009) <http://johnkey.co.nz/archives/673-ANZAC-address-at-National-Wreath-Laying-Ceremony.html> accessed 14 March 2014.

War approaches, John Key has proclaimed proudly that his government 'is developing a number of centenary legacy projects, including historical publications, digital resources and new heritage trails around Gallipoli and the Western Front'.[13]

While it is crucial to document the extent of government funding for military commemoration (evidence which contradicts the popular belief that enthusiasm for the day is a mysterious, 'organic' process), it would also be simplistic to suggest that a top-down process of government-led manipulation explains the resurgence of the Anzac legend in Australia and New Zealand. As historian Joan Beaumont has pointed out, individual initiative has also played a key role. Beaumont cites the example of Fromelles, where the persistence of a Melbourne school teacher led to the discovery of the missing graves of Australian soldiers and the Hellfire Pass cutting in Thailand, now the site of an Australian memorial museum, which was reclaimed from the jungle in the 1980s by ex-POW's with minimal government support. In a similar fashion, an individual suggested New Zealand's government-funded walking track at Gallipoli.[14]

While New Zealand might lag behind Australia in certain respects – the burying of 'the unknown soldier' at the national war memorial took place in Australia in 1993, and in New Zealand in 2004 – the centrality of the commemoration of war to both countries postcolonial identity cannot be doubted. 'The Anzac spirit' no longer applies necessarily to military heritage. It has now become a term to describe all those who serve and defend the nation. At the height of Victoria's bushfire emergency in 2009, Prime Minister Kevin Rudd compared the firefighters who stood at 'the gates of hell' to the Anzacs in their 'slouch hats' while in New Zealand,

---

13    John Key (2012) <http://www.anzac.govt.nz/today/event.html> accessed 19 February 2014. On government funding in Australia, see Marilyn Lake, 'How do schoolchildren learn about the spirit of Anzac?', in Marilyn Lake et al, *What's Wrong with Anzac?*, 135–56; in New Zealand, see Graham Hucker, 'A Determination to Remember'.

14    On New Zealand's Gallipoli walking track, see Hucker, 'A Determination to Remember', 109; also Joan Beaumont, 'Hellfire Pass Memorial Museum, the Thai-Burma Railway', in Bart Ziino and Martin Gegner, eds, *The Heritage of War: Cultural Heritage after Conflict* (Abingdon: Routledge, 2011).

Prime Minister John Key spoke of the Anzac spirit 'in Christchurch [...] as ordinary civilians risked their own lives to try and save others from the rubble'. The biblical cadences of official rhetoric at Anzac day services are also a common thread. As John Key ministered on Anzac Day 2009, 'as we lay these wreathes together let us reflect on our ties to each other and our shared pride in our country. Let us reflect on what is to be a New Zealander'. In both countries, Anzac Day carries more mass emotional resonance than Easter or Christmas.[15]

Graham Hucker has explained the significance of Helen Clark's term as New Zealand prime minister (1999–2008) in helping to articulate, fund and establish a strong focus on New Zealand's 'military heritage'. Clark's tenure as Labour PM coincided approximately with that of the conservative John Howard in Australia (1996–2007). Over a decade, the dedication of New Zealand war memorials overseas and the prominence of Anzac Day rituals at home formed the centre pin of Clark's efforts to entrench the public memory of New Zealand's wartime experience as a nation-building narrative.[16]

Like Howard, Clark's family's experiences of the First World War loomed large in her childhood. And like Howard, Clark was intent on using military experience to 'build the spirit of New Zealand' and 'strengthen national identity'. She also saw New Zealand's Gallipoli experience through the same list of values recited by Howard, and later by Kevin Rudd and Julia Gillard – courage, mateship, sacrifice and compassion. As the 2015 centenary of the Anzac landings nears, this rhetoric, recited in reverential tone, has been carried on by Clark's successor, John Key and New Zealand's Governor General, Sir Jerry Mateparae.[17]

Where New Zealand's embrace of Anzac has differed slightly from that of Australia is the placement and emphasis of the legend in national mythology. Helen Clark often described the experience at Gallipoli as 'a

---

15  Rudd's comments quoted in *The Age*, editorial (25 April 2009); Key's remarks (25 April 2009) <http://www.johnkey.co.nz/archives/673-ANZAC-address-at-National-Wreath-Laying-Ceremony.html> accessed 19 February 2014.
16  Graham Hucker, 'A Determination to Remember', 105.
17  Ibid., 106–7, 114.

defining stage in the *evolution* of New Zealand as a nation' and an important piece 'in the *mosaic* that makes up the picture the world sees when
it thinks of New Zealand'. Clark's qualified embrace of the Anzac myth
stands in sharp contrast to Australia, where the Anzac legend has become
*the* nation-defining myth, one that has given birth to the nation and yet
also expresses its contemporary *raison d'etre*.[18]

Howard's Anzac rhetoric suggested a mood of celebration as much as
commemoration, an aspect also noted by New Zealand journalist Anthony
Hubbard in 2005: 'John Howard's [speech] was full of heroic alliteration,
boasting about the deeds "that were dared and done here". Helen Clark's was
quiet and sad, grieving about the war "that broke our hearts". The Australians
boomed out their anthem. The New Zealanders murmured theirs for a
while and then it petered out'. It comes as little surprise that it was Helen
Clark who warned the Australian government about the inappropriate-
ness of John Farnham's planned performance at Anzac Cove in 2005. The
slickly produced programmes at Anzac Cove, which yet again threatened
to turn a moment of commemoration into kitsch stadium entertainment
was an anathema to Clark, which is perhaps another reminder that New
Zealand commemorates Anzac day, while Australia tends to celebrate it.[19]

One reason that New Zealand can more easily see the Anzac legend as
merely one part of the 'mosaic' of its national identity is that in Waitangi
Day, it possesses an alternative founding moment. Here, for example, is a
text from the Museum of New Zealand in Wellington, which was designed
between the mid-1980s and the late 1990s, focusing on the roles the Treaty
of Waitangi has been called upon to play.

> The Treaty of Waitangi is a living social document. Debated, overlooked, celebrated.
> A vision of peaceful co-existence, or the cause of disharmony? An irrelevancy, or the

---

18    Howard Address at Anzac Day Dawn service Gallipoli (25 April 2005) <http://
      parlinfo.aph.gov.au/parlInfo/search/display/display.w3p;query=(Id:media/pressrel/
      cbuf6);rec=0;> accessed 19 February 2014; Clark quoted in Hucker, 'A Determination
      to Remember', 114.
19    Hubbard at <http://www.stuff.co.nz/sunday-star-times/columnists/4921408/
      Nationalism-a-force-for-progress> accessed 19 February 2014.

platform on which all New Zealanders can build a future? [...] The meaning of the Treaty changes depending on who's speaking. Engage with our founding document. Here are a range of voices from past and present. The floor is open for discussion.[20]

Australia has no comparable example of such a 'founding document' or historical event, at least on its own soil. Nor is there any immediate likelihood that an alternative narrative such as the declaration of a republic is about to emerge to rival Anzac Day, either in Australia or New Zealand. Despite the existence of Waitangi Day, many New Zealanders have continued to see Anzac Day as a less problematic national day. In January 2013, Michael Cullen, New Zealand's Deputy Prime Minister, explained why Anzac Day is perceived as 'less contentious' than Waitangi Day:

> In New Zealand we could say that we have two days which are like national days. One used to be the source, 30 years or so ago, of great bitterness and division. Now, Anzac Day is a day where, despite all our differences of perspective, we remember our past. That is even though in doing so we commemorate our biggest military disaster. Our other national day, Waitangi Day, remains for many a source of argument and division rather than celebration or commemoration.[21]

Cullen's position was echoed by Jon Johansson, a lecturer in political science at Victoria University: due to 'our still contentious treaty history', observed Johansson, Anzac Day became New Zealand's 'default national day'. Nonetheless, as the social psychologist, James Liu has argued, two narratives are used to 'make sense of New Zealand's history [...] a liberal democratic and a bicultural narrative'. This remains perhaps one of the most important differences in comparison to Australia, where history is represented not through a bicultural narrative, but predominantly through a liberal democratic narrative of 'balance'. Despite Labor Prime Minister Kevin Rudd's apology to the stolen generations in February 2008, Australia still waits to be refounded in a manner that will reflect its nationhood as a

---

20 Quoted in Bain Attwood, 'Refounding the Nation: The Treaty of Waitangi and the Museum of New Zealand/Te Papa Tongarewa', *forthcoming*.

21 See <http://www.nzherald.co.nz/nz/news/article.cfm?c_id=1&objectid=10009758> accessed 19 February 2014.

genuine partnership between Aboriginal and non-Aboriginal Australians. Aboriginal people are largely invisible in the Australian federal constitution. Indeed, as I have argued elsewhere, by creating Anzac as a foundational myth of nationhood in exile from the land in which they live, Australians have turned their eyes from the true site of melancholy and loss in their history, the land itself – and the encounter between Aboriginal and non-Aboriginal people. Their emotional investment in Anzac Day is a turning away from the history of invasion, conquest and settlement on their own soil, a kind of substitute mourning for their inability to mourn the dispossession of Aboriginal people. In a very real way, Australia has continued to circumnavigate the heart of the matter. Anzac Day's success as a national day is explained as much by what is forgotten on 25 April as what is remembered. And perhaps it is here that another parallel between New Zealand's and Australia's use of the Anzac legend can be found.[22]


# Conclusion


In New Zealand, remembering Anzac Day allows both Maori and Pakeha to stand together in a common cause, one in which they died fighting together rather than fighting against one another as they did in the Maori wars. As in Australia, emphasizing the less 'divisive' history of Anzac allows the vexed

---

22    James H. Liu, 'History and Identity: a system of checks and balances for Aotearoa/ New Zealand', in James H. Liu et al, *New Zealand Identities: Departures and destinations* (Wellington: Victoria University Press, 2005), 69–87, 13; Johansson quoted in Franchesca Walker, 'Commemoration versus Nationalism', *Salient* (19 April 2010) <http://salient.org.nz/features/commemoration-versus-nationalism> accessed 19 February 2014; also see Mark McKenna, 'Anzac Day: How did it become Australia's National Day?' in Marilyn Lake et al, *What's Wrong with Anzac?*, 110–34; Mark McKenna, 'Howard's Warriors' in Raimond Gaita, ed., *Why the War Was Wrong* (Melbourne: text publishing, 2003), 167–200; Mark McKenna, 'The Anzac Myth' in *Australian Literary Review* 2/5 (2007).

history of colonialism and frontier violence to be excised from the arena of celebratory foundational history and national days. Both nations are conveniently imagined as being made elsewhere. Anzac day does not raise issues of sovereignty and dispossession (unless you are Turkish). Unlike the haunted history of colonization, it hails the spirit of thousands of men who died 'honourable' deaths in the hills of the Gallipoli Peninsula and the mud-fields of the Western Front. As Prime Minister Julia Gillard remarked at Anzac Cove in 2012, Gallipoli was 'a place hallowed by sacrifice and loss' but also 'a place shining with honour, and honour of the most vivid kind'.[23]

As both nations rush headlong towards the centenary of the Anzac landings in 2015, it appears that the remaking of the Anzac myth has managed to provide many of the things that history on their own soil can not: a history that is immutable, sacred and free of rancour and political division, a history that can justify the existence of the nation and remain relatively uncontested. The politics of Anzac Day in Australia and New Zealand today is such that no politician would dare question its centrality to the nation's identity.

23  Gillard quoted in Phillip Coorey, 'A Place Shining with Honour', *Sydney Morning Herald* (25 April 2012).

MATTHEW GRAVES

# Memorial Diplomacy in Franco-Australian Relations

## Introduction

The landmark anniversaries of the First and Second World Wars, and more recently those of the Cold War, have been used by post-war French and Australian governments as an opportunity to mark the enduring nature of wartime alliances and their continuing relevance to the political present. They have also provided a setting for bilateral or multilateral summit meetings and a platform for articulating policy agendas, both foreign and domestic. The inauguration or rededication of sites of memory, whether military (the Australian National Memorial), or civic (the École Victoria in Villers-Bretonneux, with its motto '*N'oublions jamais l'Australie*'), located extra-territorially (Gallipoli), or within sovereign boundaries (Ataturk Entrance, Albany), has long served as a platform for reinforcing relations between governments, be they present partners, estranged allies or former belligerents. They have also served as a prelude to reconciliation between states and minority groups. Such activities, however, have been pursued with greater intensity and amplitude since the advent of the 'memory boom' in the 1980s, particularly in the field of Franco-Australian relations.[1]

I have previously used the term 'memorial diplomacy' to describe the instrumentalization of sites of memory, commemorative events and national

---

1    Jay Winter, 'The Generation of Memory: Reflections on the "Memory Boom" in Contemporary Historical Studies', *German Historical Institute Bulletin* 27 (Fall 2000) <http://www.ghi-dc.org/publications/ghipubs/bu/027/b27winterframe. html> accessed 10 December 2012.

days as a vehicle for international relations.[2] It might be defined as that dimension of diplomatic practice that seeks to materialize and mobilize a shared sense of the past at the intersection of collective memory and transnational history. It involves its participants in carefully choreographed public ceremonies on the anniversaries of historic occasions at selected sites of memory, long established or of recent invention, typically on the margins of international summits or intergovernmental forums. In instrumentalizing remembrance and mobilizing history for political ends, memorial diplomacy can be considered a form of soft power, which in Joseph Nye's terms, co-opts by attraction, association and persuasion rather than by imposing compliance by military force or economic constraint.[3] Memorial diplomacy is akin to cultural diplomacy in its appeal to shared heritage and in aspects of its narrative modes, arenas and agencies – the repatriation of indigenous human remains and artefacts from archeological and ethnographic collections of museums, for instance – but in contrast to its cultural equivalent, its dominant modern idiom is war memory.

## The internationalization of public commemoration: The French perspective

While memorial diplomacy is the projection of the politics of remembrance into the domain of international relations, it rarely draws a clear line between foreign and domestic political spheres. For Nicolas Sarkozy to host Barack Obama at the sixty-fifth anniversary of the D-Day Landings

---

2    Matthew Graves, 'Displacing Geographies of Memory: The Australian and New Zealand Memorials, London' in L. E. Semler, Bob Hodge and Philippa Kelly, eds, *What is the Human? Australian Voices from the Humanities* (Melbourne: Australian Scholarly Publishing, 2012), 174.

3    Joseph Nye, *Soft Power: The Means to Success in World Politics* (New York: Public Affairs, 2004), 5.

in 2009 at the height of the new US president's popularity was to seek to bathe in the aura of statesmanship by association, for domestic as much as international consumption. But when it comes to invoking the transnational dimension of commemorative events and shared pasts, the same domestic platform may serve a foreign affairs agenda. Typically, the diplomatic agents on such occasions are national leaders or consular officials, but increasingly with the development of public diplomacy they have become devolved parliaments, regional authorities and decentralized public administrations or municipalities (via twinning agreements), museums and other institutional caretakers of public memory, but also associations of veterans, communities, minorities or victims' groups such as the British Child Migrants to Australia. Even an individual citizen can act as an agent of memorial diplomacy, as long as the object of his or her action transcends the sphere of the strictly private and engages other international agencies.[4]

The objectives of memorial diplomacy include the reconciliation of former enemies or estranged allies, the recognition of new alliances or reaffirmation of existing ones, the promotion of trade and cultural exchanges, and more nebulously an attempt to fill a perceived 'identity vacuum' in contemporary societies. It involves not just the construction of sites of memory but their actualization, and the phenomenon is not new: the first *Fête de l'Armistice*, on 11 November 1919, for example, had an inbuilt international dimension which saw the French army parade alongside its victorious allies, including British and Dominion troops. However, there is evidence of an intensification and a systematization of the set of practices which make up memorial diplomacy in the past thirty years. This has involved an unprecedented 'dilation' of the commemorative arena through the grafting of an international dimension onto established

---

4    In February 1990, Michael Mansell, a Tasmanian lawyer, successfully petitioned the Royal College of Surgeons in Dublin to return Aboriginal remains to Australia which included the head of his great-great grandfather – Memorandum submitted by the Australian government 'on the repatriation of the remains of Aboriginal and Torres Strait Islander people' <http://www.publications.parliament.uk/pa/cm199900/cmselect/cmcumeds/371/371ap76.htm> accessed 14 March 2014.

national commemorations.[5] Memorial diplomacy thus involves not so much the invention of tradition as the extension of memorial function, through the adaptation of existing sites of memory to the international political imperatives and opportunities of the day. Bastille Day was first internationalized under the second presidency of François Mitterrand for the Bicentenary of the French Revolution on 14 July 1989, when foreign heads of state were invited to Paris to attend a spectacular parade, 'la Marseillaise', designed by Jean-Paul Goude. It should be acknowledged that the internationalization of public commemorations can be a perilous exercise, stretching, and on occasions breaching, the limits of national political consensus by disrupting conventions. The invitation by President Mitterrand of the first German delegation and armoured detachment to participate in a 14 July Bastille Day parade in 1994 as part of the Eurocorps provoked an emotive protest from former president and Free French Army veteran Giscard d'Estaing: 'there are better places to stage a reconciliation, there are better occasions for remembrance'.[6]

Bastille Day on 14 July is a nineteenth-century creation, promulgated on 6 July 1880. Of the other public commemorations in the French national calendar, two were introduced in the inter-war years, two in the Cold-War period, while no fewer than six were established in the past decade alone, a sign of 'commemorative inflation' according to the Kaspi report.[7] Six new national days were created in the course of the tenure of a single president, Jacques Chirac, from 1999 to 2006, the sole creator of new commemorations

---

5    See F. Argounes, S. Mohamed-Gaillard and L. Vacher, *Atlas de l'Océanie: Continent d'îles, laboratoire du futur* (Paris: Editions Autrement, 2011).

6    Valéry Giscard d'Estaing interviewed on the evening news, 8 June 1994, was moved to tears by the recollection of the German occupation of Paris <http://www.ina.fr/video/I09169817> accessed 17 February 2014.

7    These were (respectively): La Fête nationale de Jeanne d'Arc, the second Sunday in May (inaugurated 10 July 1920); Commemoration of Armistice, 11 November 1918 (24 October 1922); The Deportation, the last Sunday in April (14 April 1954); VE Day, 8 May (2 October 1981); Les Justes de France, 16 July (10 July 2000); Abolition de l'esclavage, 10 May (Taubira Act 10 May 2001); Harkis, 25 September (31 March 2003); Algerian, Moroccan and Tunisian wars, 5 December (26 September 2003); Indochina, 8 June (26 May 2005); L'Appel du 18 juin 1940 (10 March 2006).

in the last half-century.[8] All of these have an international dimension. As Olivier Wieviorka put it: 'Jacques Chirac confirmed the internationalization of commemoration and placed it under the sign of promoting peace'.[9]

The Kaspi report (2008) is one of three official reports, including the Becker Commission (2007) and the Prost-Wieviorka report (2009),[10] to have found evidence of, and to encourage, the internationalization of France's commemorative calendar. In his review of the calendar, Kaspi recommends that the number of national commemorations should be reduced from twelve to three (Armistice Day, VE Day, Bastille Day) because of 'excessive repentance'.[11] He concludes that a 'saturation' level has been reached: 'too much commemoration perhaps undermines commemoration'.[12] His report recommends the invitation of foreign dignitaries, the representatives of Great Britain, the United States, Russia and Italy, to Armistice Day to ensure the convergence of the national and international dimensions of the event and favourably registers the international interest in the 14 July Bastille Day celebrations.[13] The committee suggested that wherever possible European unity should be made the theme of Armistice Day or VE Day commemorations: 'So defined, the event(s) would take on a European

---

8    André Kaspi, *Rapport de la Commission de Réflexion sur la Modernisation des Commémorations Publiques, sous la Présidence d'André Kaspi* (Ministère de la Défense/La Documentation Française, novembre 2008), 23.

9    Olivier Wieviorka, *La Mémoire Désunie: Le souvenir politique des années sombres, de la Libération à nos jours* (Paris: Editions du Seuil, 2010), 266.

10   Olivier Wieviorka and Antoine Prost, eds, *La Mémoire combattante, un regard international* (Centre d'études en sciences sociales de la défense (C2SD): Ministère de la Défense, September 2009).

11   Other dates are not to be suppressed, but become local, regional or exceptional. With the end of communicative memory of the Second World War in sight, a rationalization of memorial resources is seen to be more necessary than ever. See Kaspi, *Rapport*, 25.

12   Kaspi, *Rapport*, 13. Kaspi identifies the emergence of a culture of victimhood, and in response, an excess of public repentance or redemption (46), seen as a symptom of creeping 'communitarianism' and a threat to national cohesion: 'France risks forever losing her spiritual unity to become a loose aggregate of compassions' (22) [Translations by author].

13   Kaspi, *Rapport*, 17, 9.

dimension, bringing together yesterday's enemies and transcending the national to achieve an international consensus'.[14]

Chancellor Schroeder's participation in the sixtieth anniversary of the 1944 D-Day Landings in 2004 was the first by a German head of government;[15] his predecessor Helmut Kohl is said to have declined an invitation to attend the fiftieth anniversary in 1994, although contemporary sources suggested that Kohl was excluded. Schroeder had planned to honour the memory of the German dead but desisted on the day.[16] His presence was a significant but incomplete gesture of reconciliation, since no invitation was extended to the German veterans. In all, fifteen countries were represented in 2004 by twenty-two foreign dignitaries. The presence of the German Chancellor lent a spirit of multilateral *rapprochement* to proceedings, at once Franco-German and Franco-American, after the tensions of the Iraq war. The calendar of international summitry for the month reveals the dense web of diplomatic activity surrounding this single commemorative event: the D-Day anniversary, the G8 meeting, the EU summit, the US-EU summit, and the NATO summit on the transfer of sovereignty to Iraq all took place between 5 and 30 June 2004.[17]

All three reports acknowledge the internationalization of memory as a basis for memorial diplomacy. The Kaspi report sees it as plugging a breach left by the obsolescence of the grand narrative of the nation: 'today France has ceased to promote its great national myths'. The report argues that with socio-cultural shifts and syllabus changes in education, there is a perception that commemorative events are met with growing public indifference: 'national memory is no longer compelling'.[18] If so, memorial diplomacy in France has intensified just as national commemoration has lost its momentum and popular appeal.

14    Kaspi, *Rapport*, 31, 32, 30. Compare Jean-Pierre Masseret's (former Minister for Veterans Affairs) proposal to commemorate 1918 transnationally: 'around the idea of the shared history of the combatant nations' (Wieviorka, *La Mémoire Désunie*, 266).
15    *Le Monde* (3 January 2004).
16    *Le Monde* (5 June 2004).
17    *Le Monde* (2 June 2010).
18    Kaspi, *Rapport*, 24, 20.

A driving factor in the process of commemorative internationalization has been the quest for political consensus, or rather the displacement of that quest from the national to the international stage, with the explicit objective of transcending a disputed national consensus through appeals to collective history and identity, be it pan-European, Transatlantic or – in the Australian case – 'Asian', with the attendant political temptation to transcend troubled episodes in the historical record and the starker realities of international relations. The Becker commission, which was tasked with preparing the ninetieth anniversary of the Armistice of 11 November in 2008, makes special mention in its mission statement of the Commonwealth countries, pointing to the advantages of the anniversary coinciding with the French presidency of the EU: 'It is highly symbolic that the numerous commemorative events organized by the State, the local authorities and foreign governments, in particular those of the countries of the Commonwealth, should coincide with the French presidency of the Europe Union'.[19] The commission's original brief included a survey of memorial initiatives undertaken by foreign governments on French soil and in its final report it recommends that Villers-Bretonneux should be made the focal point for an international ceremony of Great War commemoration honouring the Commonwealth allies.[20]

Commemorative diplomacy operates within a given field of memory. In the analytical framework proposed by Ashplant – narratives which articulate memory, agencies (from the state to civil society), and arenas of memory (the socio-political spaces in which memories are preserved and elaborated) – the last is of particular relevance when it comes to assessing memorial diplomacy in general and the memorial politics of Franco-Australian relations in particular.[21] The geographical referent is largely secondary in Ashplant's usage as it is in Nora's definition of *lieux de mémoire*,

---

19 Jean-Jacques Becker, 'Rapport de la Commission "Becker", Pour le 90ème anniversaire de la fin de 1918' (Ministère de la Défense, 19 December 2007), 2.
20 Jean-Jacques Becker, 'La commission Becker: les missions' (Ministère de la Défense, 2007), 6.
21 T. Ashplant, G. Dawson, and M. Roper, 'The Politics of War Memory and Commemoration: Contexts, Structures and Dynamics', in T. Ashplant, G. Dawson and M.

which tends to dematerialize memorial space the better to underline its symbolic function as a floating signifier.[22] However, any diplomatic practice unfolds within – and must take account of – a given political geography. From a commemorative point of view, the Asia-Pacific space does not possess the same geopolitical valency as the Euro-Mediterranean or Transatlantic spaces, even if they share certain referents and modes of enunciation: for instance, the 'Anzac spirit' from an Australian and New Zealand perspective is analogous to the 'spirit of the Blitz' for the British or 'spirit of Verdun' for the French. In previous work, Elizabeth Rechniewski and I have proposed a complementary expression – 'field of memory' – to designate how a *lieu de mémoire* is spatially oriented and located within a constellation or network of mirror sites.[23] We argue that the performative rituals of public remembrance have both synchronic and diachronic dimensions: the recollection of the past is inscribed in a 'geography of remembrance' and construed in the political present.[24] The spatial dimension is not subordinate to the symbolic function, but conditions and structures its value. In terms of Great War and Second World War memory, France occupies a central position bridging the three geostrategic theatres of Europe, the north Atlantic and the Mediterranean basin, so that French commemorative venues have provided the *lingua franca* of memorial diplomacy, offering successive French presidents since Francois Mitterrand (and arguably Charles de Gaulle) with a high profile platform for international summitry and statesmanship. France hosts more Anzac *lieux de mémoire* than any other country, with sites dotted across 200 kilometres of northern France and Belgium, from Fromelles to Le Hamel, now joined up by the Australian

---

Roper, eds, *The Politics of Memory: Commemorating War* (London: Transaction Publishers 2004), 3–85.

22    Pierre Nora, *Les Lieux de Mémoire* (Paris: Gallimard, 1984–92).

23    Matthew Graves and Elizabeth Rechniewski, 'From Collective Memory to Transcultural Remembrance', *Fields of Remembrance. Portal – Journal of Multidisciplinary International Studies* 7/1 (2010), 8.

24    Nuala Johnson, *Ireland, the Great War and the Geography of Remembrance* (Cambridge: Cambridge University Press, 2003), 13–14.

Remembrance Trail, a Great War memorial itinerary co-funded by France and Australia for the centenary of 1914–18.[25]

The base map of memorial diplomacy is imaginative geography – the projection of the image of a country's place in the world. The digital revolution has seen an unprecedented extension of the scope of image production and mapping, and war memory has played a prominent role in this movement. In the Asia-Pacific region, as in Europe, the key anniversaries of the major twentieth century conflicts – chiefly the First and Second World Wars, but also the wars in Korea, Indochina and Vietnam – have offered governments the opportunity to underline the solidity of alliances forged in war and renewed in times of peace. This is notably the case with the commemoration of Anzac Day every 25 April in metropolitan France, but also in New Caledonia, French Polynesia and on Vanuatu by representatives of the French, Australian and New Zealand governments; or when France is invited to the annual Battle for Australia Day ceremony. This is a tradition of more recent invention under the Kevin Rudd Labor government (2007–10) during which a French consular delegation and military detachment took part in the inaugural ceremony at the cenotaph in St Martin's Place, Sydney on 3 September 2008. Obversely, the inauguration of new monuments may set the stage for the *rapprochement* of former belligerents and a pretext for the establishment or restoration of bilateral relations between governments, the first step in the reconciliation between nation-states. This was illustrated by the inauguration by Prime Minister John Howard of the Battle of Long Tan memorial in 2006, which became the symbolic theatre of the reconciliation between Australia and Vietnam, made all the more potent by its extra-territorial location.[26] The emergence of new alliances and associations (treaties, regional forums, bilateral and

---

25  'Australian Remembrance Trail across the Western Front', Department of Veterans' Affairs <http://www.dva.gov.au/commems_oawg/OAWG/war_memorials/overseas_memorials/france/Pages/western%20front%20projects.aspx> accessed 17 February 2014; see also Shanti Sumartojo in this volume.

26  Matthew Graves and Elizabeth Rechniewski, 'Australian War Memorialism and the Politics of Remembrance' in Martine Piquet et Gilles Teulié, eds, *Cultures of the Commonwealth* (Université de Paris-Dauphine, 1er trimestre 2008), 95–106.

multilateral trading agreements), the sharing of sovereignty (in the context of the European Union, for instance, but also on a memorial level in the former condominiums), the spread of diaspora, the development of 'long-distance nationalism' and war tourism have lent an international dimension to the great national shrines of remembrance.[27] The Australian War Memorial at Gallipoli is a model in this respect. It has become the symbolic cornerstone of Turkish-Australian-New Zealand relations, with the multiplication of mirror sites at Albany (Western Australia), Hyde Park Corner in London, and on Anzac Parade in Canberra, the focal point of an increasingly globalized Anzac Day, the ceremonial observance of which now extends to more than sixty countries worldwide.[28]

The trend reveals a growing recognition of the transnational dimension to memorialism, that modern histories are global and their commemoration cannot remain the exclusive possession of any single national agency. This is a realization that has been reinforced by the development of new modes of articulation, notably the multiplication of virtual sites of memory online. Just as NGOs and associations are increasingly implicated in public diplomacy as a consequence of globalization, so too representatives of government or civil society are more frequently invited to participate in the commemorative cycles of nations, as they in turn have grown more international. As part of this global trend, Australian prime ministers since Paul Keating (1991–96) have moved to expand the field of Anzac memory by extending it spatially to the Asia-Pacific region, and diachronically through the commemoration of the Second World War, the Vietnam War and latterly the Korean War, against a background of the intense debate over the militarization of public memory. In response to these developments, in the past decade French authorities have hosted the extension of Anzac Day to French overseas territories in New Caledonia and French Polynesia, but also in the former condominium of Vanuatu, in the context of the post-Muroroa *rapprochement* of French and Australian foreign policies.

---

27    See Benedict Anderson, 'Long-Distance Nationalism: World Capitalism and the Rise of Identity Politics', The Wertheim Lecture 1992 (Amsterdam: Centre for Asian Studies, 1992), 12.

28    Anzac Day at Gallipoli is increasingly multinational: in 2011, eleven countries enjoyed official representation.

# The diplomacy of war memory and 'commemorative renewal': The Australian perspective

Within the commemorative field of the Asia-Pacific region, there is no equivalent stage for the grandstanding international summits which have punctuated the diplomatic calendar in Europe in the course of the past decade: the sixtieth anniversary of D-Day (6 June 2004), associated for the first time with the commemoration of the Landings in Provence (15 August 2004); the ninetieth anniversary of Armistice Day 1918 in 2008, followed closely by the sixty-fifth anniversary of the D-Day Landing in 2009. For Wieviorka, the commemoration of D-Day, since its resurrection in 1984 in the course of the first presidency of François Mitterrand, has been a symptom of 'commemorative renewal'.[29] The 2004 commemoration, which associated the former Allied powers of 1944 (France, Great Britain, the United States, Canada, Russia, and ten other countries, including Australia and New Zealand) and their former adversary Germany, against the background of the war in Iraq and the ongoing crisis in Franco-American diplomatic relations, was qualified by one observer as simple 'mood music'[30] for the real diplomatic work. This was conducted after the Normandy ceremonies at the G8 summit in Georgia on 10 June 2004, where the Bush administration's Greater Middle East project was on the agenda, and at the NATO summit in Istanbul from 28–29 June, where the Iraq war and a 'new security era' were discussed.[31] However, as Joseph Nye points out, 'diplomacy aimed at public opinion can become as important to outcomes as the traditional classified diplomatic communications among leaders', by cultivating a diplomatic environment in which the coordination of policy is facilitated.[32]

---

29   Olivier Wieviorka, *La Mémoire Désunie: Le souvenir politique des années sombres, de la Libération à nos jours* (Paris: Editions du Seuil, 2010), 224.

30   J. F. O. McAllister, 'Mood music', *Time* (May 31 2004), 28–9.

31   Minutes of the Istanbul NATO summit, 28–29 June 2004 <http://www.diplomatie.gouv.fr/fr/actions-france_830/defense-securite_9035/otan_1134/sommets_15291/sommet-istanbul-29.06.2004_3630.html> accessed 13 September 2011.

32   Nye, *Soft Power*, 105, 107.

Prime Ministers John Howard (Australia) and Helen Clark (New Zealand) featured among the twenty-two heads of government and state and personalities from fifteen states invited to the D-Day Landing ceremonies on 6 June 2004. The same day, the Ambassador of France in Australia decorated five Australian D-Day veterans with the *Légion d'Honneur* in a ceremony in Canberra in the presence of the Commonwealth Governor-General and the Minister for Veterans' Affairs. However, the Australian and New Zealand armed forces were only engaged to a limited extent in the campaign for the Liberation of France following the strategic withdrawal of the Anzac expeditionary force to the Asia-Pacific theatre in 1942.[33] The Australian and New Zealand presence in Normandy and its ceremonial counterpart in Canberra was more a diplomatic than an historical imperative, to recall the 'fundamental values' of 1944 at a time of renewed conflict. What made their presence compulsory in geopolitical rather than historical terms, was the extension of the field of memory of Anzac diachronically from the Great War to the Second World War and beyond under the Hawke and Keating administrations, and spatially the hemispheric shift of focus away from the Euro-Mediterranean theatre of operations to South-East Asia and the Pacific. In his contribution to *What's Wrong with Anzac*, Mark McKenna retraces the history of that transition, from the commemoration of Anzac in its First World War incarnation, to the celebration of the 'spirit of Anzac' in the broader sense, encompassing Australia and New Zealand's participation in the conflicts of the twentieth century, as well as in peace-keeping operations, in both hemispheres.[34]

The modern 'resurgence' of Anzac Day as Australia's true national day is commonly dated from Bob Hawke's speech at the seventy-fifth anniversary of the Battle of Gallipoli at Anzac Cove in 1990. However, research at the Australian Prime Ministers Centre points to an earlier precedent on the eve of the first decade of the 'memory boom'. On 25 April 1979

33  Some 3,000 Australian military personnel served with British forces during the Normandy Landings, principally RAAF and RAN.

34  Mark McKenna in Marilyn Lake and Henry Reynolds et al., *What's Wrong with Anzac? The Militarisation of Australian History* (Sydney: University of New South Wales Press, 2010), 119, 123, 132.

Malcolm Fraser delivered the Anzac Day address at the war memorial in Esperance, Western Australia. His speech contained all the elements of what were to become the stock idioms of Anzac discourse: from a battle anniversary of the Great War, Anzac Day had become 'a sanctuary of the nation's reverence', for the soldiers who were 'the flower of this world's manhood' and were now presented as model Australian citizens exemplifying the 'national' qualities of 'mateship, courage, sacrifice' and whose combat in 1915 was 'the first supreme test' of the 'young nation', forged through the 'supreme sacrifice' of its youth. Fraser's speech also heralded the internationalization of Anzac Day in the recognition of 'the Allies who fought at Gallipoli' and in the aftermath of Australia's withdrawal from Vietnam and the fall of Saigon it reaffirmed his Liberal government's commitment to the ANZUS treaty: 'Australia stands by its friends and doesn't back down when the going gets tough'. Yet his speech is as interesting for where it was made as for when: located on Australian sovereign territory, far removed from the metropolitan centres of the south-east, but on the shores of the Southern Ocean, Fraser evoked France's historic presence in the region and her contribution to the founding of modern Australia through 'the arrival in 1792 of the French Frigate *l'Esperance*, which gave this port its name during the south seas search for the lost explorer La Pérouse'.[35]

Significantly, and unlike his immediate predecessor, Fraser was too young to have been a veteran of the Second World War, though old enough to remember it: indeed he confessed to having felt 'awkward' on Anzac Day.[36] That Fraser chose to construct an Anzac discourse suggests that the idealization of Anzac comes with the fading of communicative memory and the attenuation of its traumatic impact. Furthermore, it indicates that the 'resurgence' of Anzac follows the Liberals' retreat from the new internationalism in the 1970s into a more essentialist and martial narrative of

---

35   Malcolm Fraser, 'Anzac Day – Esperance' speech, 25 April 1979. National Archives of Australia, M1263/828.

36   Malcom Fraser and Margaret Simons, *Malcolm Fraser, The Political Memoirs* (Carlton: The Miegunyah Press, 2010), 131.

identity, filling the vacuum left by Whitlam's previous ill-starred efforts to implant a sense of national identity intra-territorially in democratic *lieux de mémoire* such as Eureka.[37]

## The global Anzac network and Franco-Australian shared history

Presently, the memorial geography of Anzac straddles the globe from France, Belgium and Turkey, via the Mediterranean and Middle East through Thailand, Malaysia, Korea, and Vietnam, to Papua New Guinea and New Caledonia. It is a worldwide web of sites linked by a syncretic Anzac narrative. A snapshot of Anzac Day 2011 in the Asia-Pacific region and the rest of the world reveals the extent of the network, from Prime Minster Gillard's presence in South Korea for the sixtieth anniversary of the battle of Kapyong, to former Prime Minister Kevin Rudd's attendance of the commemorations at the Australian National Memorial in Villers Bretonneux and at Bullecourt. Alongside the traditional Dawn Service at the Australian War Memorial in Canberra and in the state capitals, further ceremonies were held around the world in the presence of statesmen and women, consular officials and veterans' associations, at locations including Gallipoli, Hellfire Pass in Thailand, the Kokoda Track in Papua New Guinea, and Sandakan in Borneo. In every case, with the exception of the Anzac Day services at Australian armed forces bases, the ceremonies included diplomatic representatives from the host country and addressed an international as much as a national audience. They were held often in the context of recent or ongoing diplomatic negotiations, for example those for a bilateral free trade agreement between Australia and South Korea,

---

37    Gough Whitlam, 'Eureka: The Birth of Australian Democracy', Ballarat Fine Arts Gallery, Victoria, 3 December 1973 in *Eureka: Saga of Australian History* (Canberra: Department of Immigration, 1973).

begun in March 2009 by then Prime Minister Kevin Rudd and the South Korean President Lee Myung-Bak, or the multilateral free trade agreement AANZFTA, negotiated with the ASEAN member states, which came into effect on 1 January 2010.

Within the Anzac network, France occupies a unique geopolitical position as the principal host country at the intersection of the three major theatres of global conflict of the twentieth century, and as an associate agency actively engaged in sustaining the Anzac tradition. The growing mutualization of memorial space is acknowledged in the 'Joint statement of strategic partnership between Australia and France' signed by the French and Australian Foreign Ministers, Alain Juppé and Kevin Rudd in Paris on 19 January 2012 which provides a framework for future bilateral cooperation, including 'Cooperation in the Pacific and Indian Ocean', an area of reciprocal concern in the run-up to the referendum on the constitutional status of New Caledonia in 2014.[38] In addition to the preamble which celebrates '170 years of unbroken friendship' between the two countries (dated from the opening of the first French consulate in Australia in 1842), four of the eleven heads of the agreement directly invoke shared history and memory as a basis for bilateral cooperation, including 'Cooperation on shared memory of the First World War', which prepares the way for a joint programme of commemorative events to mark the centenary of the First World War.

There can be few more condensed examples of the invocation of historical bonds as a basis for international relations. Since 2003, France has signed eight such bilateral agreements on shared history, with Australia one of its leading partners, alongside South Korea.[39] The agreements acknowledge the growing importance of the politics of the past in international relations and seek to encourage and accompany bilateral relations with 'states and *peoples* whose military history intersects with that of France,

---

38    Department of Foreign Affairs and Trade, 'Joint Statement of Strategic Partnership between Australia and France' (2012) <http://www.dfat.gov.au/geo/france/joint_statement.html> accessed 17 February 2014.

39    The signatories are: South Korea, Australia, Morocco, Madagascar, the United Kingdom, New Zealand, Tunisia and Canada.

whether allies or adversaries' in conflicts since 1870 [emphasis added].[40] The reference to 'peoples' explicitly locates memorial politics in the field of public democracy. Australia earns special mention in this context as a country that values its First World War history and possesses a significant memorial heritage in northern France.

In the Asia-Pacific region alone, Anzac Day is now observed in nineteen countries. In the Pacific, it is commemorated on the islands of Samoa, Tonga, Cook, Niue, Vanuatu, as well as in New Caledonia and French Polynesia. In New Caledonia, Anzac Day is one of three events in the calendar of Franco-Australian public diplomacy, with Australia Day and NAIDOC week. Anzac Day is commemorated in three separate sites of memory in combined French-Australian-New Zealand ceremonies: at the memorial to the war dead in the Place Bir-Hakeim in Noumea, at the New Zealand military cemetery at Bourail, and at the monument to Allied forces in the Plaine des Gaïacs at Poya/Pouembout. Anzac ceremonies there are coordinated alternately by the Consulates of Australia and New Zealand, while French actors include representatives from the territorial government of New Caledonia, veterans associations, the municipalities of Noumea, Bourail, and Poya, and civil associations like the Kiwanis Service Club for the Centre West. To mark the ninetieth anniversary of Anzac Day in New Caledonia in 2005, the Australian Consulate published a French language commemorative brochure. The Dawn Service held there is a belated tradition, starting in 2009. In the same year, the official commemoration of Anzac Day was extended to French Polynesia, as part of the 'renewal' of a commemorative tradition in a context of enhanced military cooperation. On 24–25 April 2006, a flotilla of four Australian warships visited Noumea to take part in the Anzac Day ceremonies on the eve of a joint naval exercise, 'Southern Cross'. On 25 April 2011, it was the crew of the New Caledonian patrol boat *La Moqueuse* who represented France at the Anzac Day ceremony in Port-Vila, Vanuatu.

---

40   Ministère de la Défense, 'Mémoire partagée' <http://www.defense.gouv.fr/site-memoire-et-patrimoine/memoire/tourisme-de-memoire-et-memoire-partagee/memoire-partagee> accessed 17 February 2014.

In explaining the success of Anzac Day in New Caledonia, the Australian Consulate evokes shared episodes from the history of the First and Second World Wars: in particular the 'heavy tribute' paid by Australian soldiers in France during the Great War and the role played by Australia in rallying New Caledonia to the Free French cause in 1940, as well as the wartime stationing of New Zealand troops in the region of Bourail.[41] The political utility of adopting Anzac Day in the French territories of the Pacific should be read against the background of the troubled recent history of France's relations with the Commonwealth powers of the region: from Mururoa and the French nuclear tests in the Pacific and the sinking of the *Rainbow Warrior* to the inconclusive moves towards decolonization in the region with the repeated deferral of votes on independence in New Caledonia under the 1988 Matignon and 1998 Noumea agreements and the frustration of pro-independence movements in French Polynesia. It is significant that Michel Rocard's post-*Rainbow Warrior* bridge-mending tour of the region in 1992 included a commemorative dimension: the inauguration by the Prime Minister of a monument to the French colony of Akaroa on the Banks Peninsula, near Christchurch, New Zealand, a memorial taken to symbolize the continuity and – more tendentiously – the permanence of the French presence in the South Pacific. The diplomatic outcome of that visit, the FRANZ agreement for regional cooperation on emergency aid (France-Australia-New Zealand, signed in Wellington on 22 December 1992) constituted a turning point in Franco-Australian relations on the basis of 'the thaw in our relations brought about since the ending of French nuclear testing (in the region)'.[42] That has since become a

---

41  Australian Consulate General, Noumea, New Caledonia, 'Communiqué de presse du 10 avril 2009, 94ème commémoration de l'ANZAC Day' <http://www.australianconsulatenoumea.embassy.gov.au/nmeafrench/media212.html> accessed 17 February 2014.

42  See Assemblée Nationale <http://www.assemblee-nationale.fr/13/rapports/r1646.asp> accessed 17 February 2014. The FRANZ agreement followed the moratorium on nuclear testing in the Pacific declared by President François Mitterrand on 8 April 1992. However, a further series of tests occurred under his successor Jacques Chirac from June 1995 to January 1996, before testing was replaced by simulation.

rapid warming in response to changing geopolitical conditions (notably the spread of Chinese 'chequebook diplomacy' in the South Pacific), pointing to a convergent set of bilateral interests.

From a French point of view, active participation in the renewal of the Anzac commemorative tradition offers the best of two worlds: it projects an image of France as, to adopt Denise Fisher's terminology, 'in' the region as the last European power to sustain a global reach and a sovereign presence in the Pacific through its overseas territories; and 'of' the region an historic actor, restored to grace through the post-Mururoa political *rapprochement* with Australia and New Zealand.[43] From the Australian perspective, the nationalist revival of the Anzac tradition in the closing decades of the twentieth century took a pronounced turn towards the Asia-Pacific region under the premiership of Paul Keating. Concerns for international security after 9/11 led the Howard governments to adopt an 'ANZUS plus' outlook: cultivating the Anzac-mediated European and NATO links to the United States, France, Great Britain and Turkey, while replicating Keating's Asian tropism in relations with regional actors like Vietnam and Thailand, albeit through bilateral agreements rather multilateral forums. Howard's Labor successors have deviated only marginally from the 'ANZUS plus' line by repatriating the Second World War Anzac memory to Australian national territory, with Kevin Rudd inaugurating Battle for Australia Day in 2008 and Julia Gillard using the national commemoration of the Bombing of Darwin in 2011 as a platform to reaffirm Australia's ANZUS ties and herald the opening of a US military base in the Northern Territory.

---

43    Denise Fisher, 'France: "in", "of" or "from" the South Pacific region?' in Sarah Mohamed-
        Gaillard, ed., *Relations internationales et régionales en Océanie, Journal de la Société
        des Océanistes* 135/2 (2012).

# Conclusion

The prominent part played by commemorative politics in Franco-Australian relations suggests that an understanding of memorial diplomacy has become an indispensable complement to a critical geopolitical reading of international relations. Deconstructing the ceremonial discourse and protocols of 'shared history' exposes a dense sub-text of domestic and foreign policy interests and agendas. The internationalization of war memory provides an inter-governmental calendar rich in opportunities for the conduct of diplomacy, but it has also exposed the limits to which history and geography can be stretched in the service of international relations.

On the eve of the Great War centenary 2014–18 and the seventieth anniversaries of D-Day, V-E Day and V-J Day, the landmark anniversaries of 'a century of almost unbroken war', the diplomacy of remembrance is entering upon a new cycle of intensive activity, undiminished by the passing of the first and the fading of the second generation of world war veterans.[44] Increasingly detached from communicative memory, the acceleration of the phenomenon since the late twentieth century has been accompanied by its dilation, with the transformation of national *lieux de mémoire* into spaces of shared history and international dialogue.

The geopolitical reconfiguration of the Asia-Pacific region has extended to its commemorative spaces. The challenge facing French and Australian diplomacy, at the approach of the Great War centenary and the seventieth anniversary of the Liberation of France, is to find a way of moderating and modulating the warrior internationalism of the Anzac narrative while placing commemorative diplomacy on more consensual grounds than war memory alone, in the interests of building a more inclusive sense of shared history with allies present or estranged, past enemies and emerging rivals.

---

44    Eric Hobsbawm, 'War and Peace in the 20th Century', *London Review of Books* 24/4 (21 February 2002), 16.

ELIZABETH RECHNIEWSKI

# Contested Sites of Memory: Commemorating Wars and Warriors in New Caledonia

## Introduction

To begin with a couple of anecdotes:

In the small town of Koné on the north-west coast of New Caledonia there stood for many years a war memorial with a statue of a *poilu* – the stereotypical representation of a moustachioed and bearded French soldier of the Great War.[1] Early in 2010 the statue was vandalized and taken away for repair. Faced with holding the commemoration ceremony of 8 May, the mayor, Joseph Goromido, decided to erect a temporary replacement, a large wooden sculpture representing a Kanak warrior.[2] After all, many Kanak had fought in the Great War, as many Kanak went to fight as French citizens from New Caledonia. The ceremony went off without problem but a few days later the sculpture was daubed with red, blue and white paint, the colours of the French flag and also therefore the symbol of those opposed to the independence of New Caledonia. The following night, the Kanak flag was draped over the statue – at this point the mayor decided that what he had hoped would symbolize the unity of the communities had become the symbol of division and the statue had to be

---

[1]    'Kanak' are the Indigenous Melanesian inhabitants of New Caledonia, a word literally meaning 'hairy one'; the origin of the term is the subject of some debate. Although it is widely used for the French infantry of the First World War, it was already in use in the nineteenth century.

[2]    'Le Guerrier fait parler', *Les Nouvelles Calédoniennes* (6 May 2010).

taken down. This is not the only such incident in recent years: in August 2011 the statue of the *poilu* on the war memorial at Voh was decapitated.[3]

In 1895 a campaign was launched to build a statue to Admiral Olry, the French governor who had put down the Kanak revolt of 1877–8, a conflict that left some 1,000 Kanak and 200 Europeans dead. The imposing statue, placed in 1897 in the Place des Cocotiers, Nouméa, depicted the Admiral in a commanding pose, while a bronze bas-relief on the plinth portrayed a group of Kanak chiefs laying down their arms in submission. In 1974, as the independence movement developed, young militants of the *Foulards Rouges* [Red Scarves] faction,[4] led by Nidoish Naisseline, covered the statue with paint and demanded the removal of the bronze bas-relief, a demand that was carried out. In 2009, a petition was launched to have the statue removed to a museum as the outdated symbol of a bygone past.[5] At the end of 2012, however, the statue still stood in the centre of Nouméa.

These incidents reveal that the symbolic representations of past conflicts still carry a heavy significance to those involved in the current disputes over the future of New Caledonia. Both monuments are in a sense 'war memorials' – the one commemorating the 'official' wars into which metropolitan France drew her colonies, the other the internal conflict and repression that kept France in control. In New Caledonia, as in Australia and other colonized countries where armed conflict between settlers and Indigenous peoples took place, the question of what constitutes a 'war' and the problematic distinction between 'fighter' and 'soldier', are only recently being explicitly posed. In this country that 'more than anywhere else in Melanesia [...] was a violent frontier'[6] and yet which also lost the highest proportion of Indigenous troops who served in the First World War, nothing is more controversial than whose wars should be commemorated, and why and how they should be remembered.

3    'Une paix de courte durée', *Les Nouvelles Calédoniennes* (20 March 2012).
4    The anarchist Louise Michel, deported to New Caledonia for her actions during the Commune, had given a red scarf to one of the leaders of the revolt in 1877.
5    'Qui veut la peau de l'amiral Olry?', *Les Nouvelles Calédoniennes* (14 December 2009).
6    John Connell, *New Caledonia or Kanaky, The Political History of a French Colony*, Pacific Research Monograph 16 (Canberra: National Centre for Development Studies, Australian National University, 1987), 80.

France brought troops from many parts of its empire to fight in the Great War. Only in Algeria and New Caledonia, *colonies de peuplement* [settler colonies], however, did the Indigenous soldiers return to their place within a settler colonial framework after the war, with all that this implied in terms of their social, economic and political inequality. Examination of the nature of Kanak war service and its commemorative aftermath is of particular interest, therefore, in exploring what Noah Riesman defines as 'soldier-warrior colonialism': 'the active employment of colonized Indigenous people by the military of a colonial power, against a different imperial power'.[7] Drawing on the framework for studying war commemoration developed by Ashplant,[8] this chapter focuses on the issues surrounding the commemoration of Indigenous service in New Caledonia in a context where the former colonial powers have slowly begun to recognize the contribution that their Indigenous subjects made – willingly or unwillingly – to the two world wars. This issue is complicated in New Caledonia, as in many other ex-colonies, by the past and ongoing conflict between Kanak and settlers, the choices and narratives that accompany commemoration becoming caught up, as this chapter illustrates, in contemporary political disputes over the very future of the territory.

## Recruitment and service of Kanak soldiers in the Great War

Unlike the Indigenous peoples of Australia who were officially prevented from enlisting unless of 'substantially European descent' (although many hundreds did enroll in the First World War and thousands in the Second), the Kanak were actively recruited into war service from January 1916. Indeed there is evidence that they were pressed into it, with the chiefs

---

7    Noah Riesman, *Defending Whose Country? Indigenous Soldiers in the Pacific War* (Lincoln & London: University of Nebraska Press, 2012), 224.

8    Timothy Ashplant, Graham Dawson and Michael Roper, *Commemorating War* (New Brunswick, NJ: Transaction Publishers, 2004).

being pressured through threats and promises to send a certain number from each 'tribe' or village. John Connell writes: 'recruitment was often a combination of false promises and crude force'.[9] Over-zealous recruitment, likened by Philippe Godard to *dragonnades* [military round-ups],[10] is often cited as one of the factors leading to the revolt of 1917. Again unlike the Aborigines, the Kanak served alongside soldiers from other French Pacific colonies in a separate 'Indigenous' corps, the *Bataillon Mixte du Pacifique*, which integrated *Caldoches* (European settlers) and Kanak only in July 1918. Approximately half of those who enlisted from New Caledonia were Kanak: 'New Caledonia supplied 2,160 soldiers of whom 1,137 were colonial infantrymen. 541 New Caledonian troops were killed of whom 374 were indigènes'.[11] The death rate of the Kanak *tirailleurs* at 35 per cent was amongst the highest of the colonial troops.[12] Despite this toll, Adrian Muckle writes: 'Until the end of the twentieth century the varied experiences (of service) were largely ignored in local (New Caledonian), regional (Pacific islands) and international (French colonial) historiography'.[13]

## Mechanisms of forgetting

The reasons for this neglect can be found in a series of disjunctures and contradictions at the heart of the colonial enterprise that instituted the 'forgetting' of the participation of Indigenous soldiers in European wars.

9   Connell, *New Caledonia or Kanaky*, 74.
10  Philippe Godard, 'les opérations de recrutement prennent souvent des allures de dragonnades', *Mémorial Caledonien t. III, 1900–1919* (Noumea, Nouvelle-Calédonie: Editions d'Art Calédoniennes, 1980), 270.
11  Martin Thomas, *The French Empire between the Wars: Imperialism, Politics and Society* (Manchester: Manchester University Press, 2005), 23.
12  Sylvette Boubin-Boyer, 'D'une Guerre à l'autre', in *150 ans de mémoire collective calédonienne* (Nouméa: Musée de la Ville de Nouméa, 2003), 80.
13  Adrian Muckle, 'Kanak Experiences of World War One: New Caledonia's *Tirailleurs*, Auxiliaries and "Rebels"', *History Compass* 6/5 (2008), 1325.

This forgetting might most closely be classified in Paul Connerton's terms as 'repressive erasure',[14] and yet it was less the result, I argue, of deliberate erasure but rather the confluence of a number of factors: institutional amnesia, strategic forgetting, ideological dissonance and conflict over material interests – all underpinned by the inequality of social, economic and political power between the Europeans and the Indigenous peoples in a settler colonial society.

Both forgetting and remembering are profoundly political acts that can only be fully understood as responses to the complex demands of their contemporary contexts. And they are processes that are unevenly distributed across society: 'collective amnesia' is as unlikely to occur as the much-criticized concept of 'collective memory'; vernacular memory may survive where official memory falls silent.[15] But in modern societies, official memory is a powerful tool, bound up in the construction of national identity, that sets the agenda for national remembering and can 'crowd out' and overshadow vernacular memory. Ashplant et al., who develop a powerful framework for the analysis of the articulation of war memories, identify the key role played by the nation-state whose activities can 'impact on all other agencies, reaching down to the very process of memory formation by individuals and within families'.[16] A range of institutions – 'agencies of articulation' in Ashplant's terms – are charged with the safeguarding of memory, from the official bodies of the nation-state, its ministries and departments of veterans' affairs; and the national systems under its control, such as the education system; and institutions of civil society, such as associations of war veterans. Not all will have the same interests or promote the same message, but in a colonial society they largely reflect the power structures of that society: the Indigenous peoples do not have easy access to these institutions or influence over the dominant narratives they convey.

---

14    Paul Connerton, 'Seven types of forgetting', *Memory Studies* 1 (2008).
15    John Bodnar distinguishes 'vernacular' and 'official' memory in *Remaking America: Public Memory, Commemoration, and Patriotism in the Twentieth Century* (Princeton, NJ: Princeton University Press, 1992).
16    Ashplant et al., *Commemorating War*, 25.

Ashplant emphasizes the political significance of the power of the state and its institutions 'to recognise and name particular kinds of violence as "a war"': 'its bestowal of names upon particular wars, are fundamental to the construction (and contestation) of the national narrative and official memory'.[17] Official memory is conveyed in 'narratives of articulation',[18] in the stories that are developed around the war events that structure and give meaning to individual and collective memory and may play a role in the construction of national or racial identity. The dominant, hegemonic narratives that structured the mindset of colonial Australia and New Caledonia – those concerning national and racial identity and citizenship – were inimical to the recognition of Indigenous war service. These contradictions might be described as founded in *ideological dissonance*, when aspects of the past are 'forgotten' or obscured because they are at odds with the dominant belief systems of a society. One of those systems was of course the belief in a racial hierarchy and the superiority of European civilization – the basis of the theory and practices of White Australia and the French *mission civilisatrice*.

In New Caledonia, despite France's proclaimed commitment to bringing enlightenment and progress to her colonies, racialist and eugenicist ideas were as deeply entrenched as in other European colonies: the Kanak were the object of *'un racisme d'anéantissement'*, a racism that cancelled out their very existence, writes Alban Bensa.[19] The identity of the *colons libres* [free settlers] was intimately dependent on maintaining their distinction from the world of the Kanak and the danger of *ensauvagement* [descending into savagery] that it represented.[20] The Kanak were sometimes compared to the Australian Aborigines – both 'stagnated' at the lowest level of human development, so backward that improvement through contact with a superior race appeared impossible. Like the Aborigines, the

---

17   Ashplant et al., *Commemorating War*, 53.
18   Ashplant et al., *Commemorating War*, 20.
19   Alban Bensa, *Chroniques Kanak: L'ethnologie en marche* (Paris: Peuples autochtones et développement, 1995), 116.
20   Isabelle Merle, *Expériences coloniales: La Nouvelle-Calédonie (1853–1920)* (Paris: Belin, 1995), 360–4.

Kanak were also widely considered, in the inter-war period, to be 'a dying race'.[21] It is not that the Indigenous peoples were invisible, nor even that, in Stanner's words, 'a great silence' hung over them, but in Foucault's terms a discourse was constructed around them, a 'science', a set of 'knowledges', practices, experts and institutions defined how they should be viewed and discussed.[22] The 'flowering of eugenics' in the 1920s in America, Australia and New Zealand provided the 'scientific' foundation for the practices of discrimination and exclusion,[23] and was paralleled in France in the work of writers such as Charles Richet.

## 'Retour à la normale?'

Riesman's discussion of 'soldier-warrior colonialism' includes the claim that the service of Indigenous troops was undertaken 'with little or no consideration for the impact on Indigenous societies'.[24] Indeed, the colonial powers in New Caledonia assumed or hoped that the post war period would see a return to 'normal' relations, a process which was assisted by the neglect or deliberate forgetting of Indigenous service. The system of *indigénat* with its controls over movement, employment and denial of access to European courts, continued to govern the lives of the Kanak, who were defined as French subjects, not French citizens. Although Sylvette Boubin-Boyer writes that: '*Le sentiment identitaire d'appartenance [des Kanak] à la France sort renforcé de la guerre*' [the feeling of belonging to France is reinforced [in the Kanak] by the war],[25] there seems little evidence to support this

---

21  Merle, *Expériences coloniales*, 401.
22  Bensa, *Chroniques Kanak*, 114–16.
23  Marilyn Lake and Henry Reynolds, *Drawing the Global Colour Line: White Men's Countries and the Question of Racial Equality* (Melbourne: Melbourne University Press, 2008), 313.
24  Riesman, *Defending Whose Country?*, 224.
25  Sylvette Boubin-Boyer, *Révoltes, conflits et guerres mondiales en Nouvelle-Calédonie et sa région* (Paris: L'Harmattan, 2008), 9.

conclusion that finds few echoes in other writers. The Indigenous service-men returned to a situation little changed since before the war, and in some ways deteriorating, with conflict over land intensifying. Their service did not lead to an extension of civic and political rights to the Indigenous peoples as a whole and the veterans were often denied the benefits accorded to European ex-servicemen though they were exempted from the capitation tax. The possibility of acquiring French citizenship was held out to Kanak veterans who applied for it (in a decree of 19 April 1933), but few took up the offer, fearing perhaps to lose their customary rights. In theory they had the right to claim land in recompense for their service – in practice this was almost never granted in a context where the inexorable encroach-ment of the settlers onto Kanak land provoked ongoing dislocation and disruption of Kanak communities. Moreover the rebellion of 1917 led to severe consequences for the central-northern districts, seat of the fighting.

To return to the incident recounted at the beginning of this chapter, Koné was one of the centres of the 1917 Kanak rebellion, a rebellion that was in part provoked by causes linked to the war, notably recruitment that amounted to 10.8 per cent of the male adult population and the consequent depopulation of the villages, though there were certainly other factors at work.[26] Chief Noël Néa Ma Pwatiba, one of the local leaders of the rebellion, called on the Kanak to fight the French at home as ably as they were fighting the Germans abroad. Conflict and repression continued for seven months and led to the devastation and dispersal of population mainly from the west coast towards the east. As many as 200 Kanak, including Chief Noël, and eleven French, died in the uprising. Adrian Muckle writes that the Kanak soldiers who returned to these districts from Europe in 1919 'found devastated settlements and communities struggling to regroup after having been dispersed; others returned to villages whose numbers had been swelled by refugees and captured women and children.'[27] The events of 1917 that, in the middle of a war in which Kanak soldiers were fighting

26    Boubin-Boyer, 'D'une guerre', 80.
27    Adrian Muckle, *Spectres of Violence in a Colonial Context: The Wars at Koné, Hienghène and Tipindjé – New Caledonia, 1917* (Honolulu: University of Hawaii Press, 2012), 2.

for France, saw colonial troops on leave and Indigenous auxiliaries put down rebellious Kanak fighters – both sides with some savagery – created a complex challenge to remembrance of the Great War. If, as Ashplant suggests, war memory requires a clear narrative, then it was not to be found in these events, which instead reinforced mistrust between settlers and Kanak, and between 'loyalist' and rebel Kanak tribes, the latter depicted in the aftermath of the revolt as 'ferocious cannibals'.[28]

There were many other reasons for the neglect of Kanak war service in the inter-war period. The representations of war that became enshrined between the world wars, not only in discourse but in monumental and symbolic forms of commemoration, militated against remembrance of Indigenous service. The field of war memory was filled with hegemonic images, narratives and heroes that 'stood for' the whole: the figure of the *poilu* that adorned the Koné memorial and a number of other war memorials in New Caledonia is emblematic of the iconic figure of the First World War soldier, that of the metropolitan *Français de souche*. An imperialist metonym, imperialist in both the literal and metaphorical sense, it contributed to the symbolic exclusion of the Kanak. It was particularly unrepresentative of the men from the region of Koné who went to war, since the majority of soldiers from the north and east of New Caledonia would have been Kanak (the whites were and still are concentrated in the capital and the south of the main island). Twenty-three names figure on the war memorial in Koné, fifteen from the First World War and eight from the Second. Of the fifteen from the First World War, it appears that nine are Kanak.[29] It appears moreover that the lists of names inscribed on some of the memorials are not complete.

Not only the material, but the imaginary national landscape was colonized with such representations, while distorted or even grotesque images, such as those of the 'cannibal Kanak' who were exhibited, alongside 'other'

---

28 Adrian Muckle, 'La "dernière révolte" de Kanaky Nouvelle-Calédonie: visions de conflits passés dans un avenir commun', in *La Nouvelle-Calédonie: vers un destin commun, Nouveaux Enjeux, Nouveaux Terrains* (Paris: Editions Karthala, 2010), 45.

29 The list is available at <http://www.memorial-genweb.org>. Biographical details are not supplied for all the soldiers.

exotic flora and fauna at the *Jardin d'accclimation* at the Paris Exhibition in 1931, perpetuated denigrating images of the Indigenous peoples.[30] It is ironic that some of the 114 Kanaks sent to Europe to take part in the Exhibition (lured there with prospects of foreign travel, good pay and conditions) were soldiers who had fought in the Great War. Although fluent in French and accustomed to European ways, they were forced to dress up in scanty native garb (as imagined and supplied by the organizers) and to sing and dance in a chilly Paris spring. The show was billed as the opportunity to view '*Des Canaques: mangeurs d'hommes*' ['Maneaters'], mothers being warned, for sensational effect, to keep a careful eye on their children.[31]

The narratives of European war that included the sacrificial attack 'over the top' of the trenches, the heroic frontal assaults, the holding of territory at all cost, tended also to obscure and displace the naming of Indigenous engagements as warfare. The Kanak fighters, when they took up arms against the French, usually avoided 'battlefield' confrontations where the whites' superior weapons and numbers would be lethal. They resorted rather to guerrilla-style tactics: surprise raids, ambushes, strategic withdrawal, tactics that the Europeans saw as evidence not of innovative and adaptive strategy, but of their cunning and even cowardly nature.[32] Adrian Muckle cites the historian Sylvette Boubin-Boyer as challenging the appropriateness of the term 'war' for the events of 1917 because the Kanak did not have a regular army nor conventional weapons, and resorted to tactics of flight and ruse.[33]

---

30  Joel Dauphiné, *Canaques de la Nouvelle-Calédonie à Paris en 1931. De la case au zoo* (Paris: L'Harmattan, 1998). There was after some months an outcry against this 'human zoo' and most of the Kanak were repatriated.

31  *Le Mémorial calédonien*, t.IV (1920–39), 320–1.

32  Bronwen Douglas, 'Almost Constantly at War? An Ethnographic Perspective on Fighting in New Caledonia', *Journal of Pacific History* 25/1 (1990), 28.

33  Adrian Muckle, 'La "dernière révolte" de Kanaky', 551–2.

## The Second World War and its aftermath

During the Second World War New Caledonia sided – after some hesitation – with the Free French and in May 1941 sent 605 volunteers, including Kanak and Europeans, to fight with de Gaulle's forces in the *Bataillon des Volontaires du Pacifique*. Even more significantly in terms of its impact on New Caledonian society, the territory became the staging post for the Allied battle to reclaim the Pacific. Kanak worked on the military bases and on the war effort more generally and enjoyed relationships with Americans and New Zealanders in particular that cut across the ethnic lines established with the French colonists. The Kanak were granted French citizenship in 1946, the controls over their movement and employment were dismantled, and suffrage gradually extended, although universal suffrage was not in place until 1957. The future of the newly-designated *territoire d'outre-mer*, however, had been throughout the post war period the subject of occasionally violent dispute and confrontation between the Kanak, who are the largest ethnic group, without constituting an absolute majority, and the Caldoches. Armed clashes and violence continued into the late 1980s both between whites and Kanak (the hostage-taking at Ouvéa in 1988) and between rival Kanak groups (the assassination of Jean-Marie Tjibaou in 1989 by a rival Kanak leader). Although in response to the unrest New Caledonia was granted greater autonomy through the Matignon Accords of 1988, this has not satisfied all the Kanak parties and the territory is now on a path towards independence under the Nouméa Accord of 1998, though the terms of the endpoint of this process are still a cause of bitter division.

The conclusion cited above, that Kanak war service was ignored until recent decades, needs to be qualified: a search of the *Mémorial calédonien*, the semi-official record of the political and cultural life of New Caledonia, reveals that the service of Kanak soldiers was referred to on some significant occasions, notably during the occasional passage of a French president, with the aim of representing the unity of the population, the loyalty of the Kanak to France and their opposition to independence. On the centenary of the French take-over of the territory, in 1953, *La France Australe* editorialized that: 'The monuments raised in every village bear the names of those, white or black, Caledonians all, fraternally united, who sowed glory under our flag'.[34] It should be noted however that not all the monuments bore the names of the Kanak soldiers: that of Nouméa, with its ubiquitous *poilu*, bore the names of the Europeans but only the numbers of Kanak soldiers from each 'tribe'.[35] Similar evocations of joint patriotic efforts were made on the occasion of the visits of de Gaulle to New Caledonia in 1956 and 1966, and that of Valéry Giscard d'Estaing in July 1979 when it was the anti-independence Melanesian politician Dick Ukeiwé who stated that the monuments to the dead attested to the willingness of all Melanesians to come to the aid of France in her hour of need.[36]

Over the past twenty years there has been increasing recognition of the role of Kanak in European wars, paralleling the trend in metropolitan France towards recognition of the participation of Indigenous soldiers from her colonies in both world wars.[37] Exhibitions have been held,[38] radio programmes aired.[39] Amateur historians and motivated individuals have sought to identify and record the names of the soldiers (Schillé) while professional historians have written more extensive accounts of their war service (Adrian Muckle, Sylvette Boubin-Boyer). Commemorative plaques and monuments have been unveiled: in July 2003 a memorial was inaugurated in the cemetery of Traput to eight Great War soldiers whose names leave little room for doubt that they were Kanak: Kauma Kauma, Pulue Ozika, Hoce Mackam, Suiaeng Wahema, Goli Luenu, Hnassa Malla,

34   *Le Mémorial calédonien*, t. V (1940–53).
35   Only in 2001 were two new steles added, bearing the names of the individual Indigenous soldiers. Jacques Frémeaux, *Les Colonies dans la Grande Guerre: combats et épreuves des peuples d'outre mer* (Paris: Edns 14/18, SOTECA, 2006), 331.
36   *Le Mémorial calédonien*, t. VIII (1977–81), 232.
37   Robert Aldrich, 'Memorials to French Colonial Soldiers from the Great War' <http://cridi1418.org/doc/textes/aldrich> accessed 19 June 2013.
38   *Calédoniens dans la Grande Guerre: niaoulis et tirailleurs canaques* (Nouméa: Musée de la ville de Nouméa, 2008).
39   'Une mémoire calédonienne commune de la Grande Guerre', RFO, Histoire Pays/Pays d'Histoire (2004) <http://www.rosada.net/hpays/hpgrandeguerre.htm> accessed 19 June 2013.

Gue Luepack, Cono Naene Hnaej.[40] The return of the remains of Saiaene Wahena, killed in the attack on the village of Vesles-et-Caumont in 1918, to Lifou in 2006 was the occasion for an emotional ceremony as family and community members addressed the dead soldier who had never been forgotten.[41] In November 2009 at Plum, main base of the RIMaP-NC (*Régiment d'infanterie de marine du Pacifique Nouvelle-Calédonie*) some thirty kilometers from Nouméa, the names of the Melanesians killed in combat were engraved on a stele.[42] At Iaai, a plaque bearing the names of Kanak from Ouvéa who 'died for France' in 1914–18 was recovered from a tribe who had kept it safe and returned it to the authorities. Its restoration in 2011 provided the occasion to remember the forty-nine from the region who enlisted, and the twenty-four who died.[43]

The recognition of Kanak soldiers carries a particular resonance because of the still recent armed conflict and the contested moves towards independence. The Nouméa Accord of 1998 that set out the terms for passage towards greater autonomy or independence for New Caledonia, called for the establishment of the symbols of 'a Kanak identity and a shared future', including the name of the country, a flag, national anthem, motto, and banknotes. The issue of the flag – whether it should be the *tricolore* or the Kanak flag, or some new design – has been particularly divisive, as the incident of the Koné statue once again illustrates. In this search for a shared heritage and identity, the remembrance of Kanak soldiers who fought for France can play an important role.

Other monuments and ceremonies inaugurated in New Caledonia over the last ten years keep alive the memory of the colonial past: in 2005 a renovated stele to Colonel Gally Passebosc was re-erected in Nouméa in honour of this '*défricheur d'espace*' ['clearer of terrain'] – the youngest

---

40 'Un mémorial inauguré à Traput', *Les Nouvelles Calédoniennes* (16 July 2003).
41 'Lifou retrouve son soldat', *Les Nouvelles Calédoniennes* (15 July 2006). Some twenty bodies were returned to New Caledonia in the immediate post war period but this did not include any Kanak soldiers.
42 'La mémoire des engagés du Pacifique gravée dans la pierre', *Les Nouvelles Calédoniennes* (3 November 2009).
43 'Iaai retrouve la mémoire', *Les Nouvelles Calédoniennes* (18 June 2011).

colonel in France at the time, he was killed at La Foa during Atai's revolt of 1878–9.[44] From 2011 a ceremony has been held each year in Ouvanou, in the north-east of the Northern province, to commemorate the guillotining of ten Kanak by the French army in 1868.[45] More recently, however, more conciliatory gestures have been made in relation to the conflict between Kanak and settlers: in April 2013 the commemoration of the events at Fayaoué included family members of both the Kanak rebels and the French gendarmes killed in the hostage-taking.[46] At Bourail, the local council has proposed the erection of a monument to all those killed in the nine years of settler/Kanak conflict from the assassination of Pierre Declercq in 1981 to that of Jean-Marie-Tjibao in 1989: in all seventy-three European and Kanak victims.[47]

## Conclusion

If memorials are the most visible representations of a community's war memory, their monumental materiality does not prevent them from being the object of the most diverse interpretations and practices. The Kanak warrior that was erected on the Koné monument in place of the vandalized statue of the *poilu* carried a heavily symbolic but conflicted meaning

44    'Deux stèles pour un colonel et vingt-trois maires', *Les Nouvelles Calédoniennes* (15 December 2005).
45    'Pouébo se souvient des dix d'Ouvanou', *Les Nouvelles Calédoniennes* (23 May 2011).
46    'Main tendue à Fayaoué', *Les Nouvelles Calédoniennes* (18 April 2013).
47    'Mémorial à Bourail', *Les Nouvelles Calédoniennes* (27 January 2012). Although it is beyond the scope of this chapter to explore other attempts to symbolize reconciliation and common heritage, mention should be made of the ongoing controversy around the totemic sculpture of the Mwâ Kââ studied by Benoît Carteron: the emplacement and symbolic meanings attached to this monument have followed the political fortunes of the pro- and anti-independence parties. See 'Le Mwâ Kââ, vers la manifestation d'une appartenance commune en Nouvelle-Calédonie?', *Le Journal de la Société des Océanistes*, 134, 1er semestre (2012), 45–60.

to the local community: as soldier for France, as ruthless and savage rebel, and as warrior against colonization. In each of these roles he is diversely appreciated by the black and white populations of the area and by the pro- and anti-independentists. In an attempt at compromise, there now stand on Charles de Gaulle esplanade in Koné, erected in time for the 8 May ceremony of 2013, two statues of *poilus* placed at some distance from one another: one in white marble represents the settler soldiers; the other in wood, carrying a traditional weapon, represents the Kanak.[48] While the mayor is glad to have found a solution to the controversy, many of the comments published in the territory newspaper lament a compromise that can be seen as symbolically underlining difference rather than overcoming it. The contested fortunes of this memorial reveal the challenges involved in attempting to enrol past symbols to unify the present in a neo-colonial context, the risks of mobilizing 'an archaeology of memory in the service of a refashioned national narrative'.[49] They illustrate too the importance of studying the differential reception of commemorative activity, the ambiguous nature of symbols and the multiple and even conflicting interpretations to which they lend themselves in different contexts and to different audiences.

48 'Deux poilus en commun', *Les Nouvelles Calédoniennes* (9 May 2013).
49 Ashplant et al., *Commemorating War*, 35.

MATTHEW STIBBE

# Remembering, Commemorating and (Re)fighting the Great War in Germany from 1919 to the Present Day

## Introduction

> In German historiography the First World War has been completely overshadowed by the Second, not least because of the latter's criminal and destructive dimension: the responsibility so much clearer, the loss of lives, both military and civilian, so much greater.[1]

So writes Lothar Kettenacker, former deputy director of the German Historical Institute London, in a book review published in 2006, and undoubtedly this assessment still rings true in 2014. Only for a brief period in the 1960s, he argues, was the Great War placed in the spotlight of public debate. This was due to the 'Fischer controversy' over German war aims between 1914 and 1918, which will be discussed in further detail below. Otherwise, the Second World War seems to dominate both media representations of, and academic research into, contemporary history. Examples here include the *Historikerstreit* [historians' quarrel] in the late 1980s over the uniqueness of National Socialism, the 'Goldhagen debate' of the 1990s concerning ordinary Germans' role in the Holocaust and, more recently, the critical discussions about narratives of German 'victimhood' and collective suffering during and immediately after the Third Reich.[2]

---

1   L. Kettenacker, review of G. Hirschfeld, G. Krumeich and I. Renz, eds, *Enzyklopädie Erster Weltkrieg* (Paderborn: Ferdinand Schöningh, 2003), *Bulletin of the German Historical Institute London* 28/1 (2006), 87.

2   See for example G. Eley, ed., *The 'Goldhagen Effect': History, Memory, Nazism – Facing the German Past* (Ann Arbor: University of Michigan Press, 2000); and B.

The purpose of this chapter is not to challenge Kettenacker's argument, but rather to place German academic writing and public discourses about the Great War within the framework of broader changes in perceptions of the national past from 1919 to the present day. For the post-1945 period this will also involve making reference to German memories of the Second World War, since these memories did much to shape perceptions of the earlier conflict, both at the level of leadership, strategy and aims, and at the level of individual experience, 'heroism', suffering and endurance. In effect the Great War has been refought in Germany at many different stages in the twentieth century and beyond, reflecting shifting political priorities, generational expectations, geopolitical realities and cultural trends.[3] In what follows, these patterns will be explored further by examining the divergent ways in which the war was represented and remembered in the Weimar, Nazi, Cold War and post-reunification periods.

## The Great War in Weimar Germany

Representations of the Great War in the Weimar Republic were dominated by attempts to refute the so-called *Kriegsschuldlüge* [war-guilt lie], the claim, made in Article 231 of the Treaty of Versailles, that the Allied and Associated powers were victims of a conflict 'imposed upon them by the aggression of Germany and her allies' and were therefore justified in seeking retribution and redress.[4] A leading role was played by the German

Niven, ed., *Germans as Victims: Remembering the Past in Contemporary Germany* (Basingstoke: Palgrave Macmillan, 2006).

3    For the period up to the early 1990s see G. Krumeich, 'Kriegsgeschichte im Wandel', in G. Hirschfeld, G. Krumeich and I. Renz, eds, *'Keiner fühlt sich hier mehr als Mensch...'. Erlebnis und Wirkung des Ersten Weltkriegs* (Essen: Klartext Verlag, 1993), 11–29.

4    Treaty of Versailles, Article 231 <http://www.firstworldwar.com/source/versailles231–247.htm> accessed 14 March 2014.

Foreign Office, which set up its own War Guilt Section,[5] in 1919 and also financed semi-autonomous propaganda organizations such as the Centre for the Study of the Causes of the War and the Working Committee of German Associations.[6] As well as writing articles for the domestic and foreign press and producing literature for use in schools and universities, these bodies were involved in the collection and publication of official documents that could be used to clear Germany's name. Beneath the surface, the anti-Versailles/anti-guilt campaign also embraced an authoritarian political agenda in that it 'idealized' the Germany of the years before the revolution of November 1918, and thus by implication at least, questioned the legitimacy of the new democratic republican system.[7]

Academic historians, while supportive of these efforts, preferred to take a more backseat role. In part this can be explained by their wariness of contemporary history as a field in which 'objective' analysis of sources might be compromised through preoccupation with the fleeting concerns of the present.[8] It also reflected their tendency to leave the field of war history to military experts and in particular to the retired officers who staffed the *Reichsarchiv* in Potsdam and helped to produce its official account of the war.[9] The notion that political historians might also be concerned with military history, or – more importantly – with the concept of 'militarism' as a negative influence on German statecraft and society, was almost unimaginable before 1945.[10]

5   *Kriegsschuldreferat.*
6   *Zentralstelle für die Erforschung der Kriegsursachen*; *Arbeitsausschuss Deutscher Verbände.*
7   A. Mombauer, *The Origins of the First World War: Controversies and Consensus* (Harlow: Pearson, 2002), 50–6.
8   Mombauer, *The Origins*, 81.
9   On the Reichsarchiv see M. Pöhlmann, 'Yesterday's Battles and Future War: The German Official Military History, 1919–1939', in R. Chickering and S. Förster, eds, *The Shadows of Total War: Europe, East Asia and the United States, 1919–1939* (Cambridge: Cambridge University Press, 2003), 223–38.
10  W. Wette, *Militarismus in Deutschland: Geschichte einer kriegerischen Kultur* (Frankfurt/Main: S. Fischer Verlag, 2008), esp. 9–10.

Younger scholars, particularly those who had fought in the war, none-theless contributed to broader patriotic legends about the 1914–18 conflict such as the 'myth' of national unity in August 1914, and readily identified themselves as representatives of the 'front generation' who remained 'unde-feated in the field'.[11] Some, such as Gerhard Ritter (1888–1967), did so even though this conflicted with their own personal experience of combat on the Western Front. In 1917, for instance, having taken part in the repul-sion of two French attacks on German positions, Ritter wrote to a friend admonishing him for his naïve belief in the idea of an imminent German breakthrough: 'When every hill and every village is crawling with men, machine guns and canons, then no kind of warfare is possible apart from mind-numbing mutual slaughter'. Yet in May 1924, in his inaugural address to students at the University of Hamburg, he praised 'the heroism [and] the completely unassuming, scrupulous fulfilment of one's duty' which had supposedly characterized the indefatigable spirit of the trenches.[12]

Such comments may be regarded as fairly typical for conservative uni-versity professors, particularly around the time of the Ruhr crisis of 1923, and helped to nurture a culture of war, or at least of opposition to peace, within the German higher education system, especially from the mid-1920s on.[13] So too did the publication of numerous anthologies of letters written by patriotic student volunteers in the war, particularly those who had fought and died at the celebrated battle of Langemarck in October 1914, a battle which, in the memory culture of the Weimar years, became associated with ideals of youth, vitality and masculinity.[14]

11  C. Cornelißen, 'Die Frontgeneration deutscher Historiker und der Erste Weltkrieg' in J. Dülffer and G. Krumeich, eds, *Der verlorene Frieden: Politik und Kriegskultur nach 1918* (Essen: Klartext Verlag 2002), 311–37.

12  Quotations taken from ibid., 319 and C. Cornelißen, *Gerhard Ritter: Geschichtswissenschaft und Politik im 20. Jahrhundert* (Düsseldorf: Droste Verlag, 2001), 133.

13  See for example A. Schröder, *Vom Nationalismus zum Nationalsozialismus: Die Studenten der Technischen Hochschule Hannover von 1925 bis 1938* (Hanover: Hahnsche Buchhandlung, 2003).

14  On the 'Langemarck myth' see G. L. Mosse, *Fallen Soldiers: Reshaping the Memory of the World Wars* (Oxford: Oxford University Press, 1990), 70–3; and A. Weinrich, *Der*

Outside of academe, however, as Bernd Ulrich and Benjamin Ziemann have shown, the 'public sphere' in the 1920s remained a site of rival interpretations of the 'war experience'. Both individually and collectively, millions of ordinary veterans struggled to match their own memories of the war with one or other of the official versions being peddled.[15] At first critical-pacifist voices prevailed over conservative ones.[16] Only after 1928 did heroic discourses clearly come to dominate, culminating in December 1930 in the successful campaign mounted by nationalists and Nazis against the screening in Germany of the American film version of Erich Maria Remarque's anti-heroic war novel *All Quiet on the Western Front*.[17] Even so, the extreme right only found itself able to set the agenda because of the progressive 'fracturing of war memory' at the level of civil society under the twin pressures of a collapsing global economy and the failure of successive republican governments to create a consensus on how to deal with the war's legacy.[18] In spite of the establishment in 1925 of a national day of mourning for fallen soldiers on the second Sunday in Lent (*Volkstrauertag*), rival veterans groups continued to stage separate commemorations in the late 1920s and early 1930s, some choosing to observe the recommended date and others favouring alternative days of the year.[19] Even the official Prussian state memorial to the war dead, completed, after much delay and

---

*Weltkrieg als Erzieher: Jugend zwischen Weimarer Republik und Nationalsozialismus* (Essen: Klartext Verlag, 2013), 245–312. On students' war letters see M. Hertlin and M. Jeismann, 'Der Weltkrieg als Epos: Philipp Witkops "Kriegsbriefe gefallener Studenten"' in Hirschfeld et al., eds, *'Keiner fühlt sich'*, 205–34.

15    B. Ulrich and B. Ziemann, eds, *Krieg im Frieden: Die umkämpfte Errinerung an den Ersten Weltkrieg* (Frankfurt/Main: Fischer Taschenbuch Verlag, 1997).

16    J. Verhey, *The Spirit of 1914: Militarism, Myth and Mobilization in Germany* (Cambridge: Cambridge University Press, 2000), 211; B. Ziemann, *War Experiences in Rural Germany, 1914–1923* (Oxford: Berg, 2007), 274–5 [German original, 1997].

17    M. Eksteins, 'War, Memory and Politics: The Fate of the Film *All Quiet on the Western Front*', *Central European History* 13/1 (1980), 60–82.

18    R. Pöppinghege, '"Kriegsteilnehmer zweiter Klasse?": Die Reichsvereinigung ehemaliger Kriegsgefangener 1919–1933', *Militärgeschichtliche Zeitschrift* 64 (2005), 392.

19    See B. Ziemann, *Contested Commemorations: Republican War Veterans and Weimar Political Culture* (Cambridge: Cambridge University Press, 2013), esp. 142–7.

discussion, by the architect Heinrich Tessenow in 1931 and housed in the eighteenth-century *Neue Wache* on Berlin's Unter den Linden, 'failed to become a focus of national ritual'.[20] In a country that was becoming more divided by the day, only one political party seemed to offer a master narrative of the war which treated all (non-Jewish and non-socialist) Germans equally as participants and heroes: the National Socialist 'movement' led by Adolf Hitler.

## The Great War in Nazi Germany

In Nazi Germany, memories of the Great War were systematically manipulated to create a sense of identity between the goals of National Socialism and the aspirations of the German people. On *Volkstrauertag* in 1934, now renamed *Heldengedenktag* [Heroes' Memorial Day] the party newspaper proclaimed:

> The front experience is not just a distant memory for us, it first helped to convey an idea, and then grew beyond this into a source of strength and unity which today shapes the life and existence of the entire German nation.[21]

At the same time, the 'front experience' was used to justify the exclusion of those whom the regime considered to be 'eternal enemies' of the Reich. After 1933, for instance, the Nazis created a new monument to the assassins of the Jewish Foreign Minister Walther Rathenau in 1922, which was 'crowned [...] with reproductions of the steel helmets [...] worn by [frontline] soldiers during the First World War'. The intention was to reinforce the

---

20   L. van Ypersele, 'Mourning and Memory, 1919–45', in J. Horne, ed., *A Companion to World War I* (Oxford: Blackwell, 2010), 581. See also Ziemann, *Contested Commemorations*, 180–1.

21   From the newspaper *Völkischer Beobachter* in Ulrich and Ziemann, eds, *Krieg im Frieden*, 142.

symbolic connection between the war and 'manly' heroism, and between the Jews and the 'corrupt peace' of Versailles.[22] In 1935 Jewish soldiers' names were also excluded from war memorials, and Jewish war veterans lost their previous exemption from the government's anti-Semitic measures.[23]

Finally, Hitler's personal history as an ordinary front-line fighter in the war was repeatedly mobilized in the service of the new regime.[24] This was underscored at a carefully choreographed ceremony in March 1933 (the 'Day of Potsdam') when the ex-lance corporal solemnly shook hands with the former Field Marshal and commander-in-chief, Reich President Paul von Hindenburg, thereby marking the coming together of the 'old' with the 'new' Germany.[25] On both this and other occasions in 1933–4, public and church figures made speeches celebrating Nazism as a return to the spirit of national unity supposedly achieved when Germany went to war in August 1914.[26] In the propaganda film *Triumph of the Will* (1935), directed by Leni Riefenstahl at the 1934 Nuremberg party rally, the same point was made in the opening scene, which begins with the following textual reference to contemporary events:

On 5 September 1934
20 years after the outbreak of the world war
16 years after the beginning of our suffering
19 months after the beginning of Germany's rebirth
Adolf Hitler flew again to Nuremberg to
muster the columns of his faithful followers.[27]

22   Mosse, *Fallen Soldiers*, 169–70.

23   Ibid., 176. See also T. Grady, *The German-Jewish Soldiers of the First World War in History and Memory* (Liverpool: Liverpool University Press, 2011), 139.

24   T. Weber, *Hitler's First War: Adolf Hitler, the Men of the List Regiment and the First World War* (Oxford: Oxford University Press, 2010), 288–9.

25   I. Kershaw, *The 'Hitler Myth': Image and Reality in the Third Reich* (Oxford: Oxford University Press, 1987), 54–5.

26   Verhey, *The Spirit of 1914*, 224–5.

27   Cited in R. Griffin, *Modernism and Fascism* (Basingstoke: Palgrave Macmillan, 2007), 12.

Once the regime was firmly in place, however, the emphasis in Nazi representations of the Great War shifted somewhat from the 'renewal of the "spirit of 1914"'[28] and granting of special public recognition to veterans, such as priority seating in theatres,[29] to the more calculated goal of making the nation once again 'capable of bearing arms'.[30] In a recent study, Thomas Rohkrämer has argued that National Socialism was 'fatally attractive' to many 'ordinary' Germans, not least because of its visions of future military success and imperial conquest which would undo the 'shame' of Versailles. The reintroduction of conscription in 1935, for instance, was greeted with widespread enthusiasm. The same applied to the rapid succession of military victories over Poland, Denmark, Norway, the Low Countries and France in 1939/40.[31] As one youth later recalled of his experiences of growing up in the late 1930s and early 1940s:

> The war was a time for heroes. We all wanted to become heroes. The images in our heads came from the wars of liberation against Napoleon. They displaced all the [negative] things we knew about the 'battles of attrition' and mass slaughter of the First World War. The barrage of propaganda had its effect on us youngsters.[32]

Even traditional conservatives like the academic historian Gerhard Ritter, who had distanced himself from the populist side of Nazism in the 1930s and in particular reacted to the 'Day of Potsdam' with disgust, could not help but be impressed by the ease with which France was defeated in the summer of 1940. In a lecture to students, which twenty years later in 1960, was used by East German scholars to highlight his past and present support for 'militarism', he mapped out a future vision of a German-dominated Europe in which France would have to 'starve itself and obey'.[33]

---

28  Verhey, *The Spirit of 1914*, 4.
29  R. W. Whalen, *Bitter Wounds: German Victims of the Great War, 1914–1939* (Ithaca and London: Cornell University Press, 1984), 176–7.
30  *Wiederwehrhaftmachung.*
31  T. Rohkrämer, *Die fatale Attraktion des Nationalsozialismus: Über die Popularität eines Unrechtsregimes* (Paderborn: Ferdinand Schöningh, 2013), esp. 238–57.
32  Ibid., 254.
33  W. Berthold, '... *großhungern und gehorchen': Zur Entstehung und politischen Funktion der Geschichtsideologie des westdeutschen Imperialismus, untersucht am Beispiel von*

The events of 1939 and 1940 indeed boosted Hitler's image as a man who could 'symbolically wip[e] out the humiliation' of the Great War, especially when representatives of the French government were forced to capitulate in the same railway carriage in Compiègne where the Germans had signed the armistice in 1918.[34] Thereafter the regime's domestic popularity began to dwindle, however, reaching a low point with the defeat at Stalingrad in 1942–3.[35] Old-style nationalist critics of Hitler, including First World War veterans like Ritter, began to doubt whether the current conflict could be won, both because of the overwhelming material superiority of the enemy and because of what they now saw as the irrational, criminal and anti-national policies of the Third Reich. Ritter indeed spent the last months of the war in Gestapo custody because of his involvement in the conservative resistance circle around Carl Goerdeler.[36]

For the Nazi political and military elite, on the other hand, determination to fight on to the bitter end went hand in hand with a critique of the supposedly lifeless 'hurrah patriotism' of the 1914–18 era which – in contrast to the solid 'achievements' of the Third Reich – was now ridiculed for having failed to provide a proper organic link between people and state, or home front and fighting fronts.[37] 'Total war', as Propaganda Minister Joseph Goebbels put it in a famous speech at the Sportpalast in Berlin in February 1943, required not sham 'bourgeois attitudes' or empty, bookish 'enthusiasm' for service, but 'fanatic, determined wills', 'bitter determination' and 'a strong heart capable of withstanding every internal and external battle'.[38] The unparalleled death and destruction that resulted from the refusal to surrender in spite of increasingly hopeless odds was to ensure

---

*Gerhard Ritter und Friedrich Meinecke* (East Berlin: Rütten & Loening, 1960). See also M. Stibbe, 'The View from the Other Germany: The Fischer Controversy in the GDR', *Journal of Contemporary History* 48/2 (2013), 319–20.

34    Kershaw, *The 'Hitler Myth'*, 155.

35    Kershaw, *The 'Hitler Myth'*, 200–1.

36    Cornelißen, *Gerhard Ritter*, 335–69.

37    Verhey, *The Spirit of 1914*, 228–30.

38    J. Goebbels, 'Total War' speech, 18 February 1943 in R. L. Bytwerk, ed., *Landmark Speeches of National Socialism* (London: Texas A & M University Press, 2008), 115 and 123.

that in post-1945 Germany – unlike in Britain, France and Belgium – when people spoke of the human and material costs of war, it was almost always in reference to the Second World War rather than the 1914–18 conflict.[39]


## The Great War in divided Germany


In 1945 Germany found itself defeated and divided into four occupation zones. Its former capital Berlin lay in ruins and it was to take forty-five years before a reunified country could once again claim sovereignty over it. By 1949 two separate states had come into being: the communist German Democratic Republic (GDR) in the east, and the capitalist Federal Republic of Germany (FRG) in the west. Devastation or near devastation reigned. Yet most historians agreed that Germany still had a future. What they could not agree on was the role that memory of the Great War should play in that future.

In the GDR the focus was on the emergence of a revolutionary working-class opposition to 'imperialism' and the wars that it allegedly caused in pursuit of profit and new markets.[40] In Germany in 1914–19 this struggle was led by Karl Liebknecht and Rosa Luxemburg, who broke with the old-style Social Democratic Party (SPD) over the latter's 'opportunistic' decision to back the Imperial government's wartime mobilization measures in parliament. When the East German Marxist labour historian Jürgen Kuczynski (1904–97) published a book in 1957 arguing, against the prevailing orthodoxy, that many rank-and-file workers, and not just the SPD

39    See R. Bessel, 'Catastrophe and Democracy: The Legacy of the World Wars in Germany', in A. McElligott and T. Kirk, eds, *Working Towards the Führer: Essays in Honour of Sir Ian Kershaw* (Manchester: Manchester University Press, 2003), 15–40.
40    See for example W. Bartel, *Die Linken in der deutschen Sozialdemokratie im Kampf gegen Militarismus und Krieg* (East Berlin: Dietz Verlag, 1958).

leaders, had supported war in July-August 1914, there was a big outcry.[41] Not only did Kuczynski face internal party disciplinary measures and condemnation from academic colleagues, he was also heavily criticized in the official communist newspaper *Neues Deutschland* that published letters from 'outraged' party veterans who remembered having taken part in anti-war demonstrations in July 1914.[42] In 1960, meanwhile, the war-damaged *Neue Wache*, now in the Soviet sector of Berlin, was repaired and reopened by the East German authorities as a national 'Memorial to the Victims of Militarism and Fascism'. The remains of an unknown soldier and an unknown victim of a Nazi concentration camp were interred there in 1969, thus symbolizing the links between the First and Second World Wars, both of which had supposedly been caused by bourgeois 'imperialism'.[43]

In the FRG, on the other hand, a key aim of post-1945 representations of the national past was to demonstrate that Hitler had been an 'anomaly'[44] in an otherwise 'normal' path of historical development stretching from the Imperial government's efforts to secure European peace before 1914 to West German membership of bodies like NATO and the EEC in the 1950s. In 1951–2 Gerhard Ritter, now president of the German Historians' Association, paved the way by negotiating an understanding with his French counterparts on how recent history should be presented in school textbooks. On the question of international relations in the run up to the 'July crisis' the Franco-German historians' commission agreed that:

> The documents do not permit attributing a conscious desire for a European war to any one government or people. Mutual distrust had reached a peak, and in leading

---

41  J. Kuczynski, *Der Ausbruch des ersten Weltkrieges und die deutsche Sozialdemokratie: Chronik und Analyse* (East Berlin: Akademie Verlag, 1957).

42  See *Neues Deutschland* (14 February and 12 March 1958). Also, for broader context, M. Stibbe, 'Fighting the First World War in the Cold War: East and West German Historiography on the Origins of the First World War, 1945–1959', in T. Hochscherf, C. Laucht and A. Plowman, eds, *Divided but not Disconnected: German Experiences of the Cold War* (New York and Oxford: Berghahn Books, 2010), 34–48.

43  See for example H. Wohlgemuth, *Warum mußte der deutsche Imperialismus zwei Weltkriege verlieren?* (East Berlin: Dietz Verlag, 1960).

44  *Betriebsunfall.*

circles it was believed that war was inevitable. Each one accused the other of aggressive intentions, and only saw a guarantee for security in an alliance system and continual armament increases.[45]

The refutation of German 'war guilt' in 1914 did not mean that West German historians of the 1950s were unwilling to confront what was now conceded to be the difficult *political* legacy of 'German militarism'. Ritter, for instance, spent much of the rest of his career writing about this issue. For him, Theobald von Bethmann Hollweg, the German Reich Chancellor from 1909 to 1917, was the 'tragic' yet worthy embodiment of a particular ideal of statesmanship which still had relevance in Germany's current struggle 'against the dangers of a new form of totalitarian tyranny' emanating from Moscow and East Berlin. In 1914, he argued, Bethmann Hollweg reluctantly but courageously led Germany into a 'defensive war' and at the same time sought to harness the desire of the SPD leaders for national integration in order to create a counterweight against the extreme militarists on the right and the revolutionary socialists on the left.[46]

By the late 1950s the Ritter view was in the ascendency. However, it was opposed by a little-known West German historian, Fritz Fischer (1908–99), who in 1957 discovered a document in the East German archives in Potsdam that fundamentally altered the prevailing view of Germany's aims in the Great War. The document in question was a memorandum, dated 9 September 1914, outlining Bethmann Hollweg's plans for reshaping Europe's borders following an anticipated German victory over France and Russia. It allowed Fischer, in two articles published in 1959 and 1960, and subsequently in a book that came out in 1961, to argue that Germany had consciously risked war in 1914 in a reckless 'grasp at world power'.[47]

Fischer's book caused a storm in the FRG. By raising the issue of continuities between Germany's aims in the First and Second World Wars, it

45  Mombauer, *The Origins*, 123–4.
46  G. Ritter, 'Das Problem des "Militarismus" in Deutschland', *Historische Zeitschrift* 177 (1954), 47.
47  F. Fischer, *Germany's Aims in the First World War* (London: Chatto & Windus, 1967) [German original, 1961].

broke the 'comfortable consensus'[48] of the 1950s precisely at a time when – against the backdrop of the building of the Berlin Wall in August 1961 – the prospects for reunification and recovery of national self-confidence seemed further away than ever. For historians like Ritter, it was vital that Germans retained some pride in their past if they were going to stand up to the renewed threat from the communist east. Fischer's book, in his view and that of other conservative scholars, threatened to undermine that pride.[49]

The ensuing controversy was on one level a clash between professors, reaching its height at the German historians' congress in West Berlin in October 1964, held on the fiftieth anniversary of the First and the twenty-fifth anniversary of the Second World Wars. But what also made it stand out was the public interest it evoked. Fischer was largely shunned by his academic colleagues, but had many sympathizers in the more liberal and left-wing parts of the West German media, as well as in Britain and America The controversy was even raised in the Bundestag, the West German parliament, in 1964, when State Secretary Karl Carstens was forced to make a statement defending the withdrawal of German Foreign Office funding for a lecture tour which Fischer had arranged with universities in the United States.[50]

Fischer's visit to America went ahead anyway, and his trenchant defence of his thesis at the 1964 historians' congress was judged a success, even by some of his conservative critics.[51] Younger West German scholars now felt encouraged to challenge the hallowed beliefs of their ageing professors and a raft of new studies appeared in the decade or so after 1965 exploring the link between Imperial Germany's repressive domestic policies before 1914 and its aggressive pursuit of *Weltpolitik* [world power status] on the

---

48   Mombauer, *The Origins*, 125.
49   See also S. Berger, *The Search for Normality: National Identity and Historical Consciousness in Germany since 1800* (Oxford: Berg, 1997), 63–4.
50   H. Pogge von Strandmann, 'The Political and Historical Significance of the Fischer Controversy', *Journal of Contemporary History* 48/2 (2013), 251–70.
51   Ibid., 267–8.

international stage.[52] In the GDR, more open-minded historians also welcomed Fischer's thesis as a sign that dialogue and mutual exchange of ideas
might replace the old antagonism between Marxist and non-Marxist interpretations of the nation's past.[53] In West Germany, left-leaning politicians
like Willy Brandt, who became Foreign Minister in 1966 and Chancellor
in 1969, successfully advocated a new relationship with the East based on
acceptance of post-war geopolitical realities. The Australian historian John
A. Moses, writing in 1975, argued that West German voters' willingness to
endorse this new *Ostpolitik* was 'intimately bound up with the changes in
historical consciousness brought about [...] by the Fischer controversy'.[54]

From the late 1970s, however, the Second World War was firmly back
at the forefront of memory politics in Germany, a situation that persists
to this day. One cause was generational: men and women born between
1915 and 1925, who had fought or served in the Second World War and
in the 'reconstruction' period immediately after 1945, were now reaching
retirement age, and had time to dwell on their pasts and/or to campaign
for better pensions.[55] Another was the more conservative political climate
of the 1980s, reflected in attempts by some West German intellectuals to
seek an 'escape from the [burden of the] Nazi past' by suggesting comparisons and connections between the Holocaust and other twentieth-century
crimes, including the Gulag system in the USSR and the killing fields of
Pol Pot's Cambodia.[56] Writing in March 1989, on the eve of the seventy-
fifth and fiftieth anniversaries of the two world wars, the British histori-

52  G. Iggers, *The Social History of Politics: Critical Perspectives in West German Historical
    Writing since 1945* (Leamington Spa: Berg, 1985), esp. 25–34.
53  Stibbe, 'The View from the Other Germany', 321–32. See also M. Stibbe, 'The Fischer
    Controversy over German War Aims in the First World War and its Reception by
    East German Historians, 1961–1989', *The Historical Journal* 46/3 (2003), 649–68.
54  J. A. Moses, *The Politics of Illusion: The Fischer Controversy in German Historiography*
    (London: George Prior Publishers, 1975), 130.
55  See for example N. Kramer, *Volksgenossinnen an der Heimatfront: Mobilisierung,
    Verhalten, Erinnnerung* (Göttingen: Vandenhoeck & Ruprecht, 2011), 328–9 and
    352.
56  R. J. Evans, *In Hitler's Shadow: West German Historians and their Attempt to Escape
    from the Nazi Past* (London: I. B. Tauris, 1989).

ans Richard Overy and Andrew Wheatcroft argued strongly that it was interpretations and representations of the latter conflict which were more capable of 'produc[ing] an impassioned reaction' in Germany, a marked contrast to the situation twenty-five years previously.[57]

## The Great War in reunified Germany

In the 1990s, and particularly after the turn of the twenty first century, a noticeable trend in the 'enlarged' FRG was what Gerhard Hirschfeld refers to as the simultaneous 'historicization' and joining together of the memory of *both* world wars.[58] On one level this can be seen in the labelling of the years 1914–45 as a 'second Thirty Years' War' or 'German age of extremes' (in a conscious echo of Eric Hobsbawm's global 'age of extremes', 1914–91).[59] The eminent social historian Hans-Ulrich Wehler, for example, took this line in 2004, arguing that the 'fanatical destructiveness' unleashed by Hitler on Europe was 'to a high degree preconfigured [*vorgeprägt*] in the experience, course and outcome of the first total war'.[60] On the other hand, the gradual 'historicization' of war memory also led to a critical reassessment of German 'war enthusiasm' in 1914. The imagined unity of 'war experience' was now replaced by a multitude of in-depth studies focusing on what

57  R. Overy with A. Wheatcroft, *The Road to War* (London: Macmillan, 1989), xv.
58  G. Hirschfeld, 'Der Erste Weltkrieg in der deutschen und internationalen Geschichtsschreibung', *Aus Politik und Zeitgeschichte*, B 29–30 (2004), 3.
59  See for example H.-U. Wehler, *Deutsche Gesellschaftsgeschichte. Vol. 4: Vom Beginn des Ersten Weltkriegs bis zur Gründung der beiden deutschen Staaten 1914–1949* (Munich: C. H. Beck, 2003), 966 and 985. See also E. Hobsbawm, *Age of Extremes: The Short Twentieth Century, 1914–1991* (London: Abacus, 1994) and John Hutchinson's contribution to this volume.
60  H.-U. Wehler, Der zweite Dreißigjährige Krieg: 'Der erste Weltkrieg als Auftakt und Vorbild für den Zweiten Weltkrieg', *Spiegel special* 1 (2004), 143. Reproduced in C. Roolf and J. Thiel, eds, *Der Erste Weltkrieg 1914–1918: Quellen zur Geschichte und Politik* (Stuttgart: Ernst Klett Verlag, 2013), 106–7.

Christoph Nonn describes as the 'many fragments' of 'common people's memory of 1914–18'.[61] Benjamin Ziemann, for instance, pointed out that in the years 1939 to 1945 'soldiers from a rural Bavarian background were particularly likely to 'show aversion to the [Second World] War', reflecting not only a relative 'immunity' to National Socialist propaganda but also a decidedly negative rather than heroic recollection of the 1914–18 'war experience' in the south German countryside.[62]

From the point of view of public commemoration, a controversial message of shared suffering and grief, with the First World War again overshadowed by the Second, can be seen in the redesigned *Neue Wache* in Berlin. Following German reunification, it was recast as the 'Central Memorial of the Federal Republic of Germany to the Victims of War and Tyranny' and a specially-enlarged replica of the German artist Käthe Kollwitz's 1937 sculpture *Mutter mit totem Sohn* [Mother with Dead Son] was placed inside.[63] The new, post-1993 inscription includes, alongside a mention of the fallen soldiers of both world wars, references to those who died on the home front, in enemy captivity or as a result of forced migrations; the millions of murdered Jews, Sinti and Roma; those killed because of their ancestry, sexuality, poor state of health, religious beliefs or political views; and all women and men who lost their lives in the course of resisting dictatorship before and after 1945.

61   C. Nonn, 'Oh What a Lovely War? German Common People and the First World War', *German History* 18/1 (2000), 111.

62   Ziemann, *War Experiences*, 275.

63   B. Ladd, *The Ghosts of Berlin: Confronting German History in the Urban Landscape* (Chicago and London: University of Chicago Press, 2008), 217–24. [See also Karen Till, 'Staging the past: landscape designs, cultural identity and *Erinnerungspolitik* at Berlin's *Neue Wache*', *cultural geographies* 6 (1999), 251–83 – Ed.].

## Conclusion

This chapter has sought to show how the Great War has been remembered, commemorated and refought in Germany at many different moments during the past century. Most importantly, it has become impossible to discuss the 1914–18 conflict without stirring up memories of the Second World War, the Holocaust and the communist era in the GDR. Indeed the course of German history since 1919 is such that the Great War registers only weakly in contemporary consciousness. Compared to half a century ago, when the 'Fischer controversy' dominated the headlines, there is little interest in the war's causes or in who was to blame for its outbreak. Instead, the centenary commemorations have been pre-empted by Florian Illies's bestselling account of the year 1913 that depicts a vibrant pre-war age of great scientific and artistic promise. Even those writers and intellectuals who prophesied violence and doom in 1913, he suggests, were reflecting a crisis in their love lives or sense of personal well-being rather than a sickness in society as a whole.[64] More generally, in contrast to the place of the debate over why war came in 1914 during the Weimar, Nazi and Cold War periods, media and academic discussion of this issue in the run-up to the centenary period beginning in 2014 has given way to an emphasis on contingencies, or the alternative paths that might have been taken had Europe and the world remained at peace. Another example would be the public interest in the FRG generated by historian Christopher Clark's new account of the war's origins, with its portrayal of a Europe 'sleepwalking' its way into the year 1914, until suddenly woken up with a jolt by the assassination at Sarajevo on 28 June and the ensuing breakdown in relations between the great powers.[65]

64   F. Illies, *1913: The Year Before the Storm* (London: Clerkenwell Press, 2013) [German original, 2012].

65   C. Clark, *The Sleepwalkers: How Europe Went to War in 1914* (London: Penguin Books, 2012). A German version was published in 2013.

All this indicates that today the memory politics of the Great War are a less reliable guide to the present and 'present future' in Germany than at any time since 1919.[66] The years 1914–18 have become a mere 'historical curiosity' rather than an expression of future dreams and ambitions or a backdrop to current 'geopolitical realities'.[67] The same cannot be said for the memory politics of the great inflation of 1923, however, which continue to cast a long and somewhat dark shadow over the attempts by the current rulers in Berlin to manage the financial crisis in the Eurozone while protecting the bank accounts of German voters at home.[68]

66  Benjamin Ziemann defines the 'present future' as 'the possible worlds in fifteen or twenty years that can be envisaged in the present' – see B. Ziemann, 'Weimar was Weimar: Politics, Culture and the Emplotment of the German Republic', *German History* 28/4 (2010), 555.
67  Verhey, *The Spirit of 1914*, 230.
68  F. Taylor, 'The German Trauma', *The New Statesman* (30 August–5 September 2013), 30–4.

PART IV

# Locations of Commemoration

SARAH CHRISTIE

# The Sinking of the *Marquette*: Gender, Nationalism and New Zealand's Great War Remembrance

## Introduction

On 23 October 1915, the British transport ship *Marquette* was torpedoed in the Aegean Sea by a German submarine. Among its cargo of troops, ammunition and mules, the *Marquette* was also carrying the No. 1 New Zealand Stationary Hospital (hereafter New Zealand Hospital). Of thirty-two New Zealanders who lost their lives, ten were nurses from the New Zealand Army Nursing Service.[1] This chapter investigates how a narrative of the *Marquette* sinking was constructed, retold and commemorated as a case study for the formation and reformation of collective remembrance.

Collective remembrance is the process through which communities construct and maintain a collective memory of an event.[2] This chapter argues that the construction of the initial narrative of an event is influential to these collective memories. Narratives developed around the *Marquette* sinking were influenced by contemporaneous discourses on gender and nationalism. New Zealanders' ideals of masculinity and femininity during the Great War were intertwined with ideas of 'Britishness' and commitment to Empire. The nurses who died were paradoxically constructed as both ideal imperial women and honorary men. This memory narrative in turn influenced instances of collective remembrance. Both geographic and col-

---

1    Peter Rees, *The Other ANZACS: Nurses at War, 1914–1915* (Crows Nest: Allen and Unwin, 2008), 115.

2    Jay Winter and Emmanuel Sivan, 'Setting the framework', in Jay Winter and Emmanuel Sivan, eds, *War and Remembrance in the Twentieth Century* (Cambridge: Cambridge University Press, 1999), 6.

legial communities sought to show their connection to the event through remembrance services and monument building. However, without active retelling and 'rehearsal' a collective memory can fall into oblivion.[3] These retold memories are not fixed but become products of their contemporary setting as well as evidence of the past. As flexible narratives these retellings can be adapted and recast by communities, keeping them socially and culturally relevant. With changing ideas about gender and nationalism over the course of the twentieth century the memory and remembrance of the *Marquette* nurses has been remolded to fit new ideas of equality and post-imperial nationalism.

## Framing the *Marquette* narrative

Construction and dissemination of an event's narrative is crucial to a community's later remembrance of the event. These narratives are framed by larger discourses, justifying their inclusion in collective memory and the need for specific remembrance. The narrative of the *Marquette* was primarily created through newspaper articles that took individual memory of the event and disseminated it to a wider community. This narrative became the principal source from which communities, both local and national, formed their collective memory of the event. The sinking's trauma and drama were played out for the New Zealand public through detailed eyewitness accounts. An example was an anonymous nurse's letter published in *The Auckland Weekly News*: 'We were swamped again and again until we were exhausted. It was pitiful to see the nurses and soldiers gradually becoming tired in their frantic struggles and finally releasing their grasp upon the gunwale, floating for a few seconds and then slowly sinking without a murmur'.[4]

---

3    Winter and Sivan, 'Setting the framework', 14–15.
4    Rees, *The Other ANZACS*, 129.

Creation of collective memory involves the dual processes of remembering and forgetting, influencing inclusions and exclusions within the emerging and reiterated narrative. Processes that determined what was remembered and what was forgotten began with the survivors, with only a handful choosing to make their recollections public. Accounts were influenced by the narrator's powers of recall and self-censorship. Once in the public domain, accounts faced official censorship and editorializing by newspapers. Captain Isaacs, Quartermaster with the New Zealand Hospital, highlighted these factors in his letter home, 'The following narrative has been reported to the Press Association [...] so I hope the censor will not cut out very much'.[5]

Captain Isaacs's letter illustrates the motivation of some eyewitnesses to make their recollections of the event public. For other retellings of the event it is harder to assess an author's willingness to contribute to a public narrative. Some contributions to newspapers and magazines were anonymous while others were published extracts of letters to relatives. Newspapers then edited and contextualized the story, framing it in line with contemporary discourses of nationalism as part of an imperial ideology and gendered behavioural expectations. Regional newspapers reprinted articles from metropolitan sources. This helped to construct a nationally accepted version of events within a broader, transnational and imperial context.[6]

In New Zealand the *Marquette* sinking became synonymous with the story of the nurses. While twenty-two New Zealand men lost their lives, newspaper coverage focused on the nurses. *The Press*'s coverage was headlined: 'Disaster in Aegean Sea, New Zealand Stationary Hospital Staff – Ten Nurses Drowned – Also several male members of staff'.[7] Thus the sinking was singled out as a different kind of war tragedy due to the deaths of New Zealand women. Male death in war was tragic but accepted;[8]

---

5 John Meredith Smith, *Cloud Over Marquette* (Auckland: J. M. Smith, 1990), 34.
6 'The *Marquette*', *The Marlborough Express* (18 December 1915), 3; 'The *Marquette* Disaster', *The Colonist* (4 November 1915), 4; '*Marquette* Disaster', *Ashburton Guardian* (4 November 1915), 3.
7 'Disaster in Aegean Sea', *The Press* (3 November 1915), 6.
8 Lyn Macdonald, *The Roses of No Man's Land* (London: Macmillan, 1984), 122.

female death, however, perverted the idea that war was fought by men for the protection of women and children.[9] The accepted role of patriotic women in New Zealand, as in Britain, was as mothers to soldiers.[10] Nurses presented an ambiguous picture as women undertaking traditional caring roles but present in theatres of war. To deal with this anomaly of female war casualties, *Marquette* nurses were constructed both as exemplars of womanhood and as transcending their gender to become 'honorary men'.

New Zealand's nationalism was, during the Great War, inseparably intertwined with its identity as part of the British Empire.[11] The image of the nurses' deaths as sacrifices for an imperial cause was strengthened by their connection with the death of Edith Cavell eleven days before the sinking of the *Marquette*. Edith Cavell was a British nurse shot by the Germans in occupied Belgium for assisting stranded Allied soldiers.[12] She was constructed posthumously as the ultimate imperial heroine, her death provoking international outrage and seen by the British and their allies as one of the greatest atrocities of the war.[13] As Katie Pickles has explored, New Zealand commentators linked the two events, drawing connections based on ideas of self-sacrifice and service to others.[14] The story of the *Marquette* therefore became part of a much wider patriotic imperial

9   Katie Pickles, *Transnational Outrage: The Death and Commemoration of Edith Cavell* (Basingstoke: Palgrave Macmillan, 2007), 78.
10  Margaret Anderson, 'The Female Front: The Attitudes of Otago Women Towards the Great War 1914–1918', BA(Hons) diss. (University of Otago, 1990), 95; Susan Grayzel, *Women's Identities at War: Gender, Motherhood, and Politics in Britain and France During the First World War* (Chapel Hill, NC: University of North Carolina Press, 1999), 119.
11  Megan Woods, 'Re/producing the nation: women making identity in New Zealand 1906–1925', PhD thesis (University of Canterbury, 2002), 146 <http://indl.handle. net/10092/4827> accessed 24 January 2013.
12  Pickles, *Transnational Outrage*, 16.
13  Katie Pickles, 'Mapping memorials for Edith Cavell on the colonial edge', *New Zealand Geographer* 62/1 (2006), 4.
14  Pickles, *Transnational Outrage*, 170–1.

discourse justifying the war. The nursing journal *Kai Tiaki* decreed the event 'worthy to live in the history of Empire'.[15]

The sinking of the *Marquette* was used to reinforce patriotic rhetoric of the 'evil Hun', an enemy killing without attention to chivalric codes of conduct.[16] This discourse implied the sinking was made more tragic by the loss of female life, reinforcing Allied narratives which stressed it was 'essentially wrong to shoot a woman', narratives strongly in evidence in the reporting of the death of Edith Cavell.[17] The horror of New Zealand women killed in action added to images of Germany as an evil aggressor, evidence of an enemy who broke the code of non-violence against women. Captain Harrison's account fostered an image of German callousness, not only causing disaster but relishing it. He stated, 'As I was getting the nurses into the boat from the deck the periscope of a submarine was plainly seen about 300 yards off, and she watched through this evil eye for a long time'.[18] This image of Germans gloating over the maritime deaths of women was part of a wider surge in anti-German sentiment[19] and is echoed in reporting of the *Lusitania*'s sinking in May 1915, an event used in Britain and New Zealand to reinforce the unchivalrous behavior of Germany.[20] In contrast, New Zealand nurses, like Cavell, were represented as model imperial women through their self-sacrifice and dedication to duty.

Public narratives drew on a wider 'public cult of sacrifice', constructing the nurses' actions in a feminine discourse of maternal self-sacrifice and service for others.[21] A repeating motif of this narrative was nurses putting

15    *Kai Tiaki*, quoted in Anna Rogers, *While You're Away: New Zealand Nurses at War 1899–1948* (Auckland: Auckland University Press, 2003), 107.

16    Cate Haste, *Keep the Home Fires Burning: Propaganda in the First World War* (London: Allen Lane, 1977), 79.

17    Pickles, *Transnational Outrage*, 39.

18    'The Marquette – A Few Impressions', *The Marlborough Express* (18 December 1915), 3.

19    Andrew Francis, *'To Be Truly British We Must Be Anti-German': New Zealand, Enemy Aliens and the Great War Experience, 1914–1919* (Oxford: Peter Lang, 2012), 7.

20    'Account by Survivors', *Otago Daily Times* (10 May 1915), 5 and 'All Sorts of People', *The New Zealand Free Lance* (2 June 1915), 4.

21    Steven Loveridge, '"Sentimental Equipment": New Zealand, the Great War and Cultural Mobilisation', PhD thesis (Victoria University of Wellington, 2013), 227.

the rescue of troops ahead of their own. An anonymous account in the *Auckland Weekly News* described how some nurses had 'refused to go into the boats until most of the soldiers were saved'.[22] The author hoped these actions and the help shown to fellow injured nurses would bring 'comfort to the relatives of the nurses in New Zealand to know that they were so splendidly brave and self-sacrificing in facing death'. Stories of nurses who, in spite of serious injury and suffering from exhaustion, continued to put the needs of others first provided further evidence of self-sacrifice and justification for their construction as heroines.[23] At a ceremony for surviving *Marquette* nurses, Minister for Public Health, the Hon. George Warren Russell, illustrated how these qualities of service epitomized both a gendered and racial ideal. Events such as this, he stated, 'displayed to the world many of the finer characteristics of the British race, and none finer than the womanly qualities which were the pride of our nation'.[24]

War continued the gendered division of spaces and roles for men and women in New Zealand. The battlefield was a masculine space where displays of bravery and heroism were celebrated and proved men's commitment to their country and empire. Women's duties to nation and empire were through an extension of their maternal roles. A mother's highest virtue was to sacrifice her sons for King and Country. Women were made heroic through maternal sacrifice and through the sacrifice of their labour as caring volunteers working for patriotic causes.[25] Nurses represented and negotiated an in-between space, a composite of the battlefield and the home. While they were part of the war, there was an expectation they would be separated from the war's frontline due to their gender and role as medics. The *Christchurch Star* voiced its 'great shock' at 'women who were devoting their skill to the alleviation of pain, and working for the welfare of humanity, being among the victims of war'.[26]

---

22   *Auckland Weekly News* (25 November 1915), quoted in Smith, *Cloud over Marquette*, 31–2.
23   'Loss of the "Marquette"', *Kai Tiaki* (January 1916), 10.
24   'Arrival of the Transport "Tahiti"', *Kai Tiaki* (January 1916), 31.
25   Woods, 'Re/producing the nation', 80.
26   Rees, *The Other Anzacs*, 141.

In reality, nurses saw on a daily basis the horrible consequences of war. They witnessed shattered bodies and minds and were exposed to the dangers of enemy submarines, mines and bombing. Their roles, however, created a sphere of maternal care within the war arena. For the nurses, their service and self-sacrifice was not just for King and Country but also for 'their men'. A published letter excerpt from Margaret Rogers, one of the drowned nurses, articulated this. 'There is no romance about war', she stated, 'it spells suffering, hunger and filth, and how thankful I am every day that I came to do what I could to help and relieve our brave boys'.[27]

Nurses, both survivors and fatalities, were marked out as 'honorary men' in the *Marquette* narrative for displaying heroic qualities usually associated with male participation in war. Captain Harrison's account praised the nurses for exhibiting 'not the slightest trace of panic. Everyone of them showed a spirit that would not have shamed the bravest troops in the whole world'.[28] Nurse Jeannie Sinclair in the *Auckland Weekly News* agreed with Captain Harrison. She described the nurses' composure as they donned their lifejackets and waited in orderly fashion for lifeboats to be launched: 'There was no noise – not a single scream. I cannot think now how it was that we were so cool and collected'.[29] Lucy Delap has shown how discipline and composure during crises at sea were constructed in the Edwardian period as a value of British manliness.[30] Similar reports of calm behaviour displayed by female passengers also featured in the New Zealand reporting of the *Lusitania*.[31] Mr Russell, who had feted the nurses for their exemplary feminine qualities, was equally able to celebrate their status as honorary men: 'It was a fine thing for this country', he pronounced, 'that its women were showing the same pertinacity and bull-dog courage as our

27  'The Marquette Disaster', *Akaroa Mail* (5 November 1915), 2.
28  'The Marquette, Absolutely No Panic', *The Marlborough Express* (18 December 1915), 3.
29  *Auckland Weekly News* (16 December 1915), quoted in Smith, *Cloud Over Marquette*, 25.
30  Lucy Delap, 'Thus Does Man Prove His Fitness to Be the Master of Things: Shipwrecks, Chivalry and Masculinities in Nineteenth- and Twentieth-Century Britain', *Cultural and Social History* 3 (2006), 57.
31  'Account by Survivors', *Otago Daily Times* (10 May 1915), 5.

heroes at the Dardanelles'.[32] Women could therefore aspire to values that were part of a code of manliness if it emphasized their British civility in comparison to German barbarity.

Some newspapers used images of female heroism to challenge concepts of masculinity and shame men into enlistment. One *Evening Post* editorial challenged masculine (and British) ideas of gallantry by implying the treatment of the nurses had inverted the chivalric code for evacuating women and children first. The motif that nurses had stayed 'on decks cheering the Tommies until only a few of the men remained to help the women into the boats' should induce, the editor felt, any 'hesitating young man of New Zealand, fit and free for service' to either 'register his name for the Army [...] or he should blush for his weakness every time he sees a woman, particularly if she is a nurse'.[33] However, these versions of events challenging male survivors' masculinity were contested.

Responding to the editorial, *Marquette* survivor Lieutenant Colonel McGavin felt compelled to present his version of events, writing a letter to the Hon. James Allen, Minister of Defence, which subsequently appeared in the *Evening Post*.[34] In his letter he challenged the 'implication that the men neglected the nurses and permitted them to remain on the ship while endeavouring to save themselves'. This, he claimed, had created 'no little indignation amongst the members of my company'. While he acknowledged the courage of the nurses, his version of their bravery conforms to more conservative gender roles, depicting feminine obedience as nurses gathered at evacuation points and were helped on with life jackets and into lifeboats. He claimed nurses would not have been permitted such acts of 'theatrical' bravery but would have been 'placed in the boats by force' if they had attempted to stay.

Except for one anonymous account, the nurses did not lay claim to the myth that they had insisted on the rescue of soldiers before their own.[35]

32    'Arrival of the Transport "Tahiti"', *Kai Tiaki* (January 1916), 31.
33    For more on the contested nature of chivalry at sea see Lucy Delap, 'Thus Does Man'.
34    'The Marquette', *The Evening Post* (15 April 1916), 5.
35    *Auckland Weekly News* (25 November 1915), quoted in Smith, *Cloud Over Marquette*, 31.

In public they praised their rescuers and men who had supported them in the water.[36] In private correspondence, however, they challenged male behaviour during the sinking. Following the publication of McGavin's article both Mable Wright and Jeannie Sinclair wrote angrily to Hester Maclean, Matron-in-Chief of the New Zealand Nursing Service during the war, to challenge McGavin's recollections and complain about the treatment of nurses during the evacuation. Maclean's subsequent protest to the Minister of Defence ultimately produced no action.[37] Similar frustrations at not being able to be completely honest about the sinking are evident in Edith Popplewell's account in *Kai Tiaki*.[38]

This debate around the nurses' evacuation illustrates that molding memory narratives was not an uncontested process. The ability to shape public narratives was filtered through layers of censure, social expectations and gendered ideals of behaviour. The media's motivations to support the war and to reconfirm gender roles helped form a narrative where the nurses were the key protagonists and constructed them as tragic heroines. As 'honorary men' the nurses were allowed to exhibit bravery and courage in a sphere of war. However, this was permissible because it emphasized Britishness and was also framed as exemplifying feminine qualities of service, duty and care.

## Collective remembrance and the nurses of the *Marquette*

Communities undertake public 'rehearsal' of individual memory through ritual and through bestowing meaning on particular public places. Collective remembrance, Jay Winter explains, relies on communities

---

36  *Auckland Weekly News* (16 December 1915), quoted in Smith, *Cloud Over Marquette*, 25.
37  Rogers, *While You're Away*, 108–11.
38  'The Loss of the "Marquette"', *Kai Tiaki* (January 1916), 9.

retelling or reaffirming collective memory narratives.[39] Following the
Great War, local communities incorporated the *Marquette* into wider
programmes of remembrance, an avenue to honour and justify their war
dead.[40] In 'rehearsing' the *Marquette* narrative through collective remembrance, communities also reinforced gendered elements of the narrative
and constructions of the nurses as imperial heroines.

Waimate, like other towns across belligerent nations, sought to produce a physical marker of their memory within their community landscape.
When Waimate unveiled its memorial archway in 1923, Nurses Gorman,
Fox and Brown were included, along with Private James Bird of the New
Zealand Medical Corps.[41] The nurses' inclusion on the monument marked
their status as honorary male veterans. However, they were also marked as
different through their prominence on the plaque and their separation from
others by the use of the title 'Nurse' where others were identified only by
initials and family names. Nurse Catherine Fox, as well as being memorialized in Waimate, also appears in the Auckland War Memorial Museum
Word War I Hall of Memories.[42] Thus more than one community could
lay claim to the memory of an individual, determining who was included
or excluded in projects of remembrance.

Local memorials and events of remembrance were also part of a wider
gendered imperial framework.[43] Dedication of a memorial in 1918 at Nurse
Isabel Clark's former high school illustrates how ideas of community,
nationalism and imperial identity could be drawn together, linking both
the nurses and the communities to these larger collective identities. A large

39   Winter and Sivan, 'Setting the framework', 14–15.
40   Kenneth Inglis, *Sacred Places: War Memorials in the Australian Landscape* (Carlton,
     Vic.: Miegunyah Press, 1998), 123–96.
41   'Waimate First World War memorial', *New Zealand History Online* <http://www.
     nzhistory.net.nz/media/photo/waimate-first-world-war-memorial> accessed 23
     August 2013.
42   'Catherine Anne Fox', *Auckland War Memorial Museum Cenotaph Database* <http://
     muse.aucklandmuseum.com/databases/Cenotaph/5078.detail?Ordinal=1&c_sur-
     name_search=fox&c_firstname_search=catherine> accessed 1 April 2012.
43   Pickles, 'Mapping memorials for Edith Cavell', 11.

photograph of Nurse Clark was unveiled and draped with the Union Jack, and the 'gathering stood to sing the National Anthem *God Save the King*', further highlighting New Zealand's imperial ties.[44] The memorial service's keynote, presented by *Marquette* survivor Captain Burridge, reinforced the image of the nurses as demonstrating values of ideal national and imperial citizenship. He commended Nurse Clark's actions for showing 'no sign of hysteria or panic'. He encouraged students to remember 'that death cannot destroy her influence. An act like hers will go down in history and inspire others – those who fought and those who did not – to great things'.[45]

Collective remembrance was not undertaken only by geographical communities. The nursing community also sought to memorialize the *Marquette* nurses. In response to the news of the *Marquette* sinking, over 200 nurses in their uniforms attended a special memorial service in Christchurch on 9 November 1915.[46] These collegial communities drew connections to the same national and imperial identities as geographical communities did. Like the Anzac Days Matthew Henry has described, anniversaries of the sinking became avenues to govern contemporary conduct of citizens through celebrating exemplary behaviours.[47] In being exemplary nurses, these women had also demonstrated their claim to be exemplary national and imperial citizens, reinforcing the image of imperial heroines. In October 1919 the Trained Nurses Association arranged an 'Anniversary Memorial Service'. The memorial mirrored a funeral service with the Venerable Archdeacon Watson's eulogy drawing on the example of Christ's sacrifice.[48] The rhetoric used in the service again shows how individual remembrance was connected to ideas of national pride and an

44   Smith, *Cloud Over Marquette*, 75 and 'History of God Defend New Zealand', *Manatū Taonga Ministry for Culture and Heritage* <http://www.mch.govt.nz/nz-identity-heritage/national-anthems/history-god-defend-new-zealand> accessed 24 August 2013.

45   Smith, *Cloud Over Marquette*, 75.

46   Anna Rogers, 'In Loving Memory: The Nurses' Memorial Chapel, Christchurch, New Zealand', *The New Zealand Medical Journal* 119/1244 (2006), 2.

47   Matthew Henry, 'Making New Zealanders through commemoration: Assembling Anzac Day in Auckland, 1916–1939', *New Zealand Geographer* 62/1 (2006), 3.

48   'Marquette Disaster', *Northern Advocate* (29 October 1919), 3.

even broader sense of imperial duty, in an instructive tone. 'Many among those who were present on this occasion', Archdeacon Watson declared, 'knew well some of those nurses who had laid down their lives; knew their various talents, their various characteristics, but different though these may have been the one great gift, that of supreme self-sacrifice, had been common to all'. These sacrifices, he instructed, had been made so that the 'Empire would be a better Empire and New Zealand a better country' through people's imitation of their example.[49]

The sinking's anniversary became a date whereby nursing communities could continue to rehearse their commemoration through arranging fundraising, reunions and remembrance services. An example was the fundraising concert in 1917 in Wellington for the Nurses Memorial Fund.[50] The anniversary received a degree of institutional recognition and remained a feature in the public consciousness into the 1930s through Nurses' Day. Nurses' Day was commemorated in 1932 at the newly opened National War Memorial with a service to recognize the work of the New Zealand Army Nursing Service, with photos published in the local newspaper.[51] In 1935, the twentieth anniversary of the *Marquette* sinking, a parade was held at the Carillon in memory of the nurses who were lost at sea. The parade included the dedication of a Carillon bell, a permanent commemoration within the National Memorial to nurses' wartime service.[52] By 1945, while a concert of bell ringing was held at the National War Memorial Carillon to mark the anniversary, newspaper reports merely advertised the event, no longer espousing public instruction from these heroic deeds.[53] This diminishing attention to the *Marquette* memory illustrates the concept of 'shelf-life' for memory narratives. Winter argues that collective memory fades over time as those who found meaning in the initial event die or public expressions of the remembrance lose their significance.[54] New meaning and relevance

49  'Marquette Disaster', *Northern Advocate* (29 October 1919), 3.
50  Rogers, *While You're Away*, 113.
51  'Nurses Memorial Service', *Evening Post* (24 October 1932), 5.
52  'The Marquette', *Evening Post* (10 October 1935), 10.
53  'Carillon Recital', *Evening Post* (22 October 1945), 3.
54  Winter and Sivan, 'Setting the framework', 16 and 30–1.

must be ascribed to the narrative and the memorials by future generations in order for the collective remembrance to endure.[55] The Nurses' Memorial Chapel in Christchurch illustrates how a Memorial has been adapted, retaining meaning for successive generations.

Christchurch produced the most prominent and elaborate memorial to the nurses who drowned – the Nurses' Memorial Chapel at the Christchurch Public Hospital. This memorial reflected trends evident in other instances of *Marquette* remembrance. The chapel's foundation stone was officially laid in 1927 by the Duke of York (later King George VI), emphasizing the links between this community memorial and a wider imperial identity. Medical Superintendent Mr Fox's speech at the ceremony drew on the motifs of self-sacrifice and service to others, important aspects of the nurses' construction as imperial heroines. Interestingly the two nurses who died during the 1918–19 flu epidemic were incorporated into both the memorial and this rhetoric of sacrifice and duty.[56]

This memorial, however, has not remained a static object of remembrance. It has been changed by successive communities over time, adding new meanings to both the memorial and the memory of the *Marquette* nurses. Through broadening whom the memorial represents, the community has maintained the chapel's relevance as a site of remembrance. A series of stained glass windows was installed between 1932 and 1971 commemorating local and national pioneering nurses and nursing leaders. The chapel is now also home to a variety of memorial plaques and artifacts, commemorating men and women for their medical service both at home and abroad in times of war.[57] The most recent window is a dedication to all New Zealand nurses who served in both world wars.[58] In 1989 the national importance of this monument to women's war service was recognized with

---

55  Winter and Sivan, 'Setting the framework', 16 and 30–1.
56  'Nurses' Chapel, Foundation Stone Laid, In Peace and War', *The Press* (16 March 1927), 9.
57  'No. 7 Nurses Memorial Chapel', *The Architectural Heritage of Christchurch*, 11–16. <http://christchurchcitylibraries.com/Heritage/Publications/Christ churchCityCouncil/ArchitecturalHeritage/NursesChapel/ISBN-0959797300.pdf> accessed 16 February 2012.
58  Pickles, *Transnational Outrage*, 171.

an official heritage protection notice.[59] These additions to the memorial illustrate two trends in the recasting of the *Marquette* collective memory: a move to celebrating the nurses as professional exemplars, and to national identity replacing an imperial framework.

Lucy Delap has explored the twentieth-century rise of ideals of professionalism in shipwreck narratives. She argues that unlike concepts of chivalry, professionalism was demonstrated by either sex.[60] While contemporaries admired the readiness of surviving nurses to return to work, professionalism became more central after the war. Hester Maclean's depiction of the *Marquette* incident in her 1932 memoirs lacked the imperial bluster of earlier newspaper reports. She stressed instead the endurance and commitment of the surviving nurses, admiring the fact that 'after this sad experience, not one of the sisters wished to give up their work'.[61]

Within the last twenty years there has been a resurgence in memory-making about the *Marquette*. One explanation for this rediscovery is the renewed interest in commemorating Anzac Day and its associated symbols and stories as 'markers of nationhood'.[62] Changing gender paradigms have seen nurses become symbols for claims to greater inclusion of women's experiences in the wider Anzac heritage. Historians have recast the nurses in a national or Anzac context and emphasized their professional skills, tenacity and endurance of extreme circumstances.[63] Their position as national heroines is demonstrated in Anna Rogers' statement that while 'Gallipoli might have played a large part in forging a New Zealand character [...] the whole experience of New Zealanders suffering and New Zealand nurses tending to the suffering, in far-off lands, was a major factor'.[64]

---

59    'Nurses Memorial Chapel', *New Zealand Historic Places Trust Pouhere Taonga* <http://
      www.historic.org.nz/TheRegister/RegisterSearch/RegisterResults.aspx?RID=1851>
      accessed 23 November 2011.
60    Delap, 'Thus Does Man', 69.
61    Hester Maclean, *Nursing in New Zealand: History and Reminiscences* (Wellington:
      Tolan, 1932), 189.
62    'Anzac Day Today', *Ministry of Culture and Heritage – ANZAC.GOVT.NZ* <http://
      www.anzac.govt.nz/today/index.html> accessed 24 February 2013.
63    Sandra Coney, ed., *Standing in Sunshine, A History of New Zealand Women Since
      They Won the Vote* (Auckland: Viking, 1993), 304.
64    Mike Crean, 'Kiwi Nurses in the War Zones', *The Press* (13 October 2003), 5.

By the ninetieth anniversary the drowned nurses were remembered for their service and dedication to their profession rather than as imperial heroines, and were recast as national heroines and pioneers of New Zealand nursing. Governor-General Dame Silvia Cartwright's speech at the memorial service in the Christchurch Chapel emphasized the nurses' work ethic and their ability to maintain their professionalism under the most trying of circumstances, praising their practicality, hard work and loyalty to country and soldiers.[65] A parade of historic nursing costumes during the memorial service illustrates how remembrance of the *Marquette* nurses was being recast as a significant milestone in New Zealand's nursing history.[66] The *Marquette*'s inclusion in the Auckland War Memorial Museum's exhibit focusing on New Zealand forces in combat further demonstrates the incorporation of the nurses' story into the national narratives of the Great War.[67]

Recent retellings of the *Marquette* incident have given prominence to the question of why a medical unit was transported on an ammunition and troop ship, therefore lacking the protection of hospital ship markings. While New Zealand officials criticized this course of action at the time, it was not part of the public narrative.[68] Current narratives raise the 'mystery of why they [the nurses] were on the *Marquette* at all', emphasizing British bureaucratic bungling leading to tragedy for New Zealanders.[69] Anna Rogers goes further, describing the *Marquette* sinking as a 'scandal'.[70] Despite the nurses' increased agency due to their professionalism, they are now portrayed as victims of British Imperial decision-making rather than German aggression.

---

65   'Sinking of the Marquette remembered in Christchurch', *Kai Tiaki: Nursing New Zealand* (November 2005). <http://findarticles.com/p/articles/mi_hb4839/is_10_11/ai_n29223193/> accessed 6 March 2012.
66   'Remembrance Service for Lost Nurses', Health First: Canterbury District Health Board's Free Community Publication, December 2005, 26, 1.
67   'Scars on the Heart', *Auckland War Memorial Museum*, <http://www.aucklandmuseum.com/132/scars-on-the-heart> accessed 1 April 2012.
68   Rees, *The Other Anzacs*, 144–7.
69   Coney, *Standing in the Sunshine*, 304.
70   Crean, 'Kiwi Nurses', 5.

Interestingly, the latest incarnation of the *Marquette* story moves from a national to a wider Anzac story. Thomas Keneally's novel *The Daughters of Mars* appropriates *Marquette* events but substitutes Australian nurses as the key protagonists. Keneally reworks the narrative, incorporating some repeating elements of the story and changing others. The motif of the nurses not traveling on a hospital ship is incorporated but ascribed to the nurses informed choices, knowingly undertaking a dangerous mission out of duty to their professional commitments.[71]

## Conclusion

The framing of an event's narrative is influential in how communities construct their ongoing collective memory of an event. This chapter demonstrates how particular constructions of gender and imperial identity influenced creation of a collective memory within New Zealand about the *Marquette* sinking. Newspapers centered the experiences and deaths of New Zealand nurses in their narratives. How eyewitness testimonies were used and editorialized was important in what was included and what was forgotten. This event illustrates how intimately New Zealand identities were linked with a sense of imperial belonging and 'Britishness' during the Great War. The nurses' deaths were used to reinforce patriotic propaganda of an uncivilized enemy, drawing on gendered assumptions of non-violence against women. Connecting the *Marquette* nurses to the death of Edith Cavell reinforced this theme. Like Cavell, the nurses were constructed as exemplars of imperial womanhood, demonstrating self-sacrifice through service to others. The nurses were also portrayed as demonstrating bravery, endurance and stoic calm in the face of crisis, values essential to the manly code of British chivalry. Status as 'honorary men' was permissible as it emphasized the nurses' Britishness and strengthened their status as

71   Thomas Keneally, *The Daughters of Mars* (Sydney: Vintage, 2012), 147–76.

imperial heroines. Early instances of remembrance reflected this *Marquette* narrative. Local collective remembrance was tied to a national identity inseparable from its imperial context, thus reaffirming the nurses' exemplary roles. After a waning of interest in the middle of the twentieth century, the *Marquette* memory has more recently enjoyed a resurgence. The *Marquette* narrative has also been reshaped to fit new social discourses about gender and national identity. The representation of the *Marquette* nurses as national heroines based on their professionalism has become a way to include women in the modern Anzac narratives of the Great War.

GUY HANSEN

# Museums and the Great War: A Curator's Perspective on the History of Anzac

## Introduction

From an international perspective, it is sometimes difficult to understand the centrality of Anzac Day to Australian identity. Why would a failed military campaign fought far from Australian shores occupy such an important place in Australia's historical consciousness? In comparison, the establishment of the colony of New South Wales on 26 January 1788, now known as Australia Day, leaves many Australians underwhelmed. Similarly, the proclamation of Australia as a nation on 1 January 1901 left barely a ripple on Australia's collective memory. Anzac Day, however, continues to demonstrate its capacity to provide a shared sense of history for the nation. While many professional historians are sceptical about the mythology surrounding the Anzac legend, the power of Anzac continues to move Australians. To understand the way Anzac has come to be at the heart of Australian history one needs to examine how the history of the Gallipoli campaign is celebrated and retold in Australian popular culture. It is my contention that museums, and particularly the Australian War Memorial (AWM), are an important part of reinforcing and transmitting the Anzac myth to new generations of Australians.

The landings at Gallipoli by the Australian and New Zealand Army Corps (ANZAC) on 25 April 1915 are one of the most significant events in Australia's popular historical consciousness. In a nation with a relatively short history, the Gallipoli campaign is undoubtedly Australia's pre-eminent foundation myth. Within this myth is the heroic performance of Australian soldiers, popularly known as Anzacs (based on the acronym for

Australian and New Zealand Army Corps), which gains Australia a place at the table of nations. While some historians have attempted to deconstruct this myth, many Australians embrace the Anzac story as a central pillar of Australian identity.

How is this meme of the noble Anzac transmitted and reinforced within Australian culture? Rather than reading monographs carefully crafted by professional historians, it is far more likely Australians will encounter the history of Anzac through fictional accounts found in popular literature and film, listening to family stories and visiting war memorials and museums. As Ashton and Hamilton have demonstrated, these are the resources Australians use to construct their sense of the meaning of Anzac.[1] When seen in this light, popular narratives about the history of the Anzac legend are best understood as a set of cultural practices rather than as a type of verifiable history. In this chapter I will focus on the key role played by museums in validating the history of Anzac. This is most evident in the AWM which, in many ways, is a secular temple dedicated to the Anzac myth. As a counterpoint to this I will also discuss the *Spirit of the Digger* exhibit produced for the opening of the National Museum of Australia (NMA) in 2001.

## The Australian War Memorial

Australian military history is well represented in museums across the country. Almost every local history museum includes displays of military memorabilia. The defence forces also feature strongly in maritime and air museums. However the single most important museum exploring the history of Australia's involvement in war is the AWM. Located in Canberra, Australia's capital city, the AWM serves the dual purposes of

---

1    Paul Ashton and Paula Hamilton, *History at the Crossroads: Australians and the Past* (Sydney: Halstead Press, 2010).

military memorial and history museum. Visited by close to a million people each year, the Memorial provides a site for reflection and commemoration. When visitors arrive at the AWM they are left in no doubt of the national significance of the site. From the forecourt of the building you look down Anzac Parade, a major ceremonial avenue lined with impressive monuments marking major military conflicts. The view extends across Lake Burley Griffin to the national Parliament. This powerful visual axis gives you a sense that you are literally standing in the heart of the nation.

The AWM's two storey grey stone clad building is set into the lightly forested slopes of Mount Ainslie. From a distance it looks like a Byzantine temple or fort. The building's floor plan is based on a cross with a central commemorative area consisting of a domed chapel and walled courtyard. At the centre of the chapel is the Tomb of the Unknown Soldier. The four walls of the chapel feature mosaics depicting a soldier, sailor, servicewoman and airman. At the centre of the courtyard is a memorial pool in which burns an eternal flame. On each side of the courtyard are cloisters housing a roll of honour on which the names of 102,000 Australian servicemen and women who died in conflict are recorded in bronze.

In the wings of the AWM adjoining the central ceremonial area are a number of exhibitions that explore Australia's military history. In the entrance hall of the museum the centrality of Gallipoli campaign in Australian military history is reflected in the display of a landing boat used on 25 April 1915 riddled with bullet holes. From here the visitor moves through a series of major galleries exploring the First World War, the Second World War, the Korean War and the Vietnam War. The exhibits include uniforms, weapons, equipment and memorabilia brought back by returned serviceman. There are examples of artworks completed by Australia's official war artists as well as extensive photographic and audio-visual resources. At the rear of the AWM is the recently completed Anzac Hall featuring state-of-the-art multimedia displays. Powerful objects combined with dramatic stories are used throughout to illustrate the accomplishments of Australia's defence forces.

The overall effect of AWM exhibition galleries, particularly when combined with the building's central ceremonial courtyard and chapel, is to provide a sombre celebration of Australian military endeavour. There is a strong sense of a sacrifice and courage. The exhibitions, for the most part, avoid explicit or graphic depictions of the death and destruction that are inevitably linked to armed conflicts. Australia is presented as acting in good faith and responding to the aggression of others, whether it be the central powers of the First World War, the axis powers in the Second World War, or expansionary communism in Korea and Vietnam. Controversial topics are for the most part avoided leaving the visitor with an uncritical account of Australia's involvement in war. In terms of the type of history presented it would be best described as strongly patriotic.

As a curator and historian I have always been very aware of the powerful nature of the AWM. As a child I visited the Memorial on a number of occasions. In the chapel I would contemplate the heroic figures depicted in the ceramics and stained-glass windows. In the cloisters of the courtyard I would look for the names of relatives killed in the Second World War. In the exhibition halls I would stand transfixed in front of the battle dioramas and be amazed by the incredible collection of military technology. As I reflect on these early visits to the AWM I believe they helped encourage within me a life-long interest in history. Later, as I came to work in museums, I became much more aware of the tension between the AWM's dual role as a memorial and history museum. The question I returned to again and again was what type of history was the AWM presenting? Would it be possible, I wondered, to present a more critical account of Australia's involvement in war?

## Spirit of the Digger

In the late 1990s I was given the opportunity to explore how else a museum might present the history of Anzac. By this time I was a senior curator at the National Museum of Australia. The NMA was created by an Act of the Australian Parliament in 1980 with a strong mandate to explore Australia's indigenous, environmental and social history. Developed in the late 1990s, the museum was strongly influenced by the critique of traditional museums mounted in the writings of the new museology. The opening of the NMA in 2001 was the centrepiece of celebrations marking the centenary of the federation of Australia.

The *Nation: Symbols of Australia* exhibition, for which I was lead curator, was one of the opening suite of exhibitions at the NMA.[2] This exhibition sought to create a popular and accessible introduction to Australian history by exploring Australia's past through the lens of national symbols. Historic flags, various iterations of the coat of arms, ephemera associated with Anzac Day, and examples of Australian design provided the material culture for the exhibition. Australian language, suburban lifestyle and indigenous imagery provided further material for the NMA to explore. Each object, or set of objects, on display were selected either because of their official status as symbols of Australia or because they had gained wide popular acceptance as being quintessentially 'Australian'. Tracing the history of the development of these symbols, illustrated with examples drawn from different periods and places, provided a window on the evolution of Australian national identity. Historicizing these symbols, or sets of cultural practices, provided a range of views or voices about national identity, varying according to time and place. This allowed the exhibition to explore the question of what it means to be Australian without making a totalizing or triumphalist statement about national identity. This approach was in part inspired by Benedict Anderson's concept of nation as an 'imagined community' in which different groups and individuals are bound together within a nation. As he describes it, 'the members of even the smallest nation will never know most of their fellow members, meet them or even hear of them, yet in the minds of each lives the image of their communion.'[3]

---

2    The curatorial team for the *Nation* gallery was Guy Hansen (lead curator), Kirsten Wehner, Victoria Haskins, Libby Stewart, Nicole Livermore and Catherine Reade. Libby Stewart completed the initial research on the *Spirit of the Digger* display. Ben Wellings coordinated the development of the *Anzac Pilgrims* display that was added after the exhibition opened.

3    Benedict Anderson, *Imagined Communities: Reflections on the origin and spread of nationalism* (London: Verso, 1992), 9.

Within this framework of viewing Australian history through the symbolic vocabulary of nation, Anzac was judged the most important of all national symbols. As such, the *Spirit of the Digger* display took pride of place in the centre of the gallery. It consisted of a recreated war memorial surmounted with an iconic statue of an Australian soldier, or 'digger' (a colloquial term adopted for Australian soldiers during the First World War). Showcases built into the base of this replica memorial housed objects and text discussing the history of Anzac and the development of the digger archetype in Australian culture. An audio-visual loop showed footage of Anzac Day ceremonies from the 1920s to the present. The curatorial intent was to trace the history of the development of Anzac Day and interpret it as a symbol and social ritual. While popular with the visiting public, *Spirit of the Digger* was criticized by some commentators as being disrespectful and damaging to one of Australia's foundation myths. Exploring the response to the *Spirit of the Digger* exhibit, both popular and critical, provides an excellent case study of how the Anzac myth operates within contemporary Australian society. It also provides a cautionary tale for historians interested in deconstructing the history of Anzac.

The *Spirit of the Digger* display was inspired, in part, by Ken Inglis's book *Sacred Places: War Memorials in the Australian Landscape*.[4] As Inglis demonstrated, war memorials are ubiquitous in cities and towns around Australia. Whether they are the major monumental memorials of the state capitals or the more modest obelisks or figurative sculptures found in country towns, these memorials are literally a concrete reminder of Australia's participation in the Great War and other conflicts. Their ubiquitous and monumental nature helps reinforce popular myths of the bravery of the Australian soldier and the centrality of the digger archetype in the nation's identity. These sites of popular memory also provide 'sacred places' where the rituals of Anzac Day can be enacted each year.

*Spirit of the Digger* set out to use the recreated environment of a war memorial to provide a theatrical setting to deconstruct the history of

4   Ken Inglis, *Sacred Places: War Memorials in the Australian Landscape* (Melbourne: Melbourne University Press, 2008).

Anzac. To this end, a cast was made of the statue of a soldier featured on the Braidwood War Memorial. This is a modest memorial located on the main street of Braidwood, New South Wales, and is a classic example of the type of memorials found in country towns across Australia. Like many memorials of its type, it features an Australian soldier standing with his rifle at his side. The figure's distinctive slouch hat and .303 rifle make it an unmistakable representation of an Australian digger.

The replica of the Braidwood memorial dominated the main visual axis of the *Nation* gallery. When viewed from the ground floor entrance, the figure of the digger, which surmounted the memorial, was framed by a Federation Arch. This recreated arch referenced the many temporary triumphal arches built in cities around Australia in 1901 to celebrate the Federation of the Australian colonies. The juxtaposition of the arch and the war memorial provided a visual metaphor for the development of the Australian nation. Implicit in this positioning was the concept that, while the political union of Australia occurred in 1901, it was not until the Great War that Australia truly emerged as a nation.

It was not the display's intention, however, to reiterate the myth that the landings at Gallipoli allowed the Australian nation to prove itself on the field of battle. Rather the objective was to reveal the contingent and changing nature of the Anzac legend.[5] To achieve this goal the display explored Anzac from four different perspectives. These dealt with the history of the digger archetype reflected in media coverage of the war; the history of the development of the rituals surrounding Anzac Day; the personal stories of soldiers who died in war; and finally the changing popularity of Anzac Day over time. Each of these components challenged the notion of Anzac as immutable monolith, demonstrating instead that the Anzac tradition has evolved and changed over time.

---

5    There is an extensive literature on the evolution of Anzac Day and the Anzac myth. For example see Joy Damousi, *The labour of loss: Mourning, memory, and wartime bereavement in Australia* (Cambridge: Cambridge University Press, 1999); Jane Ross, *The myth of the digger: The Australian soldier in two World Wars* (Sydney: Hale & Iremonger, 1985); Marilyn Lake and Henry Reynolds, eds, *What's Wrong with Anzac?: The militarisation of Australian History* (Sydney: New South, 2010).

In the showcase directly below the replica memorial visitors could see a facsimile of Ellis Ashmead-Bartlett's newspaper report on the Gallipoli landing on 8 May 1915. It was in this report that Ashmead-Bartlett famously described Australians as a 'race of athletes' proclaiming that 'they had been used for the first time and had not been found wanting.'[6] Ashmead-Bartlett's glowing praise for the Anzacs, and the pride with which it was received in Australia, helped establish the concept of the Gallipoli landings as some form of blood sacrifice confirming Australia's status as a nation. Also on display was copy of Charles Bean's *Dreadnought of the Darling*, first published in 1911, in which Bean had begun constructing his archetype of the self-sufficient Australian male suffused with a strong belief in mateship. This template was to prove invaluable for Bean in his role as an official war journalist and later historian. In his writings on the war Bean was quick to identify the same qualities he had found in the Australian bushman within the soldiers of the First Australian Imperial Force (AIF). This archetype of the Australian soldier as a resourceful larrikin was further reinforced in *The Anzac Book*, also featured in the exhibit. Compiled by Bean in late 1915, this book included poems and stories by soldiers who had served at Gallipoli. Published in Australia in 1916 it quickly became a best seller and helped establish the term 'Anzac' as the common usage word for an Australian soldier.

In addition to exploring the origins of the Anzac archetype, as promulgated by Bean and Ashmead-Bartlett, the exhibition also explored the history of Anzac Day itself. Commemoration ceremonies began on 25 April 1916, the first anniversary of the landings. These events were organized both by serving military units overseas and by government and community groups at home in Australia. Over time, these events changed in format and function with the emphasis gradually shifting from remembrance and grief to a celebration of the citizen soldier. Using objects such as programmes and unit banners, the aim of the exhibit was to show that the present day rituals of the dawn service and military parade have evolved over time.

---

6    Ellis Ashmead-Bartlett, 'Australians at Dardanelles: Thrilling Deeds of Heroism' *Argus* (8 May 1915), 19.

Inspired in part by the work of Joy Damousi, the *Spirit of the Digger* display also included a number of personal stories focussed on the grief and loss associated with the death of a brother, son or husband in war.[7] Many families honoured their war dead through the display of medals and photographs in a prominent position in their homes. Examples of these domestic shrines were reproduced in the exhibition. These included official memorial scrolls and plaques, commonly known as a 'dead men's pennies', that had been issued by the Australian government to the next of kin of soldiers, sailors and nurses who died while serving in the AIF. Letters written by commanding officers of deceased soldiers to their loved ones were also reproduced. The objective in providing these individual stories was to remind visitors that the original function of war memorials was to commemorate the men and women who had died in war. Rather than focus on the abstracted notion of the Anzac as an Australian archetype, as represented in the replica digger statue, these personal stories spoke directly to the individual experience of soldiers who had died and the loss felt by their grieving families.

The final component of the *Spirit of the Digger* exhibition explored how the popularity of Anzac Day has waxed and waned. During the war, and in the immediate years that followed, Anzac Day provided an important occasion to commemorate and grieve for those who had died. In the immediate aftermath of the Great War there was widespread participation of war widows in Anzac day ceremonies and marches. By the 1930s, however, the role of women had shifted from active participant to observer.[8] The Second World War provided an impetus to expand the day to recognize the sacrifice of a new generation of Australian soldiers. Similarly, the Korean War and the Vietnam War, and each subsequent conflict, provided further recruits to participate in the annual Anzac parade. The exhibition also documented the resurgence of Anzac Day in the 1990s with the growing popularity of the Anzac Day ceremony at Gallipoli. A later addition to the exhibition, in part informed by the work of Bruce Scates, explored the growing phenomenon

7    Damousi, *The labour of loss*, 59.
8    Ibid., 35.

of Anzac pilgrims, particularly the increasing number of young Australians
who travel to Turkey to visit the landing site at Gallipoli.[9]

The exhibit also acknowledged the existence of critical voices to the
Anzac tradition. Alan Seymour's play *The One Day of the Year*, published
in 1962, which challenged the continued relevance of Anzac Day and
highlighted the drunken behaviour of ex-serviceman at Anzac Day celebrations, was featured. Also on show was a poster advertising an Anzac
Day march organized by protest group Woman Against Rape (WAR) in
the early 1980s. It was not uncommon in this period for women's groups
to target Anzac Day to draw attention to the issue of violence committed
against women during times of war. An Indigenous perspective on the
Anzac legend was presented in the form of a poem by Cecil Fisher entitled
'Black Anzac'. Fischer, who served in the Korean War, believed that the
Anzac legend did not recognize the contribution of aboriginal servicemen,
declaring that black soldiers 'never march on Anzac Day'.[10]

## The 'history wars' at the National Museum of Australia

At the same time that the NMA was developing its opening suite of exhibitions, a major debate was unfolding in the broader community about
Australian history. Now referred to as the 'history wars', this period saw
a number of commentators and politicians mount a concerted attack on
Australian historiography. The point of contention was that Australian
historians were overly negative about the past. Critics claimed that the
strong focus on violence on the frontier was unbalanced. For example in
1996 Prime Minister John Howard famously criticized historians for their

---

9    Bruce Scates, *Return to Gallipoli: Walking in the Battlefields of the Great War*
     (Cambridge: Cambridge University Press, 2006).
10   'Black Anzac' by Cecil Fisher reproduced from <http://www.abc.net.au/radiona-
     tional/programs/awaye/we-will-remember-them/3671082#transcript> accessed 17
     March 2014.

'black armband' view of Australian history. Australia's past, he argued, should be understood in terms of 'heroic achievement'. Australians, 'have much more as a nation of which we can be proud than of which we should be ashamed'. He pointed to Australia's economic development, the transition to a successful modern democracy, the rule of law, mateship, innovation and common sense as exemplifying the success of the Australian nation. While acknowledging that history should not be a source 'of smug delusions or comfortable superiority', nor 'should it be a basis for obsessive and consuming national guilt and shame'. He concluded that we 'need to recognise that our history is also the story of a great Australian achievement in which we can, and should, take great pride'.[11]

As an historian and curator working in a public institution I was very much aware of this debate. I did not realize, however, that the National Museum would become the next battlefront in the history wars. When the NMA opened to the public in March 2001, newspaper columnist Miranda Devine fired off an early salvo with a column entitled 'A nation trivialised'. Devine described the underlying message of the museum as 'one of sneering ridicule for white Australia. It is as if non-Aboriginal culture is a joke, all upside down Hills Hoists and tongue-in-cheek Victa lawn mowers'. After decrying what she saw as the lack of celebration and pride in the exhibits, Devine concluded, 'the whole museum is a lie. To find the national identity you'd be better off going to the porn museum which also opened yesterday, just around the corner'.[12] The tone and tenor of Devine's article was picked up by talkback radio host Alan Jones. On his high-rating morning programme on Sydney radio station 2UE, Jones quoted Devine's article at length saying that the museum's message was disgraceful.[13] Columnist Piers Akerman, writing in the tabloid *Sunday Telegraph*, also criticized the museum. Perceiving an inherent bias, he described the displays as paying 'more than a nod to this politically correct position'.[14]

11   1996 Sir Robert Menzies Lecture by John Howard, <http://pmtranscripts.dpmc. gov.au/browse.php?did=10171> accessed 5 February 2014.

12   Miranda Devine, 'A nation trivialised', *Daily Telegraph* (12 March 2001), 3.

13   Alan Jones, 2UE morning programme, 12 March 2001.

14   Piers Akerman, 'New museum, same old trivia', *Sunday Telegraph* (11 March 2001), 91.

For some commentators it was specifically the *Nation* exhibition's deconstruction of the history of Anzac that grated. Writing some years later, Rob Foot summarized what many conservatives saw as a lack of respect for Australian values in the exhibition. For him the digger archetype had been:

> traduced as merely an imagined icon, created by newspapers and magazines, having no reality external to what was imputed or imagined by the powers that be. 'A real character', ran the mocking commentary, having established that he had never been any such thing.[15]

Foot's critique ran deeper than challenging the historical veracity of the exhibition. Rather he took offence at what he saw as an attempt to undermine the myth of Anzac.

The condemnation that the National Museum received was balanced by considerable positive media coverage. Indeed, the vast majority of reviews and news stories celebrated the museum's opening and welcomed its contribution to Australia's cultural landscape.[16] Visitor reaction to the museum, as gauged by an ongoing survey programme, found that more than ninety per cent of visitors were highly satisfied with their visit.[17] Attendance numbers in the opening year of the museum also suggested that the museum was a success. By the time the first birthday cake was wheeled in, more than 900,000 people had visited the NMA.[18]

Positive media coverage and visitor support, however, was not enough to silence conservative critics of the museum. Within one month of the museum opening in 2001, the Museum's governing council instituted a review of its exhibitions and public programmes. The review was established under the auspices of the Department of Communications, Information,

15  Rob Foot, 'Rehabilitating Australia's National Museum' *Quadrant* Lii/10 (October 2008) <http://www.quadrant.org.au/magazine/issue/2008/10> accessed 29 January 2013.
16  Dawn Casey, National Press Club speech, 13 March 2002.
17  Dawn Casey, 'Submission by the National Museum of Australia to the National Museum of Australia Review of Exhibitions and Public Programmes', National Museum of Australia, 2003.
18  National Museum of Australia Annual Report 2001–2, iv.

Technology and the Arts. This review had a broad remit to examine the museum's exhibitions and public programmes and establish 'whether the government's vision in approving funding for the development of the museum has been realised'.[19]

The review panel's report was released on 14 July 2003 and was simply titled *Review of the National Museum of Australia* (henceforth abbreviated to *Review*). While not finding any evidence of systematic bias within the NMA, the *Review* was highly critical of some of the museum's exhibitions. This critique was built on the assumption that the primary objective of the museum should be to present the 'Australian story'.[20] The use of the singular 'story', rather than plural 'stories' was deliberate choice by the *Review*'s authors. By this they meant a coherent story of achievement that charts the development of the nation from settlement to the present day. Under this model of heroic achievement the *Nation* gallery was always going to be problematic. The *Review* described the exhibition as suffering from a 'systematic weakness'. It concluded that *Nation* 'is not good at generating compelling narratives'.[21] It recommended that the *Nation* exhibition be 'reworked to provide compelling narratives, giving priority to primary national themes. It needs to generate a broader historical sense of how individual stories fit into the evolution of nation. It needs to draw out the objects exhibited by depicting their context'.[22] This finding was accepted by the NMA's council and the museum received funding from the Howard Government for redevelopment of the exhibition space. A new exhibition entitled *Landmarks* opened in 2011.

Embedded within the *Review*'s rejection of the *Nation* exhibition was the idea that a consensus view of national identity should take priority over a pluralist or contingent model of identity:

> The Panel is inclined to read more consensus than plurality at the core of the national collective conscience. The concept of nations as 'imagined communities', which is

19   'Review of the National Museum of Australia', 74.
20   Ibid., 10.
21   Ibid., 27.
22   Ibid., 32.

drawn from Benedict Anderson's book of that title, implies that national character is a sort of fictitious construct, fluid and subject to rapid change, and therefore ephemeral. This view underestimates the deeper continuities in culture – for instance, the degree to which the portrait of the courageous warrior hero developed in Homer's *Iliad* three millennia ago has shaped later images and stories, including, in the 20th century, both the Australian Anzac legend and the American Western film genre.[23]

This quote is interesting for its misreading of Anderson. Rather than seeing national character as 'fictitious', Anderson argues that it exists as a historical construct that evolves over time. It is 'imagined' in that it is actively shared across a community even though the members of that community never know most of their fellow members. It is partial and changing in that different members bring different perspectives to the nature of collective identity. The power of nation as a concept derives from the way disparate elements can actively identify with a community of shared interest. For Anderson, a sense of nation is invented but not fabricated. In contrast to Anderson's understanding, the *Review* asserted that there is a unitary Australian national identity.

Another interesting aspect of the *Review*'s response is the direct line drawn between the *Iliad* and Anzac. Here the *Review* is expressing a desire to place the history of Australia firmly within the lineage of western civilization. It wants to celebrate the trope of the heroic warrior – the 'Anzac' – as the source of identity in Australian society. The *Review* states that this is best exemplified in the Australian War Memorial that has, 'taken our nation's most potent story, and, over more than half a century, developed its projections in a thoroughly effective manner. This has been a relatively straightforward task, given the single and narrow focus on war, and the intellectual direction provided by C. E. W. Bean's canonical history of the Anzac tradition, initiated at Gallipoli'.[24] Furthermore the *Review* concluded, 'The Australian War Memorial gains gravitas through recalling tragedy – its task is much easier here, in that the tragedy is supportive of national mythology, not at odds with it'.[25]

23    Ibid., 8.
24    Ibid., 7.
25    Ibid., 10.

At the heart of the *Review*'s approach to national history is a strong belief that institutions such as the NMA have an important role in promoting social cohesion. In an article written in defence of the *Review*, John Carroll, one of the Review's main authors, declared, 'No human society can hold together and function without what Emile Durkheim called a "collective conscience" – a strong morally charged view of the world shared by its members'.[26] For Carroll the role of institutions such as the NMA was, and is, to reinforce this 'collective conscience' by providing a positive unitary narrative of Australian history. Within this framework the Anzac legend is a positive moral influence for Australian identity, and should be celebrated rather than deconstructed.

With the benefit of hindsight I can see that the pluralist approach employed in the development of the *Nation* gallery was always on a collision course with the Howard Government's more traditional view of history. While I was aware that *Nation* would not meet the expectations of those seeking a chronological account of Australian achievement, I was confident that the exhibition would appeal to the general public. By the time the museum opened it seemed that the major ideological battles had been fought and that there was acceptance of a plural and contingent view of Australian history. As we have, seen this was not the case. The opening triggered a new phase in the history wars. Previous battles in this war included debates over the bicentenary, political correctness, contact history, reconciliation and the report on the removal of indigenous children by welfare authorities. The NMA was ideal territory for these arguments to be rehearsed once again.

For many conservative commentators, an authoritative and celebratory account of Australian history is a central tenant in their manifesto. The *Nation* exhibition, with its multi-voiced investigation of national identity and deconstruction of Anzac, was never going to be acceptable. The exhibition's appeal to the general public was in a sense irrelevant. The success or failure of the museum was not judged in terms of audience

26  John Carroll, 'A response to Bain Attwood's "Whose Dreaming?"', *History Australia* 1/2 (2004), 293.

response, but rather in terms of how it complemented the larger project of affirming the 'Australian story' – the heroic story of achievement that Prime Minister John Howard had articulated in 1996. For Howard it was important that Australians be 'comfortable and relaxed' with their past. A deconstruction of the history of the digger and the Anzac legend did not fit well with this project.


## Conclusion


As Marilyn Lake and Henry Reynolds have argued, Anzac Day can appear a monolithic institution that wields a disproportionate influence on Australian identity.[27] While Lake and Reynolds, and many other historians and commentators, rail against the militarization of Australian history, the myth of Anzac remains largely resistant to attempts to displace it from the centre of Australia's historical consciousness. In the *Spirit of the Digger* display I sought to tell the story of how Anzac Day had evolved and changed over the twentieth century; to demonstrate how it, and the rituals which surround it, have met different social needs at different times. The *Review*'s response to this display, and the *Nation* gallery in which it was located, highlighted the centrality of the Anzac legend in Australian history. While the *Review* in no way challenged the historical veracity of the display, there was a sense in which the Museum was found to have stepped over a boundary by attempting to historicize the Anzac legend. There is little evidence to suggest that a more sophisticated understanding of the history of Anzac would be accepted by the Australian public any time soon. Indeed, with the centenary of the Anzac landings due to be celebrated in 2015, there is every likelihood that the myth will continue to grow. Like a marble monument, Anzac stands in the centre of popular narratives of Australian history impervious to the debate that surrounds it.

27    Lake and Reynolds, *What's Wrong with Anzac?*

CHRISTINE CADOT

# Wars Afterwards: The Repression of the Great War in European Collective Memory

## Introduction

The past two decades have seen an increasing number of exhibitions, memorials and museums displaying Europe's history as a result of initiatives from both European institutions and member-states. The so-called 'Europeanization of memories' is often highly contested, as it goes well beyond the already contentious notion of national memories.[1] Because Great War landscapes and landmarks often escape from a narrative template that presents them as places of national triumph or heroic victories over foreign forces, they have sometimes been portrayed as 'European'. In fact, there is a gap between the practices of the custodians of First World War sites of remembrance (curators, and national or local institutions) and the academic literature, which has often developed a critical distance from the idea of a European collective memory. As such, the existence of a shared memory, in the name of the 'idea of Europe', is, like its national counterparts, also a historical product and one with different meanings in different periods, places and amongst professional networks.[2] Most of

---

1    Małgorzata Pakier and Bo Stråth, *A European Memory? Contested Histories and Politics of Remembrance* (New York: Berghahn Books, 2010); Jerzy Jedlicki, 'East-European Historical Bequest en Route to an Integrated Europe', in Klaus Eder and Willfried Spohn, eds, *Collective Memory and European Identity: The Effects of Integration and Enlargement* (Aldershot: Ashgate, 2005), 37–48.
2    Tony Judt, *Postwar. A History of Europe since 1945* (London: William Heinemann, 2005).

the commemorative projects in Western Europe promote an awareness of a European identity that begins after the Second World War, therefore silencing the First in the creation of a collective European memory. This view of the European past, privileging Western European histories, has recently been questioned by Members of the European Parliament (MEPs) and other public figures from the new member-states. Despite often being criticized as feeding a 'saturated memory', Second World War landmarks, including Holocaust *lieux de mémoires*, are often preferred as fields of research by academics working on the construction of collective memory in contemporary Europe.[3]

In this chapter, I will first focus on the historiographical processes that are at stake when one constructs a history of European integration that includes the Great War. I will also examine the extent to which there has been a 'Europeanization' of First World War *lieux de mémoire*. Secondly, this inquiry leads me to discuss the role given to museums and exhibitions to engage in such a process, examining how recent examples in European museums question the standard timeline of European integration where new European public spaces and historical memories can be encouraged and promoted.

Overall, I conclude that the Great War has been largely silenced in narratives of European integration. It has been downgraded to a pre-figuration of a general crisis of the European spirit, an episode in EU pre-history. In this way the Second World War can be presented as a starting point, rather than an interruption, in the rational and enlightened process of constructing Europe. Memory in the service of European integration is, in this way, always an 'after war' story and a narrative in which the Great War sits uneasily.

---

3    Régine Robin-Maire, *La mémoire saturée* (Paris: Stock, 2003).

# Questioning the Europeanization of Great War memories and memorials

The cultural politics enunciated by Roland Recht for the Royal Museum of Berlin in 1830 was an occasion to describe the difficulty that every history museum in Europe had been facing since their inception: how to display the voice of the universal. Museums are excellent political laboratories. Discourses about them are usually public. Historically, they helped inaugurate the concept of public space, as Le Louvre in France during the French Revolution, in allowing art works and historical artefacts to be restored and displayed for the public.[4] Museums are also spaces where visitors are encouraged to make public and critical use of their reason, but in history museums or memorials, such reasoning needs to be created from memories and narratives of traumatic and painful experiences. As such, they are very often public places of fragmentation and not just spaces that welcome universal patrimonial heritages.

Critical scholarship has shown that there is a tendency in Europe to observe strategies of historicization of conflicting pasts from actors who want to create political consensus. These strategies are either erasing traces of a criminal past or reopening forgotten histories with an attempt to create this consensus by way of symbolic recognition.[5] Museums' scientific boards as well as curators of exhibitions on the construction of the European Union (EU) have often claimed to offer new epistemological frameworks that escaped the classical forms of museums. The difficulty remains, however, that such ambitious realizations could distance themselves easily from frameworks that accompanied of the building of the nation. As Jean-Louis Déotte argued, history museums have heavy responsibilities 'as they will have to reopen files that poisoned European history'.[6]

---

4   Jürgen Habermas, *The Structural Transformation of the Public Sphere. An Inquiry into a Category of Bourgeois Society* (Cambridge: MIT Press, 1989).

5   Georges Mink and Laure Neumayer, eds, *L'Europe et ses passés douloureux* (Paris: La Découverte, 2007).

6   Jean-Louis Déotte, *Oubliez! L'Europe, les ruines, le musée* (Paris: La Découverte, 1994).

Initial studies of the Great War's impact on collective memories in
Europe were often addressed within the framework of the nation-state,
such as Paul Fussell's seminal book, *The Great War and Modern Memory*,
which described the impact of the experiences of trench warfare on four
British authors who survived the conflict.[7] From the 1970s however critics denounced the fact that at a time of intensifying European integration
museums and memorials were still being constructed as the last pristine
islands of untouched national pride or mourning.[8] We might expect therefore, following Pierre Nora's definition of *lieux de mémoire*, to identify
some *lieux d'Europe* that could be defined as peculiarities of the land and
landscape that are significant at the European level. These peculiarities,
split into what Krysztof Pomian defines as 'real topography' and 'mental
topography', are unequally distributed on European soil: most of them are
located in Western Europe.[9] Among these potentially European *lieux de
mémoire*, battlefields and war memorials are most likely to be shared by
European nation-states formerly engaged in armed conflict. Accordingly
it should be noted that commemorations of battles, presented as shared
history, are not a post-1945 phenomenon. For example, French and German
veterans (the latter bearing the Swastika flag) celebrated their pacific reconciliation through a candle-lit funerary vigil and remembrance ceremony
that took place in July 1936 in the Douaumont Ossuary, which contained
the bones of hundreds of unidentified soldiers killed at Verdun. But very
little has been said, in recent textbooks or museums, about that *veillée* as
a European or transnational *lieu de mémoire*.

In France, the First World War has been associated for a very long time
with Verdun, and the battle of 1916 has been part of a national mythology
that celebrates resistance against an invading army. This collective memory
has been recalled every Armistice Day, 11 November. For almost a century,

7    Paul Fussell, *The Great War and Modern Memory* (Oxford: Oxford University Press,
     2000 [1974]).
8    Paula Young Lee, 'In the name of the Museum', *Museum Anthropology* 20/2 (1997), 9.
9    Krzysztof Pomian, 'Europe: Topographie réelle et topographies mentales', in Stella
     Ghervas and François Rosset, eds, *Lieux d'Europe. Mythes et Limites* (Paris: Ed. de
     la Maison des Sciences de l'Homme, 2008), 32.

military parades to war memorials were organized in every village, town and city, including to the Tomb of the Unknown Soldier in Paris. French presidents have paid tribute at that site to the archetypical soldier of Verdun, the *poilu*, since 1920. For the last ten years however, new policies and political projects have shaped the Great War's landmarks making them increasingly 'globalized' and less 'state-centric'. The French Parliament approved Nicolas Sarkozy's plan to change the meaning of Armistice Day in 2012, after the last known French veteran of the Great War had died.[10] The 11th of November is now officially a day of homage to all soldiers who have died for France, including those recently killed in Afghanistan. This change has been applauded as a way of renewing the celebration of Franco-German friendship but it was also a way of implementing Sarkozy's European politics, recalling the well-known image of François Mitterrand and Helmut Kohl holding hands in a gesture of reconciliation at Verdun in 1984.

Commemorations of a shared past between former protagonists usually avoid aggressive narratives and discourses of exclusion. The comparison between the French attempt to downplay 8 May as a commemoration of victory at the end of the Second World War and the alteration of the commemoration of the Armistice in 2012 as a commemoration unique to the Great War is highly significant when viewed within an official narrative of European integration. On 7 May 1975, French president Valéry Giscard d'Estaing decided to abandon the commemoration of the end of the 1945 conflict. He sent a letter to the members of the European Council, asking that they 'turn our thoughts to what unites and bounds us', proposing to replace the anniversary of victory in Europe on 8 May with 'Europe Day', the anniversary of the Schuman Declaration of 1950, on 9 May.[11] The response was not positive. *Le Monde* published an article opposing the decision entitled '*Histoire au musée*'.[12] The same day, l'*Humanité* described the deci-

---

10  The last French First World War veteran died in March 2008. The last known Great War veteran was Florence Green a member of the Woman's Royal Air Force, who died in February 2012.

11  Serges Bernstein and Jean-François Sirinelli, eds, *Les années Giscard. Valéry Giscard d'Estaing et l'Europe, 1974–81* (Paris: Armand Colin, 2006).

12  Pierre Viansson-Ponté, 'L'histoire au musée', *Le Monde* (10 May 1975).

sion as an 'outrage to the memory of those who gave their lives'.[13] After his accession to the French Presidency, François Mitterrand restored 8 May as a French public holiday.[14]

As such, and even though 11 November is not a public holiday for any of the European institutions (nor for all the member-states of the European Union), several museums or memorials have recently been welcomed as 'Europeanized' *lieux*. Typically, museums and memorials of the First and Second World Wars were traditionally spaces of heroism where narratives regarding the dead were written according to the rules of the epidictic discourse.[15] The 'musée des engloutis', as Pierre Vidal-Naquet defines a museum or a memorial that does not forget the 'losers of history', is not the rule.[16] More recently, new memorials have been designed and celebrated as an escape from the model of the exclusive memory of the victor. Following this, one of the most famous Great War memorials in French territory, the *Historial de la Grande Guerre* in Péronne, has been described as a 'second generation war museum'.[17] As a battlefield landmark, the Somme region has often been regarded as a transnational space of mourning or as a globalized space of fighting.[18] For sociologists, the Somme region could be portrayed more accurately as French territory of British mourning.[19] Such observations can be extended to Ypres in Belgium or Gallipoli in Turkey, where the Sevres Treaty of 1923 organized the extra-territoriality of the memorial and its access roads. Most visitors to these sites are foreigners, coming from

---

13    Valéry Rosoux, 'Mémoire(s) européenne(s)? Des limites d'un passé asceptisé et figé' in Georges Mink and Laure Neumayer, eds, *L'Europe et ses passés douloureux* (Paris: La Découverte, 2007), 227.

14    Loi 23 Septembre 1981.

15    Déotte, *Oubliez!*, 1994.

16    Pierre Vidal-Naquet, *Les assassins de la mémoire* (Paris: Maspéro, 1981).

17    Sophie Wahnich and Mireille Gueissaz, eds, *Les musées d'histoire des guerres du XXe siècle, des lieux du politique?* (Paris: Kimé, 2001).

18    Historial de la Grande Guerre Exhibition Catalog, *1916, The Battle of the Somme: A World Arena* (Paris: Somogy éd. d'art, 2006).

19    Mireille Gueissaz, 'Français et Britanniques dans la Somme. Sur quelques manières de visiter les champs de bataille de la Somme hier et aujourd'hui', in Wahnich and Gueissaz, eds, *Les musées d'histoire*, 83–104.

Australia and New Zealand (Gallipoli) or the United Kingdom (Thiepval). Apart from school visits, there are very few visitors from France, Turkey or Belgium. This phenomenon also relies on national mythologies (but also sometimes on family stories), in which the First World War is constructed in some cases – such as in Australia or Canada – as a founding event, and where individual soldiers are remembered through national tales.[20] But Péronne is not Verdun, and French visitors to the *Historial* have usually no prior knowledge of the role of the Somme battles in the course of the Great War, unlike their British counterparts. Though the *Historial* consists of the juxtaposition of three narratives (French, British and German), German visitors remain negligible. For the last ten years, the Mémorial de Thiepval has been advertised as a meeting point for French and British memories. But at the time of the inauguration in 2004, the Duke of Kent hesitated to invite officials from the *Historial* to the ceremonies. These examples confirm that, far from being Europeanized, memories of wars are also wars of memories, where regional and national identities are constantly invoked when trying to build a transnational sense of place. There remains a substantial gap between the promoters of First World War landmarks and commemorations and the few studies of their audiences, pointing out the sometimes conflicting routines behind the official discourse.[21]

## Silencing the Great War in museums of European integration

The question of the EU's origin, whether it is put into words or artifacts, items or images, is inseparable from the representation of a prescribed norm of what Europe is today, or of what it should be tomorrow. The institution of the historical museum itself is used most of the time in order to initiate visitors to the historical logic that would allow them to visualize the

---

20  David W. Lloyd, *Battlefield Tourism, Pilgrimage and the Commemoration of the Great War in Britain, Australia and Canada, 1919–39* (Oxford: Berg, 1988).

21  See also Shanti Sumartojo's contribution to this volume.

enterprise of European unification throughout the display rooms. Beyond a legitimate desire to render exactly what occurred after the Second World War, the historian is confronted by a new imperative to create a public space of demonstration or exhibition. As such, the question of the patrimony that should be exhibited is a key point for most national authorities. In France, the Ministère de la Culture does not usually finance museum projects that do not exhibit artifacts as historical evidence. French museums are usually seen as an extension of textbooks, where the heavy tendency is to favour a linear history that avoids ruptures, discontinuities and heterogeneity. For scenographers, the First World War cannot appear as a 'Year Zero' in a history of European integration because the Second World War will then appear as a rupture in the construction of a rational peace process. It would become difficult to explain the irrationality of the Second World War in a museum space whose traditional role is to erase discontinuity. It would also become difficult to question the fact that the European Community has also been part of several projects, some of them elaborated during the Vichy regime.[22] Official historiographies of European integration are well connected to the conventional descriptions used by museums. Such displays present the end of the Second World War as a unique starting point for a narrative that avoids what could have been mapped or experienced before.

From the end of the nineteenth century until the end of the 1970s, the narrative structure suggested by museographers in most countries in Western Europe (the Imperial War Museum in London is an exception) was essentially a teleological vision that did not leave any room for the uncontrolled wandering of the visitor. This controlled progression towards the resolution of the enigma, what Tony Bennett calls the 'backtelling', is supposed to show the linearity of historical experience and progress.[23] A large body of literature now addresses this subject and has established museum studies as a specific field and an area that has become particularly important in historiography debates. Of course, it would be naïve

---

22    Antonin Cohen, *De Vichy à la Communauté Européenne* (Paris: PUF, 2012).
23    Tony Bennett, *The Birth of the Museums: History, Theory, Politics* (New York: Routledge, 1995).

to consider any museum as an institution of totalizing codification, as it would also reduce any history museum to an oppressive monolith. Nor do all history museums have coherent hidden agendas in actual practices. Nevertheless such tendencies have been observable in exhibitions at the *Musée de l'Europe* in Brussels or in more recent realizations, such as the *Parlementarium*, also in Brussels, which did not offer any attempt to forge non-linear communicative flows or engage with discontinuities.

The roots of European *lieux de mémoire* have long been associated with narratives of Franco-German reconciliation. Though such reconciliation could have been celebrated as a first step toward the building of a European collective history starting in November 1918, it suffered from the subsequent celebration of the end of the Second World War. Historiographical trends emphasize the Second World War as the event that spurred European integration and hence European collective history is usually dated from this moment. These trends have been shaped by the fact that research on the topic usually considers Europe as a geographical and political entity with a structure and foundations that need to be excavated and explained. Europe is often considered as a positive and existing reality with characteristics that have been waiting too long to be unveiled. Historiographical studies on European integration are squeezed between the illusion of a polity created from a *tabula rasa* with no historical foundations or comparisons and obsessive rumination on a traumatic past, dominated by murderous national passions.[24] At the same time, the boom of 'memory studies' in Europe has seen some academics denounce the difficult relationship between societies and their pasts, and the perils of a saturated memory: 'a memory that has been put to use, revised to fit the needs of the moment, and which may be just one of the perverted forms of oblivion.'[25]

For more than a decade now, institutions have been calling for new sets of narratives and new ways of displaying historical discourses on Europe

24    Henry Rousso, 'Das Dilemna eines europäischen Gedächtnisses', *Zeithistorische Forschungen /Studies in Contemporary History*, Online – Ausgabe 1 (2004), H. 3 <http://www.ihtp.cnrs.fr/pdf/HR-memeurop.pdf> accessed 19 February 2014.
25    Robin-Maire, *La mémoire saturée*, 29.

through research programmes financed by European institutions or national grants.[26] Museums and libraries are particularly targeted as possible tools that might forge a new European sense of belonging, which could and should be respectful of the historical particularities of new member-states. But very few voices have suggested that a normative point of departure could be that dark aspects of Europe's past are also plainly related to a history of European integration. Some publications have addressed the role and production of professional writers working as historians for the European Commission and the heavy tendency to use memory as a political resource.[27] As Foret and Caligaro argue 'European institutions play a part in developing historical sites of national importance into "European sites of memory".'[28]

However, the promotion of a specific 'European memory' is not always conducted 'from inside' and the notion of European integration as a progressive historical process is also part of a grand narrative that is sometimes seen as autonomous from national histories. For these projects, the use of exhibition places and museums is seen as a way to reintroduce a new sentimental attachment that is denounced as missing at the European level

26    An example is the MELA project (European Museum in an Age of Migration) funded by the 7th Framework Programme of the European Commission but also 'Towards a Common Past: Conflicting Memories and Competing Historical Narratives in Europe after 1989', funded in 2008 by the NordForsk Research board. In France a Labex grant (a cluster of 'excellence for research') has been allocated to a consortium of French units working on 'Writing a New History for Europe' [Ecrire une Nouvelle Histoire de l'Europe].

27    François Foret, 'Dire l'Europe. Les brochures grand public de la Commission. Entre rhétoriques politiques et bureaucratiques', *Pôle Sud* 15 (2001); Morgane Le Boulay, 'Investir l'arène européenne de la recherche. Le 'Groupe de Liaison' des historiens auprès de la Commission européenne', *Politix* 23/89 (2010); Oriane Calligaro, 'EU Action in the Field of Heritage: A Contribution to the Discussion on the Role of Culture in the European Integration Process', in Marloes Beers and Jenny Raflik, eds, *National Cultures and Common Identity: A Challenge for Europe?* (Brussels: Peter Lang, 2010).

28    François Foret and Oriane Caligaro, 'La mémoire européenne en action. Acteurs, enjeux et modalités de la mobilisation du passé comme ressource politique pour l'Union européenne', *Politique européenne* 37 (2012).

since the crisis of EU legitimacy that emerged during the 1970s. It has also been motivated by building a sense of European citizenship through new public spaces where art or history could be used as sites for discussion, open deliberation or confrontation.

So far however, a 'historical understanding that acknowledges the conflicts, contentions, complexity and ambiguity of Europe's past and therefore recognizes the fragility of its future' has yet to be promoted.[29] European Union historiographies usually display official narratives of the foundational period of European integration as post-1945 negotiations between men of goodwill, who wanted to include Germany in the first group of nation-states that would participate in a common European community. In Western Europe, the founding moment of European integration is usually seen as the egalitarian project of mutualizing coal, iron, scrap metal and steel between former enemies, in order to prevent them from building armies against each other. In the discourses surrounding the French and Belgian 'founding fathers' of European integration, very few references to the First World War are to be found. Visiting the house of Robert Schuman in Scy-Chazelle, one learns that he was born in Luxemburg, educated in Germany, and that he acquired French citizenship in 1919. Schuman, as many other European founding fathers in the EU official history, did not fight in First World War and had no military experience. His battlefield was figurative, crossing lines as he moved to live and study. This crisscrossing of European frontiers was instrumental in shaping his European vision. Schuman, like many of the other founding fathers, was a 'man of the frontiers' rather than an actual soldier.

Despite this, the Great War has not been entirely silenced or repressed. More accurately, it has been downgraded to a pre-figuration of a crisis of the European spirit, which was expressed more vividly by inter-war intellectuals such as Romain Rolland or Paul Valéry in France, Emile Verhaeren in Belgium, or Stefan Zweig in Austria. The work of the Czech philosopher Jan Patočka (whose work on the Great War and the crisis of the European spirit has been at the heart of *Charter 77*) remains widely unknown in the

---

29    Pakier and Stråth, *A European Memory?*, 1.

official European teleology of Western Europe. Recalling Ernst Jünger and
Theillard de Chardin's observations at the front during the First World War,
the 'solidarity of the shaken', presented by Patočka under the Soviet control
of Eastern Europe,[30] remains the only way to strive for a 'free agreement
in difference' with other shaken individuals. In an attempt to provide a
political project for the unification Europe (including its eastern part),
Patočka and his followers imagined that German and French soldiers had
felt, in the face of death, the same fate as those who had suffered human
rights violations and totalitarian existence in Central and Eastern Europe.
Despite the existence of this narrative, so far such a conceptualization of
the Great War has been blatantly ignored in the display of Europe's history in museums.

The official narrative of European integration begins in 1945, the 'year
zero' (in German, *Stunde Null*) of the history of post-totalitarian freedom
in Europe. These narratives, however, neglect the fact that Central and
Eastern European EU member-states did not experience the aftermath
of the Second World War as an era of freedom and the beginning of an
undisrupted progress. The *Musée de l'Europe* in Brussels, in a temporary
exhibition entitled 'Europe, c'est notre histoire!' reminded visitors that the
narration of the construction of Europe is always an 'after war' story.[31] The
exhibition began with a display entitled 'So many peace treaties' featuring
dozens of military boots from the Second World War and, in the next room
entitled '1945: Europe, year 0', displayed aerial pictures of an un-named
bombed city. Further into the exhibition, a room was dedicated to the fall
of the Berlin Wall and the end of the Soviet occupation in Eastern Europe.
Between the two 'events', nothing really disturbed the uninterrupted construction of an integrated consortium of countries sharing common (yet

30   Jan Patočka, *Heretical Essays in the Philosophy of History* (Chicago: Open Court,
     1996).
31   Sophie Wahnich, Barbara Lasticova, Andrej Findor, eds, *Politics of Collective Memory,
     Cultural Patterns in Post War Europe* (Wien: L. I. T. Verlag, 2008); Christine Cadot,
     'Can museums help us build a European memory? The example of the Musée de
     l'Europe in Brussels in the light of "New World" museums experience', *International
     Journal for Politics, Culture and Society* 23 (2010), 127–36.

unspecified) values, a common *tabula rasa* and a common faith in the progress of the European Union. This exhibition recalled the black-and-white picture that announced 1945 as the unique 'Never Again' in European history, relegating the First World War to the position of EU pre-history.

These observations are not isolated. In Western European memories, the victims of the Shoah have taken a more important place than other constituencies of victims, such as Communists or members of the Resistance. For twenty years studies have analysed what had been called a 'positive discrimination' in the building of the collective memory of Western Europe.[32] Therefore, questions about the relationship between First and the Second World War memories and European integration are silenced by conflicting voices that argue about a disrupted European memory divided between western and non-western European historical experiences. It is true that a visitor to the House of Terror in Budapest might find herself very disoriented when confronted with a comparison between memories of Communism from both sides of the Iron Curtain. Here, as in Prague's House of Communism, the Communist Party is not portrayed as a liberating actor. In Budapest, the exhibition compares the Stalinist and Nazi repressions on every wall of every room of the museum in scenes that pit one against the other in an attempt to stress their similarities. These new museums were built at the time of the Prague Declaration on European Conscience and Communism' that was signed by prominent European politicians in 2008. Among them was Vaclav Havel, a former co-writer of *Charter 77* with Patočka, and Joachim Gauck, who called for a 'Europe-wide condemnation of, and education about, the crimes of Communism.'[33] During the last ten years, this gap between western and non-western *lieux de mémoire* in Europe has been well addressed by researchers, especially when discussing the complexity and heterogeneity

---

32   Henry Rousso, *The Haunting Past: History, Memory, and Justice in Contemporary France* (Philadelphia: University of Pennsylvania Press, 2002).

33   'The Prague Declaration on European Conscience and Communism', 3 June 2008 <http://www.praguedeclaration.eu> accessed 19 February 2014.

of 'Central' or 'Eastern Europe's' political identities.[34] But the dichotomy we can also observe between the Second World War memory and the Great War repressed memory within the historiography of the EU remains silent.

## Conclusion

The Great War has been largely silenced in museum narratives of European integration. It has been downgraded to that of a pre-figuration of a general crisis of the European spirit in the twentieth century, and therefore has become a mere episode in EU pre-history, a situation further complicated by the division in European memory between 'east' and 'west'. The Second World War is habitually presented as the starting point of European integration, rather than an interruption in the enlightened process of building Europe so that European integration must always be an 'after war' story.

Jürgen Habermas called for museums to be a public space where visitors could also act as citizens, and in which they would be given the right to express something besides obedience to artifacts or imitation. It seems, however, that the ideal of a history museum as a zone of exchange and debate between members of various communities and experts of museum practice has so far been largely kept separate from museum projects concerning EU history. As such, memories of the First and Second World Wars could emerge as parts of common museum practices, where conflicting narratives, repressed memories and contradictory voices about European history could be displayed. In 2014, a European memory still remains political wishful thinking, rather than a proven, existing reality.

---

34    Enzo Traverso, 'L'Europe et ses mémoires. Trois perspectives croisées', *Raisons Politiques* 36 (2009); Eva-Clarita Onken, 'Memory and Democratic Pluralism in the Baltic States: Rethinking the Relationship', *Journal of Baltic Studies* 41/3 (2010).

ROMAIN FATHI

# 'A Piece of Australia in France':
# Australian Authorities and the Commemoration of Anzac Day at Villers-Bretonneux in the Last Decade

> Of History – of its depth and complexity – today, we are only shown a utilitarian use. The past has become a warehouse for identity and political resources, from which everyone draws as one pleases what can serve one's immediate interests.
>
> — HENRY ROUSSO[1]

## Introduction

War commemorations are living collective phenomena subject to change over time. They are often ritualized and may even seem set in stone to the participants. They are, however, organized, overseen and evolving activities with precise rules and *mises en scène*. This chapter considers how Australian collective remembrance of the Great War was exported to and disseminated through Villers-Bretonneux to replace and reshape local memory of the conflict. It also puts into perspective the ways in which the inhabitants of Villers-Bretonneux are involved in memory-related activities and the commemorative diplomacy deployed between Australian authorities and their French interlocutors. Finally, this chapter analyses the ways in which the Commonwealth has taken over the organization of the ceremonies at

---

1    Henry Rousso, 'Un marketing mémoriel', *Libération* (15 February 2008), author's translation.

Villers-Bretonneux on Anzac Day since 2008, using the town as a pedestal to assert an Australian national identity. It argues that the establishment of a Dawn Service at Villers-Bretonneux by the Australian government is a corollary to recent blunders at its counterpart, Gallipoli. It appears that this new commemorative service in France does not face contentious issues of ownership like it does at Gallipoli and proposes a more positive symbolism and restoration of the dignity of the Dawn Service. The time frame is deliberately short as these changes need to be analysed in depth and put into a wider context of exponential Australian First World War 'commemorativitis'.[2] The concept of the 'performance of the past' and the performative dimension of commemoration are explored in the second section of this chapter. The analytic frame provided by Winter et al. provides a valuable theoretical field for empirical studies such as this one.[3]

## Anzac Day at Villers-Bretonneux after the Second World War

The first post-Second World War Anzac Day ceremony at Villers-Bretonneux was undertaken in 1951 through the personal initiative of the Australian Ambassador to France.[4] This unofficial event attracted little attention except from a local newspaper that expressed admiration for his Austin coupé.[5] In 1952, the First Secretary of the Australian Embassy came to represent the Ambassador. Ceremonies and visits were also held nearby at Corbie, Péronne, Sailly-le-Sec and Mont Saint-Quentin.[6] There were

---

2    Antoine Prost, *Douze leçons sur l'histoire* (Paris: Seuil, 1996), 302.
3    Karin Tilmans, Frank Van Vree and Jay Winter, eds, *Performing the Past: Memory, History and Identity in Modern Europe* (Amsterdam: Amsterdam University Press, 2010).
4    *Archives Départementales de la Somme* [ADS], 24W 68, Letter to the squadron leader of Amiens' gendarmerie by M. Morel, Prefect of the Somme, 11 April 1951.
5    *Le Courrier Picard* (26 April 1951).
6    ADS 24W 68, *Préfet* to *Chef de Cabinet*, 18 April 1952.

no speeches or crowds, just a few wreaths were laid in a sober and cir-
cumspect fashion.[7] Events seemed distant; memory had faded. The previous year, the Imperial War Graves Commission judged it appropriate to
remind the *Préfet* in a few lines what Anzac Day was about.[8] However, for
the third post-Second World War Anzac Day ceremony in 1953, the letter
advising the same *Préfet* of the visit of the Australian Ambassador started
with the words 'Like every year' and the tradition was thus constituted.[9]
Subsequently, it became a ritual for the Ambassador to attend what was
now the Villers-Bretonneux Anzac Day ceremony and pay his respects
to the Australian soldiers who died on the Western Front. Progressively,
during the 1960s and 1970s, ceremonies were organized by the people of
Villers-Bretonneux under the aegis of the French-Australian Welcome
Committee and the Mayor. With the ever-growing presence of Australian
commemorative activities at Villers-Bretonneux since the rediscovery of
the Western Front in the 1980s, the local population increasingly engaged
with Australian commemorative events. In 1984, Villers-Bretonneux and
Robinvale (Victoria) were twinned, on the initiative of the Victorian town,
resulting in an increase in relationships between the communities. Initially
functioning like a very 'restricted club', the French-Australian association
opened itself up considerably.[10] The 1990s saw the consolidation of ties
between Villers-Bretonneux and Australia. One result of this was the
exhumation, in 1993, of the remains of an unknown Australian soldier
from the Adelaide Cemetery at Villers-Bretonneux. The Mayor of Villers
flew to Australia with the coffin where he joined the official party escort-
ing the Unknown Soldier to the Hall of Memory at the Australian War
Memorial where the remains were reinterred.[11]

7   *Le Courrier Picard* (26 April 1952).
8   ADS 24W 68, Letter from the Imperial War Graves Commission [IWGC] to the
    *Préfet*, 4 April 1951.
9   ADS 24W 68, Letter from the IWGC to the *Préfet*, 16 February 1953.
10  Information collected on field trip, December 2010.
11  Interview with Hubert Lelieur, December 2010.

## Creating and reshaping memory

The people of Villers-Bretonneux have become accustomed to Australian First World War commemorative events. Their awareness was especially raised under the mayorship of Hubert Lelieur between 1983 and 2008 and their participation was encouraged. However, their knowledge of the Diggers has only been recently revived and reshaped. At national level, 'the French' do not know Villers-Bretonneux nor are they aware that the Australians fought there, let alone during the Great War. The events that occurred at Villers-Bretonneux in 1918 are of too small a scale to be taught at school in the French national curriculum. Nevertheless, one might expect that at a regional level, war commemoration-related associations or French veterans would have heard of the Australian involvement in the Great War. Even this is apparently not the case. Jean-Pierre Thierry, President of the French-Australian Association of Villers-Bretonneux from 1992 to 2007, when promoting the museum and the association, wrote to presidents of like associations stating: 'very few people indeed are aware of [the Australian] participation in the Great War'.[12] Similarly, at the local level, some inhabitants were unaware that the Australians fought at Villers-Bretonneux. For instance, in 2002, Jean-Pierre Thierry wrote in a letter to a member:

> [A]fter the appalling answers to the questions we have asked the [French] pupils of Victoria School during the club fair, we have met up with the headmaster who spontaneously authorised our association to inform the [Villers-Bretonneux] children about Australia, a little before the Anzac Day ceremonies.[13]

As early as the late 1960s, adults were also taught about the Australian involvement in the Villers area during the Great War. According to the City Council's bulletin, the population has been given some short historical

---

12   Correspondence from Jean-Pierre Thierry, French-Australian Museum of Villers-Bretonneux, 15 February 2002, author's translation.
13   Letter from Jean-Pierre Thierry to the members of the Association, French-Australian Museum of Villers-Bretonneux, 2 May 2002, author's translation.

accounts to remember the past.[14] Clearly, the Australian involvement at Villers-Bretonneux was not an instinctive, ever-present memory, even for people who were born one or two generations after the end of the Great War. However, contemporary articles in the Australian press repeatedly state that the French, or the inhabitants of Villers-Bretonneux, remember Australians troops' deeds in the Great War.[15] Pride in national identity increases, it seems, when it is acknowledged by the people of another country.[16] As during the Great War, today's Australians seem self-conscious of their rank in the 'concert of nations'.

At a local level, Anzac Day, an Australian commemorative pattern, has progressively replaced a key date of the Great War in residents' memories. For the people of Villers-Bretonneux, even nearly half a century after the end of the war, the important date remained the start of the Battle of Amiens – 8 August 1918 – which pushed the front line away from the village, rather than 25 April.[17] Although on 25 April 1918, with the help of the British and the strong support of the Moroccan Division of the French Army – which is always neglected during ceremonies – the Australians entered and then occupied Villers-Bretonneux after it had been taken by the Germans the day before, for the inhabitants, the removal of the front line from their village – the Allied push in August – was more significant as their lives and belongings were no longer under threat. On 25 April, their village, streets and houses were still the scene of fighting, which was more worrisome than heartening. However, 25 April coincides with Anzac Day, an Australian event in which patriotic meanings have transcended the historical significance of the battle. Thus, with the passing of the generation who lived through the war, 8 August was forgotten by the villagers and, due to the Australian commemorative agenda, 25 April became the

14   *Bulletin officiel municipal de Villers-Bretonneux*, Issue no 1, fourth quarter 1964, 4 and 7; Issue n° 2, second quarter 1967, 5 in 1386 PER 1, ADS.

15   See *Australasian Post* (9 August 1984); 'Anzac Day goes into three days on the Somme', *The Age* (18 April 1988); 'Tour of Duty', *The Age Traveller* (2 February 2008).

16   See Jessica Pacella, 'Crikey, it's Commodified! An investigation into ANZAC Day: The next Nike?', *Social Alternatives* 30/2 (2011), 26–9.

17   *Bulletin officiel municipal de Villers-Bretonneux*, 1 (1964), 4.

day Villers-Bretonneux was liberated.[18] Australian national interventions thus transcended historical realities and recrafted traditional local collective remembrance.

Through the museum, the French-Australian Association, the City Council bulletin and the ceremonies, an Australian collective memory of the Great War, mostly designed by Australian agencies, has been imported and disseminated in the town. These agencies have orchestrated the construction of a local form of collective memory based on contemporary Australian remembrance. Annie Brassart, President of the French-Australian Association of Villers in 2008, illustrated this point when, discussing some of the inhabitants' embracement of commemorative practices: 'We must not be too idealistic about it – it is remarkable and exceptional, surprising and wonderful, but we still have to do a lot of work on the population [of Villers-Bretonneux] so they become fully aware of what it represents.'[19] Indeed, while for many years the Town Hall of Villers-Bretonneux, in association with the Australian Embassy, organized an Anzac Day luncheon in order to gather people together in a festive atmosphere, in 2001 this practice ended. Many inhabitants were coming to enjoy the 'free lunch', but were not attending the Anzac Day ceremonies. Some even took home food and drink.[20] It was in the 2000s that the previously mentioned bulletin of Villers-Bretonneux started discussing the Australians more regularly, as opposed to the anecdotal and occasional way it presented them in the early years of its circulation.

However, even if the Australian collective remembrance at Villers-Bretonneux is carefully engineered and tailored, some locals seem to embrace it. With an increased number of members and supporters, the Association was able to organize an 'Australian Week' at Villers-Bretonneux during the Anzac Day period in 2002. Its purpose was to gather people together for ceremonies, conferences, commemorative walks, concerts, a

---

18   See a commemorative documentary filmed inside the *Collège Jacques Brel* where students recite the script learned in English class <http://www.youtube.com/watch?v=rAhVsfzm9Bo&feature=relmfu> accessed 10 February 2012.

19   'The French village that will never forget', *The Advertiser Review* (19 April 2009).

20   Email to the author from the French-Australian Museum, 17 February 2012.

French-Australian Australian Football League (AFL) match and various other cultural events. With about ten different activities, the event was quite a success for a town of some 4,000 inhabitants, with 600 people attending.[21] Since then, an 'Australian Week' has been held at Villers each year, with varying levels of activity and intensity. At the local level, it is also an opportunity to organize festivities in the village. It is hard to assess what percentage of these activities is dedicated to the commemoration of the Diggers, but Australian commemorants are increasingly at the heart of the process.

Difficulties exist in estimating the number of French people involved during the Anzac Day period, but most people I have spoken with regret the mass attendance at and formalization of the event since 2008 (addressed later in this chapter) as they feel that the sense of 'community event' has been lost. For many years indeed, some Australian visitors were welcome in Villers-Bretonneux households.[22] Monsieur Tranchard, co-president of the French-Australian Association in 2013, deplored that this habit has been lost with the passing of time.[23] The impact of mass tourism at Villers-Bretonneux is evident in its museum's visitation rates, with the Anzac Day period being the busiest time of the year. This museum, run by the French-Australian Association, was inaugurated in 1975 and renovated between 1988 and 1992. Cheap airfares and the rediscovery of the Western Front, among other reasons, have contributed to an increase in visitors, with numbers sky-rocketing from 622 in 1992 – among whom forty-three were Australians – to 11,426 in 2010, of whom 9,667 were Australians.[24] The museum at Villers-Bretonneux has played an important role in popularizing

---

21    *Villers-Bretonneux infos. Bulletin municipal d'informations*, Villers-Bretonneux, 34 (2002), 11.

22    See *Villers-Bretonneux infos. Bulletin municipal d'informations*, Villers-Bretonneux, 37 (2003), 2 or 'Les Australiens chez l'habitant à Villers-Bretonneux', *Le Courrier Picard* (6 May 2006).

23    Information collected on field trip, December 2010.

24    Statistics available from the French-Australia Museum, collected December 2011.

the town in Australia.[25] With regard to the daytime Anzac Day service at
Villers-Bretonneux, between one and several hundred people used to gather
prior to the institution of the Dawn Service by the Australian government
in 2008. Since then, Dawn Services at Villers have attracted a crowd of
3,000 to 4,000 people annually, the great majority of whom are Australians.


## Australia's commemorative take-over


Ceremonies, inaugurations, erection of monuments and unveilings of
plaques have allowed the Australian authorities to forge a solid network in
northern France due to the intensity of such events since the early 1990s.
Furthermore, this network has been officially acknowledged and stimulated
by the granting of Orders of Australia. Relative to population, in the whole
of France, Villers-Bretonneux is where the greatest number of Orders of
Australia (five in total) have been awarded. In northern France, Orders
of Australia have also been given in Fromelles, Bullecourt, Hendicourt or
Beaurains. All the laureates have in common their promotion of Australian
history and memory in their community, with a high concentration of
mayors among them. For example, the citation for Hubert Huchette, Mayor
of Fromelles, states: 'For service to Australian-French relations, particularly
his contribution to preserving the memory of Australian World War One
veterans'.[26] Gratitude can be seen as an acknowledgement for the work
accomplished, but also as an encouragement to do more. Such good diplomatic relations have allowed Australia to be increasingly welcomed and
involved in northern France. Australian commemorative projects, launched
by the Department of Veterans' Affairs through the Australian Embassy in

---

25    See for example 'The French connection who recalled savage glories of past', *The Age*
      'Anzac Edition' (25–26 April 2008).
26    See <http://www.gg.gov.au/events/french-memorial-fromelles-and-investiture-
      mayor-fromelles-mr-hubert-huchette-am> accessed 7 February 2014.

Paris, are flourishing with the renovations of Monsieur Letaille's museum in Bullecourt, the up-coming renovations of the French-Australian Museum of Villers-Bretonneux and the Australian Remembrance Trail.

In 2008, the Australian government took over the organization of Anzac Day ceremonies at Villers-Bretonneux and established a Dawn Service, leaving some villagers at Villers-Bretonneux confused and disconcerted. The year 2008 was the ninetieth anniversary of the Battle of Villers-Bretonneux and the Australian government was keen to make this milestone a significant event, as it did in Gallipoli in 2005. Judging by its attendance, this was a success though it caused a commemorative quid pro quo among the French. In a local newspaper, one could read about the 'non-official' Australian celebrations of 25 April, as opposed to the 'official' French ones the following day.[27] Indeed, the service was traditionally organized by the French on the closest Saturday to Anzac Day to allow the French population to participate in the ceremony which otherwise could occur on a working weekday. That year, mostly due to the symbolism of the anniversary, the Commonwealth decided to hold its Dawn Service based on the Australian pattern. For the occasion, the Australian Embassy even deployed an outpost in the Town Hall of Villers-Bretonneux.[28] On 26 April, for what the French still called the 'official service', Alan Griffin, the Australian Minister for Veterans' Affairs, declared: 'today is an opportunity to share the French experience of this community service'.[29] This implied that the Dawn Service of 25 April was an Australian service, directed at an Australian audience. After 2008, the 'community service' disappeared and was replaced by a Dawn Service broadcast live to Australia, the format of which does not invite the French and the Australians to interact. The collaborative spirit forged through personal and diplomatic bonds which had existed for many years, and the intimate French-Australian ceremonies of Villers-Bretonneux, had ceased to satisfy the new agenda of the Australian government.

27   *Le Courrier Picard* (18 April 2008).
28   Ibid.
29   Alan Griffin MP, Australian Minister for Veterans' Affairs, *Commemorative Address, Anzac Community Service, Saturday 26th of April 2008, Australian National Memorial, Villers-Bretonneux,* 26 April 2008.

The Australian take-over of the organization of Anzac Day at Villers-Bretonneux was not only manifested in the timing of the event. Speeches delivered for the occasion have also changed. Traditionally borrowing from a form of commemorative diplomacy, the ceremonies have become an assertion of Australian identity. A preliminary comparative examination of speeches given by officials at Anzac Day ceremonies at Villers-Bretonneux and Bullecourt over the last decade testifies to this. The speeches delivered at Bullecourt have remained similar before and after 2008, in the sense that they include the French hosts. By contrast, the speeches at Villers-Bretonneux have changed considerably since the Australians organized the first Dawn Service there in 2008. Speeches of 2006 and 2007, at Bullecourt and Villers-Bretonneux, are both concise reminders of the events celebrating the French-Australian connection and are a manifestation of a commemorative diplomacy. At the Anzac Day service of 2006, held on 28 April at Villers-Bretonneux, the audience was reminded that Australia continues 'to protect the values of democracy and liberty; ideals that we share with France', and the same year, at Bullecourt, that 'what has become meaningful in the long term is the bond that has developed between the peoples of France and Australia, both of them determined to defend democratic principles and liberty'. This idea of commemorative diplomacy has been reinforced as Australia has sometimes used these villages as diplomatic pedestals.[30] In 2006, the Australian ambassador declared in her commemorative speech beside The Digger statue at Bullecourt: 'Australia's role in peace-keeping, conflict resolution and nation-building in recent times is widely acknowledged. Our contribution to peace and stability in East Timor, the Solomon Islands and Cyprus – to name a few – reflects the values of our servicemen and women of past days'.[31] This demonstrates a need and desire to be acknowledged on the international stage through an amalgam made between the Great War and modern day peacekeeping. This is reminiscent of Rousso's quote that opened this chapter denouncing the use of history for the purposes of the present.

30   [See Matthew Graves's contribution to this volume on memorial diplomacy – Ed.].
31   Speech by Penelope Wensley AO, Australian Ambassador to France, provided by the Australian Embassy.

However, from the 2008 first Dawn Service onwards, the speeches delivered at Villers-Bretonneux were about celebrating and performing Australianness and exalting nationhood and pride. In his address to the audience, in 2008 Alan Griffin declared:

> Through their exploits on Gallipoli, the men of the Australian and New Zealand Army Corps forged a reputation for courage, determination, and their willingness to stand by their mates when things got tough [...]. But the Australians showed again what they were made of [...]. They earned a reputation among allies and enemies alike as tough, courageous and determined soldiers. The Australians on the Western Front helped win some of the most important battles of the war and were awarded fifty-three Victoria Crosses for valour.[32]

In a different speech, given this time by Stephen Smith in 2010 at the Australian National Memorial at Villers-Bretonneux, one may even argue that commemoration had been pushed into the background. The association of the past with the present gives rhythm to the speech to the extent that greater emphasis is placed on the commemorants – the Australian crowd – more than on the commemorated – the soldiers. In Smith's speech, the word 'remember' appears six times when the word 'today' is mentioned eight times. 'Today' is even used in an anaphora which suggests that the present time and the visitors gathered that day are, if not at the centre of the ceremony, its main actors.[33] Smith declares 'they sought no honour'.[34] Paradoxically, the word 'honour' is the notion most referred to, appearing eleven times within a speech that is only few minutes long.

At an individual level, commemorations are a powerful means to create or remind the commemorants of their identity, as Jay Winter suggests:

---

32  Alan Griffin MP, Minister for Veterans' Affairs, 'Commemorative Address Anzac Day Dawn Service', Australian National Memorial, Villers-Bretonneux, 25 April 2008.

33  Ibid.

34  Stephen Smith MP, Australian Minister for Foreign Affairs and Trade, 'Anzac Day', Australian National Memorial, Villers-Bretonneux, 25 April 2010, <http://www.foreignminister.gov.au/speeches/2010/100425_anzac_day.html> accessed 19 September 2013.

Memory performed is at the heart of collective memory. When individuals and groups express or embody or interpret or repeat a script about the past, they galvanize the ties that bind groups together and deposit additional memory traces about the past in their own mind. These renewed and revamped memories frequently vary from and overlay earlier memories, creating a complex palimpsest about the past each of us carry with us [...]. Memories return to past experience but add their traces to the initial story.[35]

This is precisely what Smith does in his speech when dead soldiers are relegated to a pretext used to praise the attendants at the ceremony and define an Australian identity:

They volunteered to defend, and if necessary to die for, values and ideals which Australians then and now hold dear.
Values that underpin what we aspire to as a nation and as a people.
A belief in a 'fair go' for all, in not leaving behind the weak or the vulnerable.
A sense of optimism about what we can achieve through ingenuity and by working together.
A sense of humour in adversity.
An egalitarian spirit.
A defiance against the odds.
An independent nature.
The sacrifice that we honour today helped forge our national identity, helped forge our natural characteristics and helped set our national values and virtues.
As a people and as a nation we continue to draw inspiration from that sacrifice.[36]

Time and space collapse. The Anzacs are defined and so are today's Australians. As Ernest Renan asserted in relation to a Spartan ode: 'We are that which you were, we will be that which you are.'[37] Here lies the project of the present nation that defines the past in the light of the present it fantasizes living in, for its future. The entire nation is made heroic in this 'civil religion' whilst national values are ascertained.[38] Recent commemorative

---

35    Winter et al., *Performing the Past*, 11.
36    Smith, 'Anzac Day', 2010.
37    Ernest Renan, *Qu'est-ce qu'une nation?* (Paris: Éditions des mille et une nuits, 1997 [1882]), 32.
38    Ken Inglis, *Sacred Places. War Memorials in the Australian Landscape* (Melbourne: Melbourne University Press, 2008), 433.

speeches at Villers-Bretonneux suggest that commemoration has entered a new era where the commemorant is ennobled by his or her association with the Anzac legend. Moreover, with the annual live broadcast format of the Dawn Service ceremony since 2008, there has been a shift in the audience's localization. Speeches are now oriented toward an audience predominantly watching from Australia, which explains their change in nature analysed previously in this chapter. The Dawn Service has become an event, filmed as such and promoted via multiple media. Thus, from Australia, one can choose a Dawn Service: one can attend the local service in person in the morning, watch other Australian parades on the news and, after lunch, due to the time lag, watch the Dawn Service live at Gallipoli and then, an hour later, the service at Villers-Bretonneux. It is a whole Anzac Day full of Dawn Services in Australia, but also in Europe and in Asia with the Hellfire Pass Dawn Service in Thailand. Australians see Australia on different continents on that day and, during the previous and following days, every national and state newspaper is replete with articles related to the Anzacs and overseas Dawn Services and the community's pride. 'Anzac' sells and newspapers fill their editions with related themes, sometimes developed at length in special Anzac Day supplements. These are 'commodified' and expected stories, but have they become expected because of the media's attention or to cater for a popular craving? Each phenomenon has probably fed the other and contributed to the present situation.

## Gallipoli and commemorative evolution at Villers-Bretonneux

The Australian take-over at Villers-Bretonneux is also closely linked to the controversies tied to the equivalent service at Gallipoli. Since the mid 2000s, complaints about the lack of dignity of the Dawn Service at Gallipoli have increased. The party-like ceremony, the consumption of alcohol and the amount of rubbish left after the ceremony were among the main concerns.[39] Moreover, the tensions between the Commonwealth and the government of Turkey have caused contention and have attracted bad press. Still, Gallipoli remains a sacred place for many Australians. However, with ever-growing attendance at Gallipoli, a conscious decision was made by the authorities to encourage Australians to attend other overseas Dawn Services and diversify the offer of commemorative gatherings.[40] Thus, the government saw a good opportunity in organizing an official Dawn Service at Villers-Bretonneux, not to compete with the Gallipoli Anzac Day Dawn Service, but rather to avoid the series of problems that have emerged over the years at Anzac Cove.

First and foremost, the issue that has haunted the Australian collective memory since the end of the war does not exist at Villers-Bretonneux, where there is no contention over ownership.[41] Gallipoli, on the contrary, is a National Park in Turkish territory and John Howard's plan to add the site to the National Heritage List in 2003 led to a diplomatic imbroglio between the two countries and a peculiar suggestion made by MP Danna Vale in 2005 to recreate Gallipoli in Australia.[42] At Villers-Bretonneux, the cemetery of the Australian National Memorial is administered by the Commonwealth War Graves Commission (CWGC) and 'the Commission has no objection to any request to hold a ceremony at one of its cemeteries or memorials.'[43] A treaty clearly defines what the CWGC can do with the land. Regarding military cemeteries, the second article of this treaty states: 'The French government grants to the Commission, without pay-

---

39    See 'Gallipoli the rock gig – what a load of rubbish', *Sydney Morning Herald* (27 April 2005).
40    Conversation with Brigadier Malcolm Rerden, Australian Military Attaché in Rome, who participated in the organization of the 2003, 2004 and 2005 Dawn Services at Gallipoli, 6 March 2012.
41    Bart Ziino, 'Who Owns Gallipoli? Australia's Gallipoli anxieties 1915–2005', *Journal of Australian Studies* 88 (2006), 1–12.
42    Romain Fathi, *Représentations muséales du corps combattant de 14–18. L'Australian War Memorial de Canberra à travers le prisme de l'Historial de la Grande Guerre de Péronne* (Paris: l'Harmattan, 2012), n1, 179.
43    Email to author from Nelly Poignonnec, Communication and Public Relations Supervisor, Commonwealth War Graves Commission, France Area, 9 January 2012.

ment and without time-limit, the free use of the land in French territory [...]. Nevertheless [...] this land shall remain the property of the French State'.[44] Thus, the extraterritorial dimension of the ceremony is legally overcome. There no dissent over national sovereignty at Villers-Bretonneux, and Australians are welcomed by the local community. When one visits the website of the City Council, one can read that Villers-Bretonneux is 'a piece of Australia in France'.[45] Finally, the place is not claimed by the French population. Gallipoli has a national significance for the Turks as it is deeply linked to the national figure – Atatürk. This is not the case in France; the Australians can have Villers-Bretonneux as a commemorative site to themselves without attracting attention, as the town is unknown to the vast majority of French people.

Villers-Bretonneux is also less problematic symbolically. Gallipoli was the invasion of an enemy's land whilst Villers-Bretonneux was the defence of an Allied nation. Instead of invaders, Australians were liberators. The tale is much more heroic and glorious. Along the same lines, there is a transubstantiation of a defeat into a victory. The disastrous 25 April 1915 is turned into a triumphant 25 April 1918. In addition, at the battle itself at Villers-Bretonneux, the Australian infantry retook what the British had lost to the Germans the day before, a positive symbol in terms of national identity-making.

The ceremony at Villers-Bretonneux appears to restore the dignity of the Dawn Service allegedly lost at Gallipoli. Official evidence suggests that a service at Villers-Bretonneux prevents the crowds of young backpackers from attending. As Bart Ziino demonstrates, youth have been identified in the media as a threat to the Dawn Service at Gallipoli.[46] Attending the

---

44    Treaty series N°39 (1953) *Agreement between the Governments of the United Kingdom of Great Britain and Northern Ireland, Canada, Australia, New Zealand, The Union of South Africa, India and Pakistan of the one part and the Government of the French Republic of the other part regarding British Commonwealth War Graves in French Territory.*

45    <http://www.villers-bretonneux.com> accessed 9 January 2012.

46    Ziino, 'Who Owns Gallipoli?', 9.

Dawn Service at Gallipoli has been described as a 'rite of Australianness'.[47] It is a popular destination, and one can find all-inclusive tours from London, which sometimes combine tourist visits and activities in Turkey. Such tours are convenient and affordable. Conversely, Anzac Day tours in the Somme are still in embryonic form. To get to Villers-Bretonneux at dawn, backpackers starting their journey in Paris, in all probability, would have to rent a car and pay for accommodation either in Paris or around Amiens, which can be expensive as there is currently no youth hostel in the region. Backpackers are welcome at the service, it being a public event, but the effort and the cost to attend the ceremony act as a deterrent. On the other hand, 'youth' is represented by organized parties of schoolchildren under their teachers' supervision. The Australian Embassy in Paris has succeeded in crafting an 'honourable' Anzac Day for large crowds without 'desacrifying' the cemetery as is the issue often raised for Gallipoli.[48] Admittedly, Villers-Bretonneux is also turned into a giant television studio set with many cameras, one of which is overhead, rigged onto a crane to take aerial shots. However, the transmission trucks remain relatively hidden. Even the bins and the toilets are away from the graves and the gathering site. The organization of the ceremony is a logistical challenge, taking about five days to set up the material for the ceremony. Starting from 19 April, the cemetery is progressively fitted with portable toilets and tents, chairs, sound and light devices and their scaffolds, platforms and stages.[49]

---

47   Bruce Scates cited in Mark McKenna and Stuart Ward, "'It was really moving, mate": the Gallipoli Pilgrimage and Sentimental Nationalism in Australia', *Australia Historical Studies* 129 (2007), 148.
48   'RSL chiefs dismayed by Gallipoli rubbish', *The Age* (27 April 2005).
49   Information collected on field trip at Villers-Bretonneux, 19 to 25 April 2011.

# Conclusion

This ongoing commemorative phenomenon at Villers-Bretonneux demonstrates how Australian authorities have reframed the Anzac Day service in the township. They have imposed their commemorative needs and practices to the detriment of the local French population whose memory of the Great War has been substituted by the official Australian collective remembrance of the conflict. The Commonwealth has taken advantage of an Australian popular craving for First World War memory-related activities and has considerably influenced the Anzac Day service at Villers-Bretonneux, in part to compensate for perceived problems with regard to the Gallipoli Dawn Service. Reignited by collective remembrance and visitors, the significance of the Western Front was later promoted by the government. Prime ministers have come to Villers-Bretonneux, both Bob Hawke and then Paul Keating. But it was John Howard, who also visited the town, who contributed the most to its popularity.

Part of this is linked to his family history and part of it is due to his conception of the Anzac story within Australia's national identity.[50] It was during the Howard years that the government – with the help of the Australian War Memorial – caught up with and then surpassed the popular demand for the Western Front. The project of an Australian Remembrance Trail, specifically designed for Australians, is yet another example. A clear indication of how important and consensual the remembrance of the Western Front has become over the last decade was demonstrated when, following a change of government in Australia in 2007, the Remembrance Trail project of the Howard government was continued by the Australian Labor Party (ALP). Subsequent ALP governments have endorsed the Anzac legend as a national story as tailored by Prime Minister Howard into a comprehensive national historical narrative. Opposing voices, like

---

50 John Howard, *Lazarus rising: A personal and political autobiography* (Sydney: Harper Collins Publishers, 2010), 6–7.

that of Paul Keating, have become a minority.[51] The example of the Western Front suggests that it has become impossible for an Australian government in office to disregard the legend, so popular and significant it has become within the Australian community.

Australian collective remembrance of the Great War was exported to and disseminated through Villers-Bretonneux via several agencies, the effect of which replaced and reshaped local memory of the conflict. Since 2008, the Commonwealth has taken over the organization of the Anzac Day ceremonies at Villers-Bretonneux traditionally organized by the French villagers. Though the Australian commemorative diplomacy at stake here is deployed overseas, its primary purpose serves the domestic Australian community as the town is transformed into a pedestal to assert an Australian national identity. Here, commemoration is politics in action.

---

51    James Curran, 'Keating's ancient history', *The Australian* (14 November 2008).

SHANTI SUMARTOJO

# Anzac Kinship and National Identity on the Australian Remembrance Trail

## Introduction

The Australian Remembrance Trail (ART) stretches from Ypres in Belgium, to the battlefields of the Somme in northern France. A coherent line of discrete sites on a map, the Trail has been the focus of Australian government funding in anticipation of large numbers of Anzac 'pilgrims' visiting the area during the Great War centenary commemorative period that begins in 2014. At once a tourist attraction and the locus of memorial diplomacy and 'people-to-people' links, the Trail is an important site of national remembrance and a means by which Anzac national identity is constructed, reinforced and performed.

This chapter explores how the ART conditions manifestations of 'Australianness'. It illustrates how commemorative practices within the sites' material environments help shape Anzac nationalism and how this is understood by an audience already primed as a national one. This analysis includes both 'top-down' official practices and 'from-below' vernacular ones that augment each other to make the sites powerful locations for reinforcing a version of Australian national identity based on 'values' linked to martial service and sacrifice. Furthermore, these practices are enhanced by commemorative performances that fold events at the sites into larger narratives of Australians as members of the same national 'family' and also infuse individual family histories with national narratives.

As this chapter will explain, this process contributes to a vision of Australia as a nation with kinship at its core, one that can sit uneasily with the 'civic' qualities with which Australia is usually associated, and that have been identified as central to its contemporary multicultural identity. This version of Anzac nationalism performed at commemorative sites also potentially limits discursive possibilities for Australian national identity. Rather than opening up multiple narratives through the possibility of a range of uses or practices, as some other national sites have been shown to do, this chapter will show how the Trail has instead contributed to a narrowing of the Anzac narrative, and Australian identity more broadly.

## The Australian Remembrance Trail

By 2013, planning for the development of the Australian Remembrance Trail was well underway, with some projects already completed. The $10 million that had been allocated to develop the Trail in the 2009–10 Federal budget was part of a much bigger $83 million budget for an overarching Anzac Centenary programme which included facilities and activities in Australia and overseas.[1] In 2013, the Minister for Veterans' Affairs, MP Warren Snowdon, reported to Parliament on the progress of the Centenary programmes, identifying its expansive remit to commemorate 'service and sacrifice by Australian men and women in all wars, conflicts and peacekeeping operations in which Australia has participated'. This meant programmes and activities that reached far beyond the First World War, located around Australia and overseas.[2]

However, the ART is specific to the Great War, and in Department of Veterans' Affairs (DVA) material, two aspects of the investment in the

1    ABC News Online, '$83m package for Anzac centenary plans' <http://www.abc.net.au/news/2012–04–24/govt-to-announce-anzac-centenary-plans/3967968> accessed 15 August 2013.
2    Warren Snowdon, Ministerial Statements – Anzac Centenary', page 3539, *Hansards House of Representatives* (16 May 2013) <http://parlinfo.aph.gov.au/parlInfo/search/display/display.w3p;query=Id%3A%22chamber%2Fhansardr%2F135b167f-578d-4414-a5b0-b2a35bc1cc32%2F0204%22> accessed 13 June 2013.

Trail received particular emphasis. The first was that the achievements of Australians on the Western Front had been 'far greater' than those at Gallipoli, which had until now 'overshadowed' the war in France and Belgium.[3] The Trail was envisioned as a correction to the overwhelming emphasis on the Dardanelles campaign, and a way to highlight the Western Front as 'Australia's most significant contribution to victory in the First World War'.[4] To redress this oversight, a list of changes to twelve memorial sites that '[built] upon existing efforts of French and Belgian communities to commemorate Australian service' was undertaken.[5] By emphasizing local commemorations, 'some of which date back to the 1920s', Australian government claims about the importance of the Trail have been legitimized and strengthened by local 'grassroots' activity. The 'people-to-people' links implicit in this exchange also underpin the memorial diplomacy that surrounds such sites.[6]

DVA material describing the improvements to the Trail highlights the importance of the individual experience, a focus on the personal that resonates with the larger approach to Anzac national identity that I discuss below. For example, to help visitors to the ART, the Australian government has developed a 'comprehensive and easily accessible set of materials and options to inform and guide visitors of all ages, levels of fitness and varying amounts of time to travel [...] the interpretive materials presented assume no prior knowledge of the subject and will be available in a mix of traditional and digital formats'.[7] The ART appears to be designed to function as a 300 kilometre-long display, punctuated by local museums, toilet and picnic facilities and 'ample opportunity for contemplative reflection'.

3    'Australian Remembrance Trail along the Western Front', Department of Veterans' Affairs <http://www.dva.gov.au/commems_oawg/OAWG/war_memorials/overseas_memorials/france/Pages/western%20front%20projects.aspx> accessed 13 June 2013.

4    Ibid.

5    Ibid.

6    Matthew Graves and Romain Fathi address aspects of this relationship in their contributions to this volume.

7    'Australian Remembrance Trail', Department of Veterans' Affairs.

To accompany the Trail, an extensive website called the 'Virtual Visitors' Centre' was also planned. Thus, the ART can be understood as akin to an extensive, open-air museum, with landscape and architectural aspects that underpin its commemorative meanings.

The memorial sites on the Trail are typified by architectural approaches that have been designed to sanctify the death of the individual by linking personal 'sacrifice' to national glory. Two of the largest, the Thiepval Memorial and the Australian National Memorial at Villers-Bretonneux, were created in the 1930s by Sir Edwin Lutyens, one of a number of architects engaged by the Imperial War Graves Commission (IWGC) to design memorials and cemeteries on the Western Front. Lutyens adhered to an 'abstract monumental design' or 'open-air cathedral' that used the sky as a dome and that included elements such as the War Stone (its name was later changed to the Stone of Remembrance), a semi-religious element recalling an altar, an 'architectural expression of an imperishable mass, which perpetuates commemoration in all eternity'.[8] At Villers-Bretonneux, the formal layout of headstones in rows, the symmetry of the central tower and flanking wings, and elements such as the Cross of Sacrifice reflect Lutyen's monumental preferences. The almost overwhelming numbers of names inscribed on the memorial's enclosing walls forge an intimate link between visitors and the memorialized dead. However, the architects commissioned by the IWGC did not all interpret the balance between the national and the personal or familial in the same way. Lutyen's colleague Herbert Baker, for example, advocated spaces based on 'traditional English burial places' that included gardens and enclosed spaces offering shelter and privacy for visiting relatives.[9]

The IWGC (that later became the Commonwealth War Graves Commission) graveyards also featured rows of headstones of standard size and shape, many of which included text by Rudyard Kipling: 'A soldier of the Great War known unto God'. These stones were meant to invoke the

---

8    Jeroen Geurst, *Cemeteries of the Great War by Sir Edwin Lutyens* (Rotterdam: 010 Publishers, 2010), 22.

9    Geurst, *Cemeteries*, 26 and 69.

equality of soldiers and officers in death, creating commonality amongst those who were killed, regardless of rank, religion or country of origin. Sir Frederic Kenyon, the Director of the British Museum, in his report to the IWGC entitled 'How the Cemeteries Abroad Will Be Designed', explicitly linked the design of the proposed cemeteries with collective sacrifice and remembrance:

> The sacrifice of the individual is a great idea and worthy of commemoration; but the community of sacrifice, the service of a common cause, the comradeship of arms which has brought together men of all ranks and grades – these are greater ideas, which should be commemorated in those cemeteries where they lie together, the representatives of their country in the lands in which they served.[10]

Although the intention appears to have been to conflate the fallen soldiers and a 'community of sacrifice', in practice the headstones also create connections between visitors and the individual dead. Some of these inscriptions are very sad, as in these examples from Villers-Bretonneux, that express deep personal loss and family tragedy: 'in memory of my beloved son who gave his life that we might live'; 'sadly missed by his sorrowing wife and family'; 'an affectionate husband and father who lived as he died, for others'. In the official DVA material about the history of the Villers-Bretonneux site, one family connection in particular is invoked that explicitly links personal grief and military service. That the then Queen should be included as an example of the 'community of sacrifice' both personalizes the commemorative narrative, and renders it abstract, collective and imperial:

> On 22 July 1938, Queen Elizabeth laid a bunch of poppies, given to her by a local schoolboy, at the unveiling of the Australian National Memorial at Villers-Bretonneux. Was she thinking of her own brother, Fergus Bowes-Lyon, 'missing' at the Battle of Loos in 1915?[11]

---

10    Frederic Kenyon, *War Graves: how the cemeteries abroad will be designed. Report to the Imperial War Graves Commission by Sir Frederic Kenyon* (London: His Majesty's Stationery Office, 1918), 6.

11    'Site 9: Australian National Memorial – Villers-Bretonneux, France' <http://www.ww1westernfrNnt.gov.au> accessed 13 June 2013.

Interpretive material written and erected by the Australian government at Trail sites provides further examples of the 'personalization' of the First World War, including family relationships. Photographs, of individuals or of personal effects such as identity discs, signal the presence of the individual soldier at the centre of the Anzac story. The narrative of the battle is often told from the perspective of individual soldiers, such as 'Sergeant Simon Fraser, 57th Battalion, Australian Imperial Force, from Byaduk, Victoria', who helped rescue the wounded from no-man's-land. His story is depicted in Peter Corlett's *Cobbers* (1998) statue that stands at the VC Corner site, in the Australian Memorial Park near Fromelles. The figurative statue is in the form of an Anzac 'Digger', based on Fraser, carrying an injured comrade.

Another Peter Corlett figurative statue, *The Bullecourt Digger* (1992), looks out over the memorial site at Bullecourt, 'gazing out towards the enemy trenches'.[12] The interpretive material at this site reveals the artist's intimate connection to Bullecourt: his father had fought there. Corlett described his reaction in terms of a profound emotional connection: 'I stood in the field and touched the cairn upon which my sculpture will eventually rest and felt a wave of emotion run through me. I felt my Dad's presence and everything went quiet'. In an intimate act that underscored his family connection to the site, Corlett used a photograph of his father to model the face of the 1917 soldier that his sculpture depicts, 'trying to capture in it "the fresh face of a young man about to set off on a great adventure"'.[13] On the other hand, for one travel writer visiting sites on the Trail, it was not the intimate knowledge of a particular Anzac soldier that was emotionally affecting, but rather the 'anonymity of these lost sons, brothers and husbands' that brought on 'the tears the Western Front demands of all visitors'.[14] In both these accounts, the individual soldier, defined by his family relationships, anchored an emotional experience of the Trail.

12    This text is taken from the 'Bullecourt Digger' interpretive sign at the Australian Memorial Park in Bullecourt, France.

13    Ibid.

14    Shaney Hudson, 'A walk among giants', *Sydney Morning Herald* (22 April 2012) <http://www.smh.com.au/travel/a-walk-among-giants-20120419-1x9it.html>

## Anzac commemorative practice

If material aspects of ART sites enable and encourage forms of remembrance, then those activities also help to shape commemorative sites; in other words, physical sites and the practices that take place in them are co-constituting. This approach to space aligns with phenomenological approaches that emphasize activity and practice as the 'primary drivers' for any landscape.[15] Such practices are employed by Australian visitors to Anzac sites, including participants in Anzac Day ceremonies, who are often described as 'pilgrims'. This term conflates the religious, personal and the national, but retains the emphasis on the individual experience.

The figure of the pilgrim has been present in the narrative of Anzac commemoration since soon after the war ended. According to Ken Inglis, Australian official war historian C. E. W. Bean anticipated that Gallipoli would be come a site of pilgrimage, and the first organized group arrived in Turkey in 1924.[16] Some individuals managed to visit before then, usually bereaved parents seeking information on where their child had died, but by 1931, organized groups from Australia were visiting sites on the former Western Front, including the areas where the Australian National Memorial would be unveiled only a few years later. Some early pilgrims, aware that most Australians could not afford to travel to Australian First World War sites in Europe and Turkey, shared their experiences with others to help comfort bereaved families. For contemporary Australians, therefore, the vicarious experience of gravesites overseas has a longstanding history.[17]

---

accessed 14 June 2012. Visitors to Gallipoli also commonly report emotional reactions – see Mark McKenna and Stuart Ward '"It was really moving, mate": The Gallipoli Pilgrimage and Sentimental Nationalism in Australia', *Australian Historical Studies* 38/129 (2007): 141–51.

15　Mick Abbott, 'Activating Landscape', *Landscape Review* 14/1 (2011), 25.

16　Ken Inglis, *Sacred Places* (Melbourne: Melbourne University Press, 1998), 257.

17　See Bart Ziino, *A Distant Grief: Australians, War Graves and the Great War* (Crawley: UWA Press, 2007), 173. See also McKenna and Ward, '"It was really moving, mate"'. Guy Hansen discusses contemporary Anzac pilgrimage in his contribution to this volume.

Contemporary visitors are still understood as pilgrims, and the use of this term has the effect of linking this practice to those of earlier visitors. Foreign Minister Bob Carr asked about this practice in his Anzac Day 2013 address at Villers-Bretonneux: 'Why do Australians make the pilgrimage, in increasing numbers, to remember tragic events that happened nearly one hundred years ago, so far from home?' For Carr, the answer was expressed in terms of values and characteristics personified in the figure of the individual soldier. In his speech, he used snippets of personal diary entries and letters home from individual Anzacs, such as 'all my mates are here' and 'how lucky we are in Australia', to tell a story of a much larger national group.[18]

There is also evidence that the individual emotional experience of 'pilgrimage' helps to construct participants' sense of national identity. For example, echoing a common attitude, in 2009 Donna Turnbull told *The Herald Sun* that 'My dad was in the services so I feel a big affiliation with [the Diggers]. We go to a dawn service every Anzac Day. You aren't an Aussie if you don't come'.[19] Caroline Winter's research on Australian tourism in the Somme region of France suggests that almost sixty per cent of visitors to Thiepval and Villers-Bretonneux, two ART sites, had family members who had served in the Great War. Many were also either seeking the names of their own relatives or were visiting on behalf of someone else; remembrance of an individual Digger remains an important reason that many people visit the region.[20]

The centrality of the names of the victims, repeatedly mentioned by visitors, officials and media reports, links the sites on the Trail to ways

18    Bob Carr, 'Anzac Day address: Dawn Service, 25 April 2013' <http://foreignminister. gov.au/speeches/2013/bc_sp_130425.html> accessed 14 June 2013.

19    Belinda Tasker, 'Thousands attend Anzac service in Villers-Bretonneux, France', *The Herald Sun* (25 April 2009) <http://www.heraldsun.com.au/news/breaking-news/ thousands-attend-anzac-servce-in-france/story-e6frf7jx-1225703889035> accessed 16 April 2012. For more on Anzac pilgrimage, see Bruce Scates, *Return to Gallipoli: Walking the Battlefields of the Great War* (Cambridge: CUP, 2006).

20    Caroline Winter, 'Commemoration of the Great War on the Somme: Exploring personal connections', *Journal of Tourism and Cultural Change* 10/3 (2012), 248–63.

of understanding Anzac nationalism as framed by a narrative of kinship. Name listing is common in memorial design, and was used by Lutyens at Villers-Bretonneux, Thiepval and other Great War sites, as discussed above. Seemingly innumerable names on large memorials can overwhelm visitors, emphasizing the futility of the losses. However, there is also evidence that use of long lists of names can connect the individual 'pilgrim' to a relative.[21] Certainly, the much smaller number of names on headstones connect visitors to the individual dead, as in this description of a visit to Adelaide Cemetery, near Villers-Bretonneux:

> To actually see his [the visitor's uncle's] grave and read his name [...] made me well up with tears again. I just stood transfixed and felt sorry for him [...] I thought it was a shame that he had died a terrible death alone in a foreign country away from his family and that he had been there alone for 85 years.[22]

The emotional immediacy of the family relationship is striking, as the visitor's relative is described as alone and far from home, despite the many years since his death. Here, the physical environment of the gravesite combines with family connections in a set of ritual Anzac practices that, according to Jay Winter, 'rehearses and recharges the emotion which gave the initial memory or story embedded in it its sticking power, its resistance to erasure or oblivion. Hence affect is always inscribed in performative acts in general and in the performance of memory in particular [...]'.[23] As Winter suggests, the personal emotional aspects of the pilgrim experience – and the rituals that many engage in – are vital in helping Anzac nationalism to 'stick'.[24]

---

21    Maya Lin, the designer of the Vietnam Veterans' Memorial in Washington, DC, took Thiepval as her inspiration. Edwin Lutyens was also responsible for designing Thiepval, which lists names of over 73,000 British dead or missing. See Mark Facknitz, 'Getting it right by getting it wrong: Maya Lin's Misreading of Sir Edwin Lutyens' Thiepval Memorial', *Crossings: a counter-disciplinary journal*, 7 (2005), 47–69. Thanks to Quentin Stevens for pointing out this connection.

22    Quoted in Scates, *Return to Gallipoli*, 107.

23    Winter, 'Introduction: the performance of the past', 12.

24    See McKenna and Ward on 'sentimental nationalism', op cit. Also see Hillman in this volume on sentimental 'supra-nationalism' in European narratives of the Great War.

These charged rituals contribute in turn to the impact of the physical sites, activating them as specifically commemorative.

The figure of the individual Anzac embedded in family relationships goes beyond reports of individual experiences, however. It also informs national ceremonies. Winter argues that 'the performative act of remembrance is an essential way in which collective identities are formed and reiterated', and in Anzac Day services, the individual experience of emotional connection is magnified into a national experience.[25] Seal reminds us that 'the dawn service is the tangible representation of the Anzac mythology, combining its main constituencies of interest – military, religious and civic'.[26] The rhythm of the readings, hymn singing, official speeches, a minute's silence and a bugler playing the Last Post are all familiar elements of this Australian ritual, even as they have gradually changed over time. However, instead of the 'civic' quality that Seal identifies, Anzac commemoration can also be understood as a ritual of kinship based on the figure of the individual as a member of a larger national family. For Winter, this performance 'is both a mnemonic device and a way in which individual memories are relived, revived and refashioned. Through performance, we move from the individual to the group to the individual [...]'.[27] This framework is part of Anzac Day services, with the notion of the family forming a central animating theme in media reporting on Anzac rituals.

For example, coverage in *The Australian* newspaper of the 2010 Dawn Service conflated the official and the personal by focusing on the family history of Australian Foreign Minister Stephen Smith, who had two great uncles who died on the Western Front. The report underlined the combination of the official and the personal by quoting a line from Smith's speech: 'there was hardly an Australian family that wasn't touched by the tragedy'

---

25   Jay Winter, 'Introduction: The performance of the past: memory, history, identity' in Karin Tilmans, Frank Van Vree, Jay Winter, eds, *Performing the Past: Memory, History and Identity in Modern Europe* (Amsterdam: Amsterdam University Press, 2010), 15.

26   See Graham Seal, '"... and in the morning...": Adapting and adopting the dawn service', *Journal of Australian Studies* 35/1 (2011), 49–63.

27   Winter, 'Introduction: The performance of the past', 11.

of the First World War.[28] Similar references to the strength of personal connection to the Great War or to the soldiers buried at Villers-Bretonneux
are commonly emphasized in Anzac Day ceremonies there, as well as in
media reporting on those events, echoing the emotion that McKenna and
Ward and Scates relate in their analyses of the Dawn Service at Gallipoli.[29]

By framing Anzac history as family memory, the narratives implicit in
these performances are insulated from critical analysis. As Winter insists,
'Memory is history seen through affect. And since affect is subjective, it is
difficult to examine the claims of memory in the same way as we examine
the claims of history'.[30] Anzac ritual performances are reported or broadcast
to a much larger national audience, presented as an event significant for *all*
members of the Australian family, even those who are not actual participants
in the ceremonies. The Australian Remembrance Trail, with its multiple
sites of national family pilgrimage and physical features such as lists of
names and rows of headstones, demonstrate intimate kinship connections.
Furthermore, the ART not only frames these performances, it also helps
to construct them as a central part of the narrative of Anzac nationalism.

## Anzac kinship and Australian national identity

The scope of these rituals, both personal and national, with the figure of
the individual pilgrim and his or her Anzac family relationships in a central
role, points to a version of the nation based on kinship. Eriksen argues that
'kinship terminology' helps to 'transfer the sentiments and commitments of

28  'Villers-Bretonneux personally poignant', *The Australian* (26 April 2010) <http://
    www.theaustralian.com.au/in-depth/anzac-day/villers-bretonneux-personally-poign-
    ant/story-e6frgdaf-1225858137047> accessed 10 Apr 2012.

29  Bruce Scates, 'The first casualty of war: A reply to McKenna's and Ward's "Gallipoli
    pilgrimage and sentimental nationalism"' *Australian Historical Studies* 38/130 (2007),
    312–21.

30  Ibid.

citizens from their personal experiences to that abstract and imagined community called the nation.'[31] Indeed, kinship is a central organizing feature of Anthony Smith's 'ethnic' nationalism.[32] Framing Anzac commemorative practice as a loose form of national kinship ritual helps to reveal some of the tensions and elisions in the larger Anzac narrative.

Perhaps most importantly, the notion of Anzac kinship deviates from the 'civic' nationalism that Australia is usually understood to enjoy. At the core of Australian 'civic' nationalism is multiculturalism, based on a model of liberal citizenship that not only accommodates new immigrants, but also provides the basis for their recognition and participation in national life. According to the 2011 policy statement, 'Australia's multicultural composition is at the heart of our national identity and is intrinsic to our history and character.'[33] In this version of the national story, what ties Australians together is a common commitment to national institutions that are underpinned by a set of inclusive democratic principles, a set of 'shared rights and responsibilities that are fundamental to living in Australia.'[34]

The Anzac narrative is not necessarily incompatible with this model of democratic liberal citizenship. Tim Soutphommasane, for example, argues that it provides the symbolic resources for 'a distinctive brand of egalitarianism, a robust democracy supported by an Anzac myth' of larrikinism, suspicion of authority and resourcefulness that C. E. W. Bean identified in his war reporting.[35] Furthermore, the government-commissioned report outlining the national programme of Anzac commemorative activity described the 'Anzac spirit' as a set of aspirational attributes that are

---

31    Thomas Hylland Eriksen, 'Place, kinship and the case for non-ethnic nations', *Nations and Nationalism* 10/1–2 (2004), 49–62.

32    Antony Smith, *Ethno-Symbolism and Nationalism: A Cultural Approach* (Abingdon and New York: Routledge, 2009). Eriksen also outlines Smith's position in Eriksen, 'Place, kinship'.

33    'The People of Australia: Australia's Multicultural Policy', Department of Immigration and Citizenship <http://www.immi.gov.au/media/publications/multicultural/pdf_doc/people-of-australia-multicultural-policy-booklet.pdf> accessed 3 July 2013.

34    Ibid.

35    Tim Soutphommasane, *Reclaiming Patriotism: Nation-building for Australian Progressives* (Melbourne: Cambridge University Press, 2009).

compatible with an inclusive and democratic Australia: 'courage, bravery, sacrifice, mateship, loyalty, selflessness and resilience'.[36] This focus on values, often expressed in terms of commitment to the nation and to one's comrades, is very general and therefore easily mobilized to include the many Australians *without* family roots in the First World War. However, Anzac becomes less generalized when considering its practices of commemoration. In particular, the reoccurring use of symbols of the nation as a family, as well as material support for these symbols by successive Australian governments, are expressed in rituals and environments designed to link the individual and the nation through a story of sacrifice and kinship specific to wartime service.

This narrowing of the symbolic repertoire occurs through activities of individual commemorants and pilgrims, as well as through state-sponsored events. Thus, one of the main sites on the ART, the Australian National Memorial at Villers-Bretonneux, acts as a stage for Anzac ceremonies that involve French and Australian officials (local and national), members of the Australian Defence Force and schoolchildren. As Romain Fathi details in his contribution to this volume, on these occasions, the Memorial is transformed into a literal stage, with cameras, lights and public amenities erected in the days preceding the event. In Australia, the Somme site acts as a backdrop to national ritual practices that are repeated in television coverage throughout the day of dawn services in Australia, Papua New Guinea, Thailand, Turkey, the United Kingdom and Ireland, as well as France.[37] In this instance, Anzac nationalism is highly structured and official, but also popular with visitors and the larger Australian audience – the Gallipoli

---

36   The National Commission on the Commemoration of the Anzac Centenary, *How Australia may commemorate the Anzac Centenary* (Canberra: Department of Veterans' Affairs, 2011), vi. See also Frank Bongiorno's contribution to this volume on the implications of Anzac's current inclusivity.

37   This performance is also one that enjoys official guidelines, through DVA guidelines that underscore official involvement in Anzac commemorations. See <http://www.dva.gov.au/COMMEMS_OAWG/COMMEMORATIONS/COMMEMORATIVE_EVENTS/Pages/index.aspx> accessed 11 February 2014.

and Villers-Bretonneux services were the most popular programmes on
ABC News 24 in 2012.[38]

Anthony Smith emphasizes the role of sites such as these in highlighting the importance of kinship in national identity:

> the cenotaphs and cemeteries of the many soldiers who fell in battle defending the
> homeland possess an additional aura of sanctity and [...] are commemorated in
> public ceremonies. But the more immediate and personal attachments and memories
> are those generated by the last resting-places of our kin. Multiplied across the land,
> these memories hallow every town and village graveyard; the memories, symbols and
> traditions of each contribute to the sanctity of 'our' land [...].[39]

Here, commemorative sites are sacralized by the graves of national family
members, and the Australian Remembrance Trail can be understood as
comprised of burial sites for soldiers who are concurrently national and
individual. It is this embedding of family relationships into a larger national
narrative that makes the Trail a powerful symbol that stretches across a
foreign landscape, a reimagined 'crimson thread of kinship' that connects
Australians to each other.[40] That Australian 'land', in this case physically
located in France and Belgium, should be so far from Australia does not
interrupt the commemorative logic or its practices, or its capacity to construct Australian-ness as based on the idea of a common family. The metaphor of Anzac kinship constructs the nation as a large extended family,
separated by distance and time, but still loyal and committed. This way of
thinking about nationalism is popularly compelling and easily understood,
providing 'security and a feeling of continuity [...] an abstract version of

---

38   'ABC News 24 the one to watch' <http://about.abc.net.au/2012/04/abc-news-24-
     the-one-to-watch/> accessed 19 June 2013.
39   Anthony Smith, *Ethno-symbolism*, 95.
40   Henry Parkes, then Premier of NSW, used this phrase at the first federation confer-
     ence in 1890 to describe the link amongst the states and territories that later became
     Australia. See <http://www.naa.gov.au/naaresources/publications/research_guides/
     fedguide/chronology/chron5.htm> accessed 11 February 2014.

something concrete which every individual has strong emotions about'.[41] The notion of an Australian family is also appealing and successful because it hints at ties that go far deeper than the bloodless 'civic' loyalties of liberal citizenship and democratic institutions.

## Conclusion

This chapter has argued that commemorative sites on the Australian Remembrance Trail, including design elements such as long lists of names and uniformly shaped headstones, help shore up a version of the Anzac narrative that draws on metaphors of kinship for its popular impact. This occurs through practices of Anzac commemoration that conflate the personal and the national, using the stories and experiences of individuals and their relatives to underpin a powerful narrative of an Australian Anzac 'family'. ART sites are seldom subject to practices beyond these rituals, which enjoy strong official support and popular engagement.

Sites along the Australian Remembrance Trail could have a role to play in alternative constructions of the Anzac story, especially if they can accommodate new or multiple ways of thinking about contemporary Australians. Such places, for example, help to connect Australia to Europe, through memorial diplomacy and the personal exchanges that inevitably accompany travel and pilgrimage. Furthermore, attempts to tell the stories of non-Anglo Anzacs are increasing, and contribute to calls to recast Anzac as a civic deal based on a set of common values to which all Australians might be able to subscribe. There are, in other words, possibilities for Anzac nationalism to include a wide range of people in its Australian family.

41   Thomas Hylland Eriksen, *Ethnicity and Nationalism: Anthropological Perspectives* (London: Pluto Press, 1993), 108.

However, ritual performances on the Australia Remembrance Trail are linked to specific landscapes and practices that so far remain resistant to transformation, or even complexity of use. The Anzac sites on the ART are subject to a narrow range of activities based almost entirely on particular commemorative rituals. These are comprised of state events that are tightly controlled or individual practices that usually adhere to well known patterns of remembrance. Even though these rituals have great value and meaning for their participants, the reoccurring theme of family and kinship works to limit those who participate and how they do so. One stated reason for government investment in the ART – that that the Trail can serve as a corrective to the dominance of Gallipoli in the Anzac story – is intended to draw more pilgrims to France and Belgium. In doing so, ART sites might yet see a wider range of ways of remembering, once a wider range of visitors use them.

# Notes on Contributors

FRANK BONGIORNO is Associate Professor in History at Australian National University and has broad interests in Australian history. He is the author of *The People's Party: Victorian Labor and the Radical Tradition 1875–1914* (Melbourne University Press, 1996); *A Little History of the Australian Labor Party* (University of New South Wales Press, 2011), which was written with Nick Dyrenfurth; and *The Sex Lives of Australians: A History* (Black Inc., 2012). He is co-editor of *History Australia*, the Australian Historical Association's official journal.

CHRISTINE CADOT is Associate Professor in Political Science at the Université Paris VIII. She is the author of *L'Europe imaginée. Lecture iconoclaste de la construction européenne* (Presses de Sciences Po, 2014). Her research focuses on the study of the historiography of the European Union, particularly on the development of master narratives of the European Union in museums and exhibitions.

SARAH CHRISTIE is a PhD candidate in History at the University of Otago, New Zealand. Her research interests are gender, empire and culture, and women's labour history. As part of her master's research at the University of Canterbury she studied single women missionaries and ideas of whiteness and reform in the imperial context. Her current work explores gender relationships within the context of New Zealand's post-war labour relations, focusing on clerical workers and equal pay.

ROMAIN FATHI is a PhD candidate at Sciences Po and the University of Queensland. He is the author of *Représentations muséales du corps combattant de 14–18: The Australian War Memorial de Canberra au prisme de l'Historial de la Grande Guerre de Péronne* (L'Harmattan, 2013).

MATTHEW GRAVES is a senior lecturer and researcher in British and Commonwealth Studies at Aix-Marseille Université – LERMA, a Fellow of the Royal Geographical Society (Political Geography Research Group) and an alumnus fellow of the Australian Prime Ministers Centre. His research focuses on 'shared history', commemorative politics and geographies of remembrance in twentieth- and twenty-first-century Europe and Australasia, as well as nineteenth-century speculative geographies and blueprints for political and social reform. His is currently writing a study of memorial diplomacy in the Asia-Pacific region based on research undertaken at the Australian Prime Ministers Centre, Museum of Australian Democracy.

GUY HANSEN is an historian and curator. He is currently Director of Exhibitions at the National Library of Australia. Prior to working at the NLA, Guy was Head Curator in the Australian Society and History Programme at the National Museum of Australia. He was the lead curator on many exhibitions including *Nation: Symbols of Australia* (2001), *Captivating and Curious* (2005) and *League of Legends* (2008).

ROGER HILLMAN teaches Film Studies and German Studies at Australian National University. His research focuses on issues of music and history in European cinema, especially their relationship to memory studies. He is the author of *Unsettling Scores: German Film, Music, Ideology* (Indiana University Press, 2005), and closer to the chapter in the present volume, of 'A Transnational Gallipoli?' in *Australian Humanities Review* 51 (November 2011).

JOHN HUTCHINSON is Reader in Nationalism in the Department of Government at the London School of Economics, where he teaches courses on theories of nationalism and on warfare and national identity. He has published several books on nationalism, most recently *Nations as Zones of Conflict* (Sage, 2005), and he is joint editor of the journal *Nations and Nationalism*. He is currently completing a monograph on nationalism and war.

JAMES W. MCAULEY is Professor of Sociology and Director of Research, School of Human and Health Sciences at Huddersfield University. He is also a Director or board member of the Academy of British and Irish Studies, the Institute for Research in Citizenship and Applied Human Sciences, and the Centre for Research in Social Sciences. He is the author of many articles and chapters examining the politics of identity in Northern Ireland as well as the monograph *Ulster's Last Stand? (Re)constructing Ulster Unionism after the Peace Process* (Irish Academic Press, 2010).

MARK MCKENNA is an Australian Research Council Fellow in Australian History at the University of Sydney. His most recent book, *An Eye for Eternity: The Life of Manning Clark* (Melbourne University Publishing, 2011), won the 2012 Prime Minister's Prize for Non-Fiction.

ANDREW MYCOCK is Reader in Politics at the University of Huddersfield. His research and teaching focus on post-empire citizenship and national identity, particularly in the UK and the Russian Federation, and the impact of citizenship and history education programmes. He has published widely on the 'politics of Britishness', history and citizenship education, and democratic youth engagement. He is co-convenor of the Academy for British and Irish Studies based at the University of Huddersfield and the Political Studies Association's Britishness Specialist Group.

ELIZABETH RECHNIEWSKI is an Honorary Senior Lecturer in the School of Languages and Cultures at the University of Sydney. She is Chief Investigator on the Australian Research Council Discovery Project *Judging the Past in a Post-Cold War World*. This project develops her research in the area of memory and commemoration: over the last decade she has published widely on remembrance of twentieth-century war in Australia, France and New Caledonia, including the commemoration of the role of indigenous soldiers in these countries. Recent articles include: 'Remembering the Battle for Australia', *Portal* 7/1 (2010); <Forgetting and Remembering the Darwin bombings>, *e-rea* 10/1 (2012); and <The Memorial Path from Darwin to Cowra>, *JOSA* 44 (2012).

MATTHEW STIBBE is Professor of Modern European History at Sheffield Hallam University and a specialist in twentieth-century Germany. His most recent work includes *Germany, 1914–1933: Politics, Society and Culture* (Pearson, 2010) and (edited with Kevin McDermott) *The 1989 Revolutions in Central and Eastern Europe: From Communism to Pluralism* (Manchester University Press, 2013). He is currently a member of the research network *Das 20. Jahrhundert erzählen: Zeiterfahrung und Zeiterforschung im geteilten Deutschland*, based at the Friedrich-Schiller-University, Jena, which aims to explore the inter-connections between East and West German historiography on twentieth-century themes during the Cold War era.

SHANTI SUMARTOJO is a Research Fellow in the School of Architecture and Design at RMIT University in Melbourne. She is the author of *Trafalgar Square and the Narration of Britishness, 1900–2012: Imagining the Nation* (Peter Lang, 2013). Her current research includes projects on the geographies of Anzac nationalism, memorial planning in capital cities and the role of public art in shaping urban experience.

LAURENCE VAN YPERSELE is full Professor of Contemporary History at the Catholic University of Louvain (Belgium). She is also member of the *Historial de la Grande Guerre* of Péronne (France). Her research focuses particularly on Belgian memory of the Great War. Her monographs include *Le roi Albert, histoire d'un mythe* (Quorum, 1995; et Labor, 2006); *Questions d'histoire contemporaine: conflit, mémoires et identités* (PUF, 2006); and *Je serai fusillé demain. Les dernières lettres des patriotes belges et français fusillés par l'occupant, 1914–1918* (Racine, 2011).

BEN WELLINGS is Lecturer in the School of Social Sciences at Monash University and a Visiting Fellow at the ANU Centre for European Studies. He is the author of *English Nationalism and Euroscepticism: Losing the Peace* (Peter Lang, 2012). In addition to the politics of Great War commemoration, his research interests include Britain's relationship with the European Union and the connections between nationalism and European integration since 1919.

# Index

# CULTURAL MEMORIES

## SERIES EDITOR

Katia Pizzi

Director, Centre for the Study of Cultural Memory

Institute of Modern Languages Research, University of London

*Cultural Memories* is the publishing project of the Centre for the Study of Cultural Memory at the Institute of Modern Languages Research, University of London. The Centre is international in scope and promotes innovative research with a focus on interdisciplinary approaches to memory.

This series supports the Centre by furthering original research in the global field of cultural memory studies. In particular, it seeks to challenge a monumentalizing model of memory in favour of a more fluid and heterogeneous one, where history, culture and memory are seen as complementary and intersecting. The series embraces new methodological approaches, encompassing a wide range of technologies of memory in cognate fields, including comparative studies, cultural studies, history, literature, media and communication, and cognitive science. The aim of *Cultural Memories* is to encourage and enhance research in the broad field of memory studies while, at the same time, pointing in new directions, providing a unique platform for creative and and forward-looking scholarship in the discipline.

Vol. I    Margherita Sprio
          Migrant Memories: Cultural History, Cinema and the Italian Post-War
          Diaspora in Britain
          2013. ISBN 978-3-0343-0947-9

Vol. 2    Shanti Sumartojo and Ben Wellings (eds)
          Nation, Memory and Great War Commemoration: Mobilizing the
          Past in Europe, Australia and New Zealand
          2014. ISBN 978-3-0343-0937-0